POWER KNOWLEDGE

An Introduction to

Political Philosophy

GIUSEPPE ROTOLO

Kendall Hunt

publishing company

Cover images © Shutterstock.com

Kendall Hunt
publishing company

www.kendallhunt.com
Send all inquiries to:
4050 Westmark Drive
Dubuque, IA 52004-1840

Copyright © 2019 by Kendall Hunt Publishing Company

Text + website ISBN 978-1-5249-5811-4
Text ISBN 978-1-5249-5812-1

Published in the United States of America

Contents

Preface

Writing a preface or an introduction to a book is probably my least favorite part of the entire writing process. These sections in a book are possibly the ones that the reader usually skips and that, as a student, seemed to me very much superfluous. Moreover, they always betray the text of the book itself. In fact, they say something *about* the book and therefore, they don't say *what is* in the book and this makes them often slightly off focus. For these reasons, I will use this space to do two things that really have nothing to do with prefacing or introducing the volume that you hold (in whatever format) in your hands. I will give you a brief *personal history* of this text, and I will thank the people that in a way or another have contributed to the birth of this book. So, if you are looking for *content* turn the page, skip this part, and start reading the text itself. If you want to know how this text happened to exist, instead, please continue reading.

The story of this book is a multiple one. I can say that it is possible to tell it at least in three different ways. (1) This book exists because one day, while I was sitting in my office at Middlesex County College, a nice lady knocked and asked if she could come in. She introduced herself and asked if I was interested in writing a book for Kendall-Hunt. After a brief discussion, I agreed to meet again to formalize the whole thing by signing a contract. I have always wondered why this lady came to me, but I have decided not to ask, I am sure that all of the reasons that I have imagined are much more self-esteem building than the truth. The name of the lady in question is Sue Saad, and she is been following the project from the very beginning of the process. She is the first person that I need to thank. (2) In another sense, this book was born more than twenty years ago. In the vibrant environment that was the university that I attended, it was impossible not to be passionate about political issues. It was also impossible not to engage in discussions and activities that had a great political significance within the local community where I lived. Those discussions with friends and colleagues really formed me and they still reflect in my words and thoughts today. (3) The final version of the story of this book can be connected, without a doubt, with the fact that at a certain point in my life, I ended up emigrating from Italy and immigrated in the United States. This experience was also very formative; it was in fact the stark contrast in political and social discourse between the two countries that reignited my sleeping interest for political philosophy. Trying to make sense of these differences, it has been useful when thinking of political issues *in general*, meaning as not tied to a specific geographical area or historical period.

These are the stories. Now I must thank the people that have contributed to the conception, birth, and development of this book.

I already mentioned Sue Saad, the acquisition editor at Kendall-Hunt. Without her, literally, this book would not be here. The same can be said for Karen Hoffmann, Senior Applications Coordinator at KH, she has been pushing me to the finish line since the first day she was involved with this project. Both of them had to deal with my lateness in more than one occasion, but they never stopped being supportive.

I also need to thank some of my philosophy colleagues here in the United States, in particular, Brandyn Heppard for his help and the stimulant conversations. He is definitely the reason why the chapter on Plato is as long as it is. I also want to thank my students: their questions and interest about the topic has urged me to be as clear as I can be while writing this book. I really tried to make this read as vibrant and easy to read as possible, hopefully I succeeded at least partially.

I also need to thank two *institutions*: Middlesex County College for it has been my place of work since I moved in the United States and it has provided me with the right cultural and intellectual environment to work on this book. In addition, thanks to Doylestown Public Library are in order: more than half of this book was physically written there. At times I wished the air conditioning in there was not as cold as it was but all in all, it was a wonderful experience writing in such a peaceful library.

Finally, I need to thank my family and especially my wife Antoniette and my kids Antonino and Tessa. Without them and their love, I wouldn't have written any of this.

PART 1

THE ANCIENTS

Premise to Part 1

The philosophy of the ancient Greeks had a very manifest political component after the Pre-Socratics. From the Sophists to the Cynics, they all tried to formulate some sort of theory about the way in which we should live in a community: some of them advocated for a life of relative detachment from the political institutions and other individuals, others theorized that the political institutions serve only the powerful, some advocated for a massive political involvement of the individual, others, finally, tried to understand which one is the best or the perfect form of government.

In this part of the book, we will focus on the political component of the philosophy of Plato and Aristotle. Their political views can be considered, at the same time, the baseline and the point of arrival of the Ancient Greeks sociopolitical thought. We will see, also, that they will serve as a steppingstone, or as a bounce wall, for many of the other philosophers that we will encounter in this book.

Specifically, we will see how Plato and Aristotle try to deal with all sorts of political issue. First, they try to understand which one the best form of government could be. We take for granted, in fact, that democracy is the best form of government for the people living in a State. The ancients challenge this idea and explore all sorts of possibilities from historically incarnated ones, like monarchy or oligarchy, to utopian ones, like the one presented by Plato in his Republic.

Secondly, the ancients try to establish what is should be, if any, the goal of government. Should the State be concerned with the wealth of the people? Should the government be preoccupied with Ethics and moral choices or should it just worry about the safety of its subjects? Should politicians be the *best* among the citizens, or should they be just professionals that treat the welfare of the state as job?

Finally, they will try to answer the question: Do we really need a government? Why do we even have one?

CHAPTER 1

The Ideal Government

1 Plato (427–347 BCE), the Ideal Political Community and Practical Government

For centuries, the political component of Plato's philosophy (Platonism) was minimized. Only during the twentieth century, we finally "discovered" how prominent politics was for Plato's life and theory.

Tracing his autobiography, Plato, in the *Seventh Letter*, explicitly says that politics was his main passion throughout life. Moreover, it becomes clear that the entire philosophical production of Plato can be considered centered around politics. This is probably one of the main differences between Plato and Socrates: the latter never actively participated to the political life of Athens, and actually thought that politics was against his nature. Plato, instead, was attracted by politics since he was young, as he says in the *Seventh Letter*:

✳ *In the days of my youth my experience was the same as that of many others. I thought that as soon as I should become my own master I should become a politician.* (Plato, *VII Letter, 324b–c.*)

Plato, though, does not participate to the political life of the city: he is taken aback by the corruption and the customs of politicians and by the discovery of the unjust nature of the laws in Athens and in other places. He concludes, by observing the political corruption that culminated with Socrates being sentenced to death that before one can truly wish to do politics meaningfully, there would be the need to completely reform the system. Hence, his attraction to philosophy and the idea that the only way in which politics can become respectable is through philosophy:

[. . .] *yet as regards political action I kept constantly waiting for an opportune moment; until, finally, looking at all the States which now*

5

exist, I perceived that one and all they are badly governed; for the state of their laws is such as to be almost incurable without some marvellous overhauling and good-luck to boot. So in my praise of the right philosophy I was compelled to declare that by it one is enabled to discern all forms of justice both political and individual. Wherefore the classes of mankind (I said) will have no cessation from evils until either the class of those who are right and true philosophers attains political supremacy, or else the class of those who hold power in the States becomes, by some dispensation of Heaven, really philosophic. (*Ibidem,* 326a–b.)

Plato believes that we need to move from rhetoric to true philosophy if we want to really *do* politics: only philosophy can be considered a safe passageway to access values like Justice and Good that are the foundation for any form of politics and government that we can call authentic.

1.1 The Republic and the Relationship between Ethics and Politics

Before we move ahead with the analysis of one of the main works of Plato directly related to politics and social issues, *The Republic*, we need to explain in which way we should read this work. There are, in fact, some preliminary clarifications that are needed in order to understand the letter and the spirit of this masterpiece of ancient political thought.

In *The Republic*, Plato establishes first and foremost that in his philosophy Ethics and Politics are united and, therefore, trying to decide if the Republic is about *Justice* or the *Ideal State* is a pseudo-problem. From the perspective of Plato (or of Socrates), there is no real distinction between ethics (the problem of Justice) and Politics (the Ideal State), we separate them, sometimes, just out of convenience. The rules of law are the same for the city, the social classes, and the single individual. To be more precise, these rules are laws of personal moral conduct: politics has its foundation in ethics and not vice versa. Because the city and the individual should be governed according to the same rules, Plato, in his analysis, makes it clear that the State is the magnified image of the individual and that he wants to find and shape *the perfect State and the perfect Man.*

1.2 From the Analysis of Justice to the Organization of the City and Back

The first book of the Republic starts with the analysis of the concept of Justice and the criticisms that the Sophists (that in the dialog are represented by Thrasymachus) have of it. Plato is conscious of the fact that to recuse these criticisms he needs to pose radical questions and to give radical answers: *What is Justice (what is its nature, its essence)? Which value does it have for men? Does Justice have a real value or is it just useful tool, a convention, a mere legality?*

Here is the exchange between Socrates and Thrasymachus:

> *"Hearken and hear then," said he. "I affirm that the just is nothing else than the advantage of the stronger. Well, why don't you applaud? Nay, you'll do anything but that." "Provided only I first understand your meaning," said I; "for I don't yet apprehend it. The advantage of the stronger is what you affirm the just to be. But what in the world do you mean by this? I presume you don't intend to affirm this, that if Polydamas the pancratiast is stronger than we are and the flesh of beeves is advantageous for him, for his body, this viand is also for us who are weaker than he both advantageous and just." "You're a buffoon, Socrates, and take my statement in the most detrimental sense." "Not at all, my dear fellow" said I; "I only want you to make your meaning plainer." "Don't you know then," said he, "that some cities are governed by tyrants, in others democracy rules, in others aristocracy?" "Assuredly." "And is not this the thing that is strong and has the mastery in each—the ruling party?" "Certainly." "And each form of government enacts the laws with a view to its own advantage, a democracy democratic laws and tyranny autocratic and the others likewise, and by so legislating they proclaim that the just for their subjects is that which is for their—the rulers'—advantage and the man who deviates from this law they chastise as a law-breaker and a wrongdoer. This, then, my good sir, is what I understand as the identical principle of justice that obtains in all states the advantage of the established government. This I presume you will admit holds power and is strong, so that, if one reasons rightly, it works out that the just is the same thing everywhere, the advantage of the stronger."* (Plato, *Republic*, I 338c–339a.)

Where should we stand regarding this argument? Are there any confutations of Thrasymachus' argument? Plato believes so and begins a meticulous analysis of the concept of Justice.

Because Justice can be found in one individual (the Just man) or in a State (a Just State or Government) and because it is more evident when it is shown (or when it is lacking) on a bigger scale, it is better, according to Plato, to analyze it on the State level. The idea is that if we understand how Justice works and what it is on the level State, we will be able to apply the same principles when we talk about individuals. Premised this, Plato starts his analysis of the State.

Why and how is the State born? Is a State necessary? The State is born, Plato says, because nobody is *autarchic*, no one can be "enough" for oneself.

✳ We need many things and each one of us needs many other people to be "in charge" of these things. We are not born all exactly the same, and this natural uniqueness is what leads different individual to choose different professions and to make society necessary for the satisfaction of our material needs (farmers, artisans, traders). Only different people can tend to different professions correctly. In other words, according to Plato, in order to be doing your profession in an adequate way, to be good at it, you need to be born with a natural talent for it.

> "The origin of the city, then," said I, "in my opinion, is to be found in the fact that we do not severally suffice for our own needs, but each of us lacks many things. Do you think any other principle establishes the state?" "No other," said he. "As a result of this, then, one man calling in another for one service and another for another, we, being in need of many things, gather many into one place of abode as associates and helpers, and to this dwelling together we give the name city or state, do we not?" "By all means." "And between one man and another there is an interchange of giving, if it so happens, and taking, because each supposes this to be better for himself." "Certainly." "Come, then, let us create a city from the beginning, in our theory. (Ibidem, Book II 369b–c.)

In a State there are other "positions" that are needed beside the ones of professionals useful to satisfy the essential needs of our life; there is also the need of a class of Warriors and one of Guardians: the first ones to protect the City during times of war and to help the City conquer new territories that are needed to keep up with its always growing needs, and the second ones to be in charge of the city laws and to make sure that everything is working properly in our society. These people also, will need to have the appropriate traits. Plato says that they will need to be like a good breed of dogs: they will possess the virtues of mildness and pride, they will be agile and physically strong, valiant and lovers of knowledge. These traits are necessary for someone to be part of the class of the Guardians or the Warriors (there are some differences between the two, but we will see these variances later) and a special education is therefore needed when it comes to them: the class of the producers (the people that work the "regular" professions) do not need to be educated too much because their professions are easy to learn by example and need more practice than anything else. The Guardians of the City (and the Warriors as well) instead need a strict education, Culture (Poetry and Music) and Gymnastics are the perfect tools to edify the soul and the body. This idea is pretty common in Greece during Plato's times, but he reforms it in a significative way. Poetry, for example, if it needs to be useful to the education of the young Guardian, it needs to be purified from anything that it is deemed indecent or false. The same needs to happen when it comes to Music: basically, Plato wants to put in place some sort of censorship that should decide what is appropriate or not, what will be good poetry or music, banning anything else. At the same time, Gymnastics will be moderate and will follow the education of the soul: in fact, a good soul can make good the body, but not the opposite.

The reason why Plato insists upon these disciplines (Music and Gymnastics) has to do with the idea that they can develop specific elements of our souls: Music shapes and makes the rational part of the soul stronger while Gymnastics, through the body, shapes and makes stronger the part of the soul that deals with feelings and emotions—like courage (Plato calls this part of the soul *spirited*). Together these two parts of the soul create the perfect harmony in people's behavior.

As we mentioned before, there is a difference between the Warriors and the Guardians; Plato, at the beginning of the Republic, calls the people in these

Why Is Music Considered a Discipline That Can Develop the Rational Part of Our Mind?

It might seem strange to us that Plato (and the Greeks in general) considered music a tool for the development of rationality. If anything, we think, music appeals to our emotional being, it makes us happy, sad, excited, nostalgic, in some sort of irrational way. While for the Greeks, evidently, all sorts of emotions can be evoked by music, the study of it elicits rational reasoning. Why? Because the way the Greeks made music was similar to the way they did mathematics: music, for them, is the product of a calculation. The perfect harmony of different tones, of silence and sound, the perfect symmetry of rhythm etc. are not dictated by emotions or emotional expressions but are the product of an attentive mathematical study. Understanding music, and its quantitative value, was understood as very difficult because it dealt with "elements" that were not immediately relatable to the material world, but that did influence it. The creation of music, the Greeks thought, is an abstract form of rational thinking that can produce specific emotional responses. This is why Plato, for example, want to censor specific kinds of music that by design will produce "negative vibes" that are in contrast with the project of governing docile individuals. We might think that this is a foreign and archaic way to look at music, but if we analyze our recent history, we can see that the same reasoning was applied, for example, during the years following 9/11 2001. All "rebellious" music was banned from radio stations and concerts of bands like Rage Against The Machine (a band very critical of the political views and actions of the United States, with a catalog of songs like "Township Rebellion" or "Guerrilla Radio") were cancelled all over the United States. There is more: for decades now, the music industry has been interested in finding a scientific connection between specific tunes, tones, rhythms and some parts of our brain, in order to create songs that will produce specific emotional reaction. Adjusting the pitch or the note of a song, they think, might be key to the commercial success of it.

classes in the same way (they are all Guardians), but then he makes a distinction between the *real* Guardians and the Warriors: the first ones need to be in charge of the state and the second ones need to obey. The real Guardians will be the one in charge of the State and we will know who they are because they have exhibited the most love for the City and have done the best for it consistently. These real Guardians, Plato says, are the true Philosophers and can be considered to be a separate class. In the end, we have, in our Ideal City, three separate classes: the *Producers* that are in charge of the essential, we can say almost biological needs of the society; the *Warriors* that are in charge of the security of the City and of any actions regarding war; and, finally, the *Philosophers* (*Guardians*) that are in charge of governing.

These classes (of which a lot has been said by Plato's scholars) can be considered, depending on the point of view, open (true social classes) or closed (social castes). In fact, we have seen how to be part of class we need to have specific dispositions, better yet predispositions, that we can develop through education. This means that if you are born with the producer predisposition you cannot "climb" your way up to be a philosopher: from this perspective the Ideal City is rigidly divided in *castes*. On the other hand, there is no "genetics" involved: the son or the daughter of a Warrior, for example, has absolutely no guarantee to be part of the same class. Human beings are uniquely positioned, independently from their blood ties: so, from this perspective the Ideal City is divided in *classes.* The differences between this classes (we will call them this way from now on) are marked not just by the role that every individual has within the City, but also by what is permitted or prohibited to the individuals that belong to these classes.

For example, to the first class, the one to which farmers, artisans, and merchants belong to, it is conceded to possess goods and to accumulate some wealth (not too much, but not too little either). The Guardians (philosophers and warriors), instead, will be prohibited to possess any goods or to accumulate any sort of wealth: they will live in shared houses and share meals in a communal place. They will receive the necessary things to live (food, water, clothing, etc.) from the other citizens as a form of payment for what they do. These limitations are necessary, according to Plato, if we want to advance the good of the City over the happiness of a single class of individuals. So, while the first class will work to accumulate some wealth and to become moderately rich, the Guardians will make sure that no changes will be introduced to the perfect State (if it needed changes it would have not been perfect!) that would risk ruining it. The Guardians will also make sure that the first class does not become too rich or too poor, that the State does not become too big or too small, and that the nature of the individual does correspond to the functions that they exercise in society; The Guardians, finally, will supervise the education of the best of the new generations so these young people will not change the constitution of the State. To summarize here is the outline of the Ideal State up to this point: a place where individuals live and exercise their functions according to their intimate nature. Now, Plato writes, we can go back to investigate a bit more the nature and value of Justice and see how it is connected with the perfect State/City.

The State described by Plato, in order to be perfect, has to be based on four cardinal virtues: *Justice*, of course, but also *Wisdom*, *Fortitude*, and *Temperance*. The Ideal state has wisdom because the Philosophers (that are governing) manage the State so that it works the right way when in contact with other States and when it deals with its own citizens: the state has wisdom because it is governed by the Guardians. Fortitude (a form of Courage we can say) is the ability to keep the right opinion when it comes to dangerous things (and sometimes even non-dangerous ones). This means that fortitude is the virtue that prevents us to surrender ourselves to pleasures, pains or fears, or passions (feelings). This virtue is typical of the warriors and the State is strong (has fortitude) because of this class. Temperance is some sort of order or discipline over pleasures or desires. It is, using Plato's words, the ability to submit the worst part of something to the best part of something (in the case of our souls, he would say temperance consists in submitting the irrational part of it—the worst—to the rational part—the best). This virtue can be found especially in the producers' class, but it is present in all aspects of the State. Thanks to temperance the inferior classes submit themselves to the superior ones and harmonize perfectly with them. Finally, justice. This virtue is nothing but the main principle on which the entire Ideal State is build: everyone *must* do only those things that by nature, and therefore by law, is called to do. When every citizen and every class of citizens exercises its functions the best way possible, then the life of the State evolves in perfect fashion and therefore we have a *Just State*.

Justice regulates the State so that everyone is bound to do by law what he or she can do best by nature. People will be redirected if they feel that they should do something different from what they are good at, but, to tell the truth, according to Plato, the possibility that someone would try to do that is miniscule: through propaganda and education everyone will, in a Just—perfect—State, do what they are best at.

In addition, because—as you will probably remember—the state is just a magnified version of the individual soul, justice should have the same role within the individual and everything that we have described on a State level has to correspond something of an individual level: the different virtues, for example, will be expression of different Souls that inhabit the individual. People are a mixture of rational and emotional, and all like physical pleasures: who people are it is determined by which part of their soul is predominant.

If the rational part is predominant, they can become (through education) Guardians, if they are more *Spirited* they can become Warriors, if they like physical pleasures over anything else they should be Producers (as long as they possess temperance).

"Just too, then, Glaucon, I presume we shall say a man is in the same way in which a city was just." "That too is quite inevitable." "But we surely cannot have forgotten this, that the state was just by reason of each of the three classes found in it fulfilling its own function." "I don't think we have forgotten," he said. "We must remember, then, that each of us also in whom the several parts within him perform each their own task—he will be a just man and one who minds his own affair." "We must indeed remember," he said. "Does it not belong to the rational part to rule, being wise and exercising forethought in behalf of the entire soul, and to the principle of high spirit to be subject to this and its ally?" "Assuredly." "Then is it not, as we said, the blending of music and gymnastics that will render them concordant, intensifying and fostering the one with fair words and teachings and relaxing and soothing and making gentle the other by harmony and rhythm?" "Quite so," said he. "And these two thus reared and having learned and been educated to do their own work in the true sense of the phrase, will preside over the appetitive part which is the mass of the soul in each of us and the most insatiate by nature of wealth. They will keep watch upon it, lest, by being filled and infected with the so-called pleasures associated with the body and so waxing big and strong, it may not keep to its own work but may undertake to enslave and rule over the classes which it is not fitting that it should, and so overturn the entire life of all." "By all means," he said. "Would not these two, then, best keep guard against enemies from without also in behalf of the entire soul and body, the one taking counsel, the other giving battle, attending upon the ruler, and by its courage executing the ruler's designs?" "That is so." "Brave, too, then, I take it, we call each individual by virtue of this part in him, when, namely, his high spirit preserves in the midst of pains and pleasures the rule handed down by the reason as to what is or is not to be feared." "Right," he said. "But wise by that small part that ruled in him and handed down these commands, by its possession in turn within it of the knowledge of what is beneficial for each and for the whole, the community composed of the three." "By all means." "And again, was he not sober by reason of the friendship and concord of these same parts, when, namely, the ruling principle and its two subjects are at one in the belief that the reason ought to rule, and do not raise faction against it?" "The virtue of soberness certainly," said he, "is nothing else than this, whether in a city or an individual." (Ibidem, Book IV 441d–442d.)

Clearly, justice is the disposition of the soul that superintends all other dispositions and that makes sure that every part of the soul will do what it is supposes to do. Justice is there to restore the natural order of things inside of human beings and outside of them: Justice will lead to beauty (harmony is considered the major element of beauty for the Ancient Greeks), and health of the soul, while injustice leads to ugliness and illness of the soul. *Justice, in a formula, regulates the functions of the happy soul and the happy State.*

1.3   The Social Consequences of the Ideal State

The Ideal state, in order to be functioning correctly, according to Plato, needs the entire society to work in the same direction: we saw how the existence a Just State is based on the idea that everyone is supposed to be in its place and do whatever the individual nature dictates. Even though Plato is describing an ideal State, he is conscious that this *Utopia*, to work, needs to have a social make up that is very different from the one that is typical in Athens in the fifth century BC. We have already mentioned that the subdivision of all population in classes/castes leads to a series of rules about what the citizens can and cannot do regarding property; now we will look at other social "consequences" of this way of organizing society.

The first consequence, we can say, it is revolutionary for the time in which Plato writes: he proposes that the women that are part of the class of the Guardians share with their men the same responsibilities and education. This is really hard to imagine for an Athenian of the fifth century BC considering that women rarely left their houses and that their job was limited to the administration of the house and to take care of the children. Women, at that time, are banned from any cultural or political activity; they are also prohibited from participating in any activity regarding war.

> *"Then there is no pursuit of the administrators of a state that belongs to a woman because she is a woman or to a man because he is a man. But the natural capacities are distributed alike among both creatures, and women naturally share in all pursuits and men in all—yet for all the woman is weaker than the man." "Assuredly." "Shall we, then, assign them all to men and nothing to women?" "How could we?" "We shall rather, I take it, say that one woman has the nature of a physician and another not, and one is by nature musical, and another unmusical?" "Surely." "Can we, then, deny that one woman is naturally athletic and warlike and another unwarlike and averse to gymnastics?" "I think not." "And again, one a lover, another a hater, of wisdom? And one high-spirited, and the other lacking spirit?" "That also is true." "Then it is likewise true that one woman has the qualities of a guardian and another not. Were not these*

the natural qualities of the men also whom we selected for guardians?"
"They were." "The women and the men, then, have the same nature in
respect to the guardianship of the state, save in so far as the one is weaker,
the other stronger." (Ibidem, Book V 455d–456a.)

Because women and men share the same nature, women will be educated
exactly in the same way: they will exercise, like men, in the gym and will eventually serve as politicians or go to war.

A second consequence, strictly connected to the first one, is the elimination of the family as an institution for the class of the Guardians: women,
just like men, will be concerned exclusively with the administration of the
State. If we ended here our analysis, it would seem like Plato is this illumi-
nated, almost feminist, author that is rethinking the role of women in Greek
society. Unfortunately, if we think this way, we are far from the truth. Firstly,
we have to remember that Plato is describing an Ideal state that has very
little chances (if any) to be realized. Secondly, the language used by Plato still
denotes a conception of women that is very far from the one that recognizes
equality between the two genders. For Example, the traditional family will
still exist in the lower classes (all but the Guardians will still have families);
also, Plato clearly states that women *of* the Guardians and the offspring
of the Guardians will be shared. The language used by Plato betrays him:
women and children are grouped together as property even in the Ideal State.

Weddings will be regulated by the state and declared sacred. The criteria
of these regulations will be pretty simple: the best of men and the best of
women will be coupled to copulate so the race of people resulting from these
acts will be better and better. The State will make sure that this people will
procreate as much as possible. Their sons and daughters will be raised and
nurtured, the sons and daughters of the people that are not the best will not.
All this will be done without the knowledge of common people and even the
coupling will be apparently drafted at random, while in reality the drafting
process will be manipulated to guarantee to best results possible.

The children will be taken away from the parents immediately after birth.
All the children that will be born between the seventh and the tenth month
starting with the date a man and a woman have celebrated their wedding (and
consummated it) have to be considered by these men and women as sons and
daughters. At the same time, these children will call father and mother to
the men and women that got married (and consummated their marriage)
between the tenth and the seventh month prior to their birth. Consequently,
the people born in the same period will call each other brothers and sisters.

At first glance, these rules of the platonic State seem to be absurd and cruel.
But if we look more carefully we can see how these rules are in line with the
intent to build an ideal, perfect, State, and that they are less cruel and absurd
than what they seem. Plato wants to take away from the Guardians a specific

private family to give them a vast *public* one. We know very well that material goods (wealth in general) is a divisive factor among men (this is why the Guardians are prohibited to have property), but also that the peculiar *thing* that is "family" provokes human egoism. If family also becomes communal, the Guardians will not have anything of which to say, "it is mine!", or better, they will be able to say, "it is mine!" about everything: every child, everything that is within the state will be shared. These are the logical reasons why Plato believes that such extreme measures are needed, but although we can understand these reasons, we cannot a-critically accept them.

From our modern perspective, there is one fatal flaw at the center of the methodology that Plato uses to try to create a city united like a family where there is little to no egoism: he believes that the collectivity is more important that the single individual, and he does not understand that a man is a *single unique individual* that cannot be mortified even to create a perfect society. Our uniqueness, our being specifically who we are, is indispensable to give meaning to our life.

1.4   The Philosopher King and His Education

We have already seen how Plato believes that in order to be a true Guardian, to be in charge of the State, people need to exhibit specific natural characteristics: they need to be equipped with true philosophical nature (we also saw how Plato does not care for differences in gender: both men and women can be philosophers, so we should probably talk of philosopher kings and queens). Therefore, among the young people in the ideal city, we will select the ones that seem to be philosophically gifted and we will further their education. In fact, the educational sequence proposed for the upper class (music and gymnastics) will be just the beginning of the cultural journey of the future philosopher/guardian: these two disciplines produce good results but don't give the youths the knowledge of the Good, which is the proper aim of the philosophical education. To get to the maximum knowledge (philosophical knowledge of the Good) there are no shortcuts, but only the long road that will show the young people the existence of true reality, a reality that is not perceivable, but that is where the absolute Good is hidden. This long road passes by mathematics, geometry, astronomy, and harmony (as a musical science that is). At the end of this progression, the young philosophers will be challenged with what Plato calls *Dialectics* (we would call it philosophy today) which will lead them to knowledge of the supreme Good. Plato's identifies a real "road map" for these gifted individuals: at twenty years old they start being educated as "philosophers," when they are thirty, it will be decided who, amongst them, has real Dialectic nature, and after five years of Dialectical studies only the fitted ones will start "working" in the real world again by being generals or assuming minor roles in the government of the city. They will do this until they are fifty years old: at that point they can finally become head of the state, real Guardians.

The Philosophers/Guardians that have experienced the supreme Good would probably want to live in contemplation of it the rest of their life. So why should they abandon this life of contemplation and endure a life of "servitude" in the name of the State? Because, Plato says, they have contracted a debt with the State: they were able to find the Good thanks to the education given to them by the State, and now they realize that they need to give back. Some will govern and some will teach, but all of the philosophers will work to make sure that this perfect machine that is the State will keep on working the right way avoiding any corruption that could be fatal to the only system that can create a happy, truly Just society. Stop 9/14

1.5   The Degenerate States and Their Form

In Plato's philosophy, the creation of a perfect State relies on the existence of a relationship between virtue and happiness, and on the fact that happiness is the natural effect of virtue. Virtuous people (philosophers) will make the State virtuous and therefore happy, which in turn will make citizens happy. The same reasoning can be applied to the form of government that we can consider degenerated and therefore not desirable: these States are degenerated because they have substituted Virtue (as supreme value) with something else, and non-philosophers are at the helm of them. The result? States where the citizens are not happy, and the individuals degenerate in typologies that are less than desirable.

Plato identifies four forms of government that he considers corrupted. He describes them in order of degeneration (from less to more degenerated and dangerous).

1. *Timocracy*: It is the form of government that has, as its foundation, *honor*. In this form of government, what makes people choose public life is the want of being recognized, to be considered honorable, and therefore, ambition is the engine of public life. In their private lives, citizens start to be more and more attracted by money and wealth, even though they tend to hide it. Timocracy incites the Spirited part of the soul (one of the two a-rational ones) to take charge and to vanquish the Rational one. Citizens of this state are slaves to their emotions.

2. *Oligarchy*: It is the form of government that values *wealth* more than anything else, and the wealthiest of the people administer the State. Essentially, this form of government is what we would call *Plutocracy* today. This form of government is worse than Timocracy because it substitutes Virtue with something superficial and *material* like wealth (timocracy substituted virtue with ambition, but at least ambition is not a material

Like the world today

good). Only rich people govern, the Good and its virtues disappear, and poverty and the poor are seen as the worst of all people. Under an oligarchical government, the conflict between the poor and the rich becomes fatal, and this conflict cannot be solved: in fact, there are no superior values to appeal to move onward. The citizens of this State spend their lives trying to make more and more money and being dominated by the inferior part of the soul the appetitive part.

3. *Democracy*: It is the form of government that, in Plato's hierarchy, precedes and prepares Tyranny. What Plato calls democracy has to be understood as *demagogy* or the populistic aspect of democracy. In this form of government, the insatiable appetite for wealth leads the oligarchy to care just about making even more money, while the young are left without any moral education: the new generations lose any form of temperance and are preoccupied just with seeking any sort of pleasure. This way, the wealthy people that are in power end up weakened (morally and physically) and soon the poor realize that it might be time to overthrow the old political class. As soon as the lower class finds itself finally in power, they will proclaim the equality of all citizens and install a popular government. The State, according to Plato, is now full of freedom, but this freedom without any sort of moral values leads, inevitably, to chaos. Everyone lives according to his or her own personal code of conduct, people can decide not to participate in the administration of the state. Justice becomes very tolerant: the verdicts emitted by the judges are seldom enforced. Who wants to be a politician does not need to have the right nature and temperament, the right education and experience; who wants to govern does not need any competence. All he or she needs is to proclaim himself or herself a *friend* of the people.

    In this form of government, the young people are attracted only by pleasure and desire. False truths impede the possibility of reasonable discussions about everything that can aid the current state of affairs. Through these false truths, and the incorrect reasoning that directly derives from them, respect is banned because is considered foolery, temperance is expelled with insults and considered as lack of virility, and moderation regarding spending is considered stinginess. At the same time, negative qualities are considered good: arrogance is called frankness, anarchy is called freedom, excessive public spending is said to be liberalism and insolence is called courage. This way, the life of the people voided of meaning, without law or order, it is absolutely devoted to pleasure seeking.

4. *Tyranny*: It is the form of government that Plato despises the most and that he considers the most dangerous. Deriving directly from democracy, Tyranny uses the "excess of freedom" and turns it into its opposite: serfdom. The passage from democracy to tyranny happens when a group of people, using the freedom conceded to them by the system, impose

their will through words or actions and do not tolerate whomever speaks against them. They use any mean to take away from the wealthy and the powerful resources, making sure that the people benefit, partially, from this, while keeping most of the wealth and the power. When among these people is born a man that is able to impose himself as a leader recognized by the general population (a demagogue), he will eventually become a tyrant. This means that he will be able to (and will exercise this power) wrongfully accuse his adversary, to exile them or to kill them. At this point, this individual will either transition effectively from leader to tyrant or he will be killed by his adversaries. The tyrant will be, at first, kind and gentle, but soon he will remove the mask: he will declare war constantly, so the State will constantly need a commander in chief; then he will "purge" the state by eliminating all the people and rules that can contrast his power: and of course the best people and the best rules will be the ones that will be eliminated. This way the tyrant will end up living amongst inept people and will be eventually hated even by them. Under tyranny, not only the leader is a tyrant, but the citizens of such states are also tyrannical: the unbridled freedom (that it is in reality anarchy) leads them to surrender to those desires that are present in all of us, but that thanks to education and reason we are able to dominate. Controlled by these desires, tyrannical people lose every residual temperance, and want to extend their dominion over all people and gods. These people hit rock bottom, according to Plato, when they completely give in to drunkenness, sex, and depression. Clearly, these kinds of men are unable to have true relationships with other people: they are only able either to command or to obey and abandon all people that they encounter right after they get what they want from them.

To summarize, tyranny, for Plato, is the form of government of absolute servitude: not just the serfdom of the people to the tyrant, but total serfdom of reason to low instincts; the exterior servitude is just the consequence and the manifestation of this internal servitude.

One more time, through this list of degenerate states, Plato affirms the principle that any State, any government, is the blown-up picture of men soul: its virtues and vices and, therefore, its happiness or unhappiness. In all the degenerations of the State that we have seen, rationality progressively loses his preeminence generating a disruption of the equilibrium necessary to live a good life. Under the tyrannical state (and for the tyrannical man) the disruption has become a complete breakdown of the balance of the soul: the lowest desires are now emerging as the leading forces of the soul to the point that men become beasts. The tyrannical man is a man that we can consider spiritually and socially ill, and tyranny has to be considered, consequently, an ill form of government.

1.6   The Analysis of the Historical Constitutions: The Statesman

Plato, having drafted for us an ideal form of organization, an ideal government, declares it achievable only in our hearts: he truly believes that society, in order to work properly, should follow the ideal principles that are articulated in the *Republic*, but he is also conscious of how difficult it would be to actually have people living according to these principles. In addition, the Academia had, as its main purpose, to prepare and educate the future political class: to create a new political elite for a new kind of government, therefore Plato has the need to draw a political model that would be historically reachable.

For this project, Plato is not reconsidering his ideal of State and Man, rather he is taking in consideration some more factors: in order to think of a State that is attainable, he says, we should think not only of how men should be, but also of how they are. The first step of this work of mediation between *Ideal Politics* and the *Historical Reality* results in Plato's dialogue *The Statesman*.

This Dialogue presents Socrates trying to define what a Statesman is and what kind of "art" it takes to be a statesman. Almost immediately we are presented with a dilemma that gives us a good understanding of how the inquiry is not anymore purely ideal, but very "historical": *Should the Statesman be above the law or should the law be paramount?*

Obviously, the dilemma would have not made sense in the ideal state described by the *Republic* because in that context the Statesman (the Philosopher) and the law would have never been in any form of contrast. The Law, after all, is just the way in which the Philosopher brings to the city the Good that he has found during his years of dialectical studies. In the *Historical State*, though, things could be different: there are no such individuals as the Philosophers described by the Republic, therefore, we need to explore the possibility that some contrasts between the Statesman and the Law could arise; and if contrasts do arise we need to know if the Statesman is bound by the law or if he should be above it and able to modify it.

Just to be clear, Plato, here, does not say that the ideals of the *Republic* are wrong or that we should give up on them. On the contrary, he declares that the best form of government would be the one that where the statesman can govern with "Science and Virtue" and be above the law. The law, in fact, is abstract and impersonal, and therefore, often inadequate for the art of governing. At the same time, though, Plato recognizes that this kind of men (virtuous and wise) are not only exceptional and rare, but pretty also much nonexistent. For this reason, in the *historical state* the law has to be paramount and it is necessary that the Constitution has to be written and inviolable.

Stranger

Thus, we say, the tyrant has arisen, and the king and oligarchy and aristocracy and democracy, because men are not contented with that one perfect ruler, and do not believe that there could ever be any one worthy of such power or willing and able by ruling with virtue and knowledge to dispense justice and equity rightly to all, but that he will harm and kill and injure any one of us whom he chooses on any occasion, since they admit that if such a man as we describe should really arise, he would be welcomed and would continue to dwell among them, directing to their weal as sole ruler a perfectly right form of government.

Younger Socrates
Certainly.

Stranger

But, as the case now stands, since, as we claim, no king is produced in our states who is, like the ruler of the bees in their hives, by birth pre-eminently fitted from the beginning in body and mind, we are obliged, as it seems, to follow in the track of the perfect and true form of government by coming together and making written laws. (Plato, *Statesman* 301c–e.)

Aside from the re-evaluation of the position of the statesman in relationship to the law, Plato feels also the need to reassess the different forms of government analyzed and declared degenerated forms of the Ideal State in the *Republic*. These forms of government are presented in *The Stateman* as necessary because it is manifest the fact that we cannot reach the perfect form of government: once again, there are no extraordinary men to rely on to build the ideal state.

What we call the *Historical Constitutions*, the forms of government that we actually find in reality, can be considered *imitations* of the ideal form of government previously delineated. If only one man is governing, and he is imitating the ideal Statesman we have *Monarchy*; if, instead, it is the multitude of rich people to govern and to imitate the ideal statesman we have *Aristocracy*; finally, if it is the entire population to govern and to imitate the ideal statesman we have *Democracy*. These three forms of government are expression of Justice and Good until who governs respects laws and customs. The moment the law is not respected three degenerate form of government are born: Monarchy becomes Tyranny, Aristocracy becomes Oligarchy, and Democracy becomes Demagogy. These corrupted forms of government will lead to the terrible consequences described in the *Republic*.

If we look at all six of these forms of government, Plato tries to establish a hierarchy in order to see which one of them is the best and which one is the worst:

Stranger

Before, when we were in search of the right government, this division was of no use, as we showed at the time but now that we have set that apart and have decided that the others are the only available forms of government, the principle of lawfulness and lawlessness bisects each of them.

Younger Socrates
So it seems, from what has been said.

Stranger

Monarchy, then, when bound by good written rules, which we call laws, is the best of all the six; but without law it is hard and most oppressive to live with.

Younger Socrates
I fancy it is.

Stranger

But just as few is intermediate between one and a multitude, so the government of the few must be considered intermediate, both in good and in evil. But the government of the multitude is weak in all respects and able to do nothing great, either good or bad, when compared with the other forms of government, because in this the powers of government are distributed in small shares among many men; therefore of all these governments when they are lawful, this is the worst, and when they are all lawless it is the best; and if they are all without restraint, life is most desirable in a democracy, but if they are orderly, that is the worst to live in; but life in the first kind of state is by far the first and best, with the exception of the seventh, for that must be set apart from all the others, as God is set apart from men. (Ibidem, 302e–303b.)

What Plato is saying here is that if we are to live in a world where these possible forms of government are realized correctly, we don't want to live in a democracy, because in democracy very little is accomplished, and the advancement of society is very slow. But in the off chance that we are living in a world where these forms of government are not necessarily perfectly realized, living in a democracy is the best situation: very little harm can come from it.

At this point, Plato has clarified for us the relationship between the States-man and the law, and the hierarchy of the different forms of *Historically existent* constitution. What he does next is to establish what sort of "art" (what sort of ability) it takes to be a statesman. The activity proper of the states-man can be easily distinguished from the activities that might seem related to politics, but that are in reality only subordinated to it, according to Plato. For example, rhetoric is different from politics (and this distinction is crucial to understand the difference between Democracy and Demagogy) because the former translates in activity of persuasion, while the latter is the activity that *decides* if it is convenient to persuade. According to Plato, this fact shows clearly how politics is superior to rhetoric. The same kind of reasoning can be made for the art of war: this art is preoccupied only with doing and winning wars, but it does not deal with the decisions pertaining the convenience of going to war or not. Going to war or keeping the peace is a decision that pertains only to politics. Same goes with the activities proper of judges and courts: they apply the laws, while politics makes them.

In general, we can say that the role of all these arts (Rhetoric, War, Judicial) is to apply a scale, a measurement that was established by the chief art: Politics. What is then the core of the Statesman art? What is its objective? Its objective is to establish what is opportune, convenient, and important for the life of the City. To do so, the Statesman will need to harmonize heterogenic (and sometimes opposite) elements to achieve unity and to create a functioning government:

Stranger

This, then, is the end, let us declare, of the web of the statesman's activity, the direct interweaving of the characters of restrained and courageous men, when the kingly science has drawn them together by friendship and community of sentiment into a common life, and having perfected the most glorious and the best of all textures, clothes with it all the inhabitants of the state, both slaves and freemen, holds them together by this fabric, and omitting nothing which ought to belong to a happy state, rules and watches over them. (Ibidem, 311b–c.)

Toolbox

Now and Then

It is important to understand the radical differences that there are between the concept of politics that we have, and the platonic understanding of politics.

1. According to Plato, politics (at least ideally, the politics of the *Republic*) should not be concerned necessarily with the economic well-being of the people, but rather with the well-being of their souls; therefore, politics has to be philosophy, it has to be a life-long training toward perfection.
2. In ancient Greece, at least until the classical period, the State and the law of the State were the paradigm of every being: the individual equated to the citizen, and the value and the virtue of the individual were the value and the virtue of the citizen. The *polis* was the maximum expression of life for the Greek man.
3. Our understanding of politics is quite different: The State is not in charge anymore (at least apparently) of regulating *all* aspects of the life of its citizens. Individual and citizen are not exactly the same anymore. The State is not interested any longer in the life of the mind of its citizens, at least not in the sense described by Plato: the consciousness of each individual is now in charge of many decisions that Plato would have wanted the State to take. Today the economy and the common aspiration to be wealthy influence so radically the political theory and praxis that a good government is synonymous with a system that permits a steady and gradual increment of goods and material wealth. This, as you now know, was exactly what Plato thought to be the origin of all evil when it came to government. We are the direct heir of a different political tradition that we will analyze in the following chapters.

2

Political Virtues

2 Aristotle: Politics as "Philosophy of Human Things"

Aristotle (384–322 BCE) conceives Politics as the science that deals with human conduct and with the goals that, through this conduct, humans want to achieve either as individuals or as a group. He will eventually subdivide Politics in ethics and politics proper (State theory). Ethics, in fact, it is subordinated to Politics in the Aristotelian system because of the typical Greek conception of individual existence as realized completely only within the political horizon of the City: the individual man exists only in function of the City and not vice-versa.

Politics carries out a function of leadership: it is Politics that has to determine which sciences are necessary for the City and to what point are these sciences needed. In Aristotle's system, the values of the single human being are always subordinate to the one of the State: The *Polis* is the only place, the only horizon where human values can exist. Aristotle will argue that even though the Good of the single individual and the Good of the State share the same nature (both, as we will see, consist in *Virtue*), the Good of the State is more important, more beautiful, and divine. The reason for this is quite simple: if we look at human nature we can immediately see how a human being is *unable* to live independently from other human beings, to live isolated. A human being has the need, to become who/what is supposed to be, to have relationships with other fellow humans in every moment of her existence.

Firstly, Aristotle writes, human beings are naturally divided in males and females. These two kinds of beings unite to form the first basic community that we can observe, the *Family*, to procreate and to satisfy the most basic needs (we will see how the concept of family that he has in mind is slightly

25

different from ours). Families, however, are not self-sufficient and this is why there is the need for a bigger community that can guarantee the satisfaction of our needs. This is why we need a *Village*.

Family and Village are sufficient to satisfy the need of our life almost in a biological sense (offspring, shelter, food, basic exchange of goods), but they are not enough to give us the platform, the conditions, for a *perfect* life. This form of life, that we can call *moral* life, can be guaranteed only by laws, political offices, and, in general, by the complex organization of a State. Only within the state, the individual, thanks to laws and political institution, is given a chance to exit his natural *egoism*, and to live a life according to what is objectively good, rather than according to what is subjectively good. The State, from this point of view, comes last chronologically, but it is first ontologically: The State is the whole of which family and village are the parts, and the whole is what gives meaning to the parts. In other words, we can say that historically families and villages existed before the State, but the State is necessary for the full realization of families and villages. A human family can reach its human *potential* only thanks to the State.

> *The partnership finally composed of several villages is the city-state; it has at last attained the limit of virtually complete self-sufficiency, and thus, while it comes into existence for the sake of life, it exists for the good life. Hence every city-state exists by nature, inasmuch as the first partnerships so exist; for the city-state is the end of the other partnerships, and nature is an end, since that which each thing is when its growth is completed we speak of as being the nature of each thing, for instance of a man, a horse, a household. Again, the object for which a thing exists, its end, is its chief good; and self-sufficiency is an end, and a chief good. From these things therefore it is clear that the city-state is a natural growth, and that man is by nature a political animal, and a man that is by nature and not merely by fortune citiless is either low in the scale of humanity or above it (like the "clanless, lawless, hearthless" man reviled by Homer, for one by nature unsocial is also 'a lover of war') inasmuch as he is solitary, like an isolated piece at draughts. And why man is a political animal in a greater measure than any bee or any gregarious animal is clear. For nature, as we declare, does nothing without purpose; and man alone of the animals possesses speech. The mere voice, it is true, can indicate pain and pleasure, and therefore is possessed by the other animals as well (for their nature has been developed so far as to have sensations of what is painful and pleasant and to indicate those sensations to one another), but speech is designed to indicate the advantageous and the harmful, and therefore also the right and the wrong; for it is the special property of man in distinction from the other animals that he alone has perception of good*

and bad and right and wrong and the other moral qualities, and it is partnership in these things that makes a household and a city-state. Thus also the city-state is prior in nature to the household and to each of us individually. For the whole must necessarily be prior to the part; since when the whole body is destroyed, foot or hand will not exist except in an equivocal sense, like the sense in which one speaks of a hand sculptured in stone as a hand; because a hand in those circumstances will be a hand spoiled, and all things are defined by their function and capacity, so that when they are no longer such as to perform their function they must not be said to be the same things, but to bear their names in an equivocal sense. It is clear therefore that the state is also prior by nature to the individual; for if each individual when separate is not self-sufficient, he must be related to the whole state as other parts are to their whole, while a man who is incapable of entering into partnership, or who is so self-sufficing that he has no need to do so, is no part of a state, so that he must be either a lower animal or a god. (Aristotle, *Politics* A 2 1252b–1253a 29.)

This excerpt from Aristotle *Politics* is considered to be one of the most radical defenses of the State done by any ancient philosopher. Aristotle proclaims the state to be natural and he is convinced, just like most Greeks at the time, that the only kind of society that had goals that were not purely biological was the *polis* through the state. This is the reason why Aristotle declares men to be *political animals*, rather than social animals.

2.1 The Nature of the Family and the Justification of Inequality

The family is, for Aristotle, the original foundation that makes up the City, and it is constituted by four elements: (a) the relationship between man and wife, (b) the relationships between father and sons, (c) the relationship between master and slave, and (d) the art of getting what one needs and, in particular, the art of getting wealth.

The administration of the family needs to be conducted appropriately and to do so, it requires adequate tools, both animate and inanimate: workers and slaves are necessary to administrate correctly the family unit. The worker is, according to Aristotle, like a tool that precedes and directs other tools, and he can be used to produce objects and material wealth. The slave, on the other hand, is not used to produce *something*, but he is considered a tool useful to the life of the master. The slave is a tool that is necessary for the master to fulfill his potential as a perfect human being: only because slaves can perform all sorts of physical menial actions, the master can spend his days doing *politics*. But, who are these slaves? And how can Aristotle justify the existence of an institution like slavery that establishes that a man can be a "living possession" of another man?

Some philosophers in ancient Greece do question slavery as a permissible institution, but Aristotle doubles down on it by declaring it not only permissible, but also natural. When we look at the totality of the Aristotelian system, it seems strange that he would be in favor of slavery, and we can be tempted to disregard this view as a glitch, a mysterious incoherence within the thought of the philosopher. The truth is, if you like, much more unpleasant: this way of thinking is perfectly normal at the time of Aristotle's life, and while some philosophers go against the grain of the prejudices of the society where they live, Aristotle, in this case, does not. It is not a coincidence that the philosophers that are openly against slavery were the Sophist, those philosophers that were proposing concepts that were alien to the Greek culture at the time (Atheism, epistemological and ethical Relativism, etc.). Aristotle, like most of the Greek philosophers and citizens, was a conformist and, as said before, thought of slavery as a natural institution. Let's take a look at his reasoning.

Sophism: The Unconventional Philosophy

Sophism is a very controversial kind of philosophy that arises in Athens in the V century. Socrates, even though he uses its rhetorical technique sometimes, believes that its way of thinking is plainly misleading, when not purely dangerous. Plato thinks that it is not even real philosophy, and Aristotle and the subsequent ancient philosopher relegates it as to a lower status discipline. What is so condemnable about this philosophy? Simply the fact that the Sophists broke all the rules of the conventional Greek thought of the time. Greek society, as much as it was the cradle of our democracy and of western though in general, was very conservative when it came to its core values. There were certain traditions that were considered untouchable, even by the most progressive thinkers of the time. But the Sophists decided to challenge these traditions: the Greeks were, customarily, very religious and the belief in the gods was pervasive; the Sophists declare the gods to be an invented (by the powerful) invisible police that is in place to make people behave in a certain way. In a time where Socrates is looking for the truth, and where Greek culture in general is establishing the objective moral truths that will become the norm in western civilization, the Sophists say that morality is convention and that it is relative to the individual beliefs. Moreover, they believe that all knowledge is relative and that there is no such thing as Truth. You can see how this way of thinking could be shocking to the people living in Athens at that time. At the same time, it should not come as a surprise that they were also going against other, less theoretical traditions, like slavery or misogyny. Challenging the norm, at that time, relegated them for a long time to the status of false philosophers, and still today they are considered the odd ones even though their ideas are probably more modern than the ones of other classic philosophers.

It is obvious, for Aristotle, that the soul and the intellect, by nature, control the body and the appetites. In the same way, it is natural that those men in which the intellect is predominant must control the living beings in which the intellect is not predominant. This is the reason why, for example, men must dominate women (another prejudice of the time stated that in men there was more intellect and reason than in women):

> *the male is by nature superior and the female inferior, the male ruler and the female subject. (Ibidem, A 5, 1254b 13–24.)*

Even more evidently, according to this reasoning, all those men that nature has gifted with vigorous bodies, but weak intellect must be, *by nature*, worse and only able to obey, and therefore slaves:

> [. . .] *therefore all men that differ as widely as the soul does from the body and the human being from the lower animal (and this is the condition of those whose function is the use of the body and from whom this is the best that is forthcoming) these are by nature slaves, for whom to be governed by this kind of authority is advantageous, inasmuch as it is advantageous to the subject things already mentioned. For he is by nature a slave who is capable of belonging to another (and that is why he does so belong), and who participates in reason so far as to apprehend it but not to possess it; for the animals other than man are subservient not to reason, by apprehending it, but to feelings. And also the usefulness of slaves diverges little from that of animals; bodily service for the necessities of life is forthcoming from both, from slaves and from domestic animals alike. (Ibidem, A 5, 1254 16–26.)*

This way of thinking, aside from justifying the unjustifiable, is problematic even for Aristotle. Consider, in fact, that most of the slaves at the time, came from war: one of the terrible consequences of losing a war was that all prisoners and sometimes the entire people of a City would be enslaved. Aristotle knows, though, that war can be unjust, and that a prisoner can be noble (and intellectually gifted), and a fellow Greek completely undistinguishable from the other men gifted with intellect. In all these cases, slavery is *not* justified by nature. So, who can be enslaved? *Barbarians*, by nature are inferior to Greeks, therefore they can be enslaved. Once again, a prejudice of the time (that all non-Greek people were less rational—if rational at all—than Greek people) permeates Aristotle philosophy. We could be tempted to say: Aristotle was a proponent of slavery, a misogynist, a racist, why should we even look at his philosophy? It is important to understand that while Aristotle is, in our eyes, all the things that we have said, he is also a product of his time just like we are a product of ours. To judge him (and ban his philosophy) according to the standards of today would be anachronistic: judging practices that were normal over two thousand years ago according to our moral and social principles would be not only unjust, but also intellectually improper. This does not mean that we should condone or celebrate Aristotle's view of slavery, misogyny or racism. It simply means that we can read and understand the context in which Aristotle operates and identify his shortcomings, and, at the same time, appreciate his work when he is, *de facto*, foreseeing and shaping the future: the influence that Aristotelian thought has had in Western culture is worth understanding.

Aristotle continues the analysis of the family taking in consideration the ways in which we acquire goods and wealth. He believes that there are three ways of doing so: (a) a *natural* way, that he considers immediate, which consists in activities such as hunting, fishing, herding animals, and cultivating; (b) an *intermediate* way, that he calls mediate, that consists in bartering goods with equivalent goods; and (c) an *unnatural* way that consists in the activity doing business through money, and it uses all possible techniques to increase wealth without any sort of limit. Our Philosopher deems this last way of acquiring wealth and goods dangerous and wrong: this way of doing business puts no limit to the growth of wealth, and whoever partakes in such activity ends up losing sight of the real goal of business that should be to satisfy real needs and not to accumulate wealth. Who does accumulate wealth mistakes a simple mean for an end. Aristotle clearly says:

> [. . .] *some people suppose that it is the function of household management to increase property, and they are continually under the idea that it is their duty to be either safeguarding their substance in money or increasing it to an unlimited amount. The cause of this state of mind is that their interests are set upon life but not upon the good life; as therefore the desire for life is unlimited, they also desire without limit the means productive of life.* (*Ibidem*, A 9, 1257b 38–1258a 2.)

A healthy economy, instead, tries to acquire what is required to satisfy our natural needs which have limits given by nature. Therefore, Aristotle believes that moneylending and any other form of money investment that is intended just to produce more money is wrong and unnatural. Aristotle is warning against making money the center piece of our life: money should be a mean, not the goal of our entire life.

2.2 Citizenship and Citizens

After the analysis of the family as the building block of the state, Aristotle skips the examination of the Village (the second element that constitutes the state) and presents us the issue of the state from another perspective. Considering that the state is made of citizens, Aristotle says, we should try to establish what makes a citizen.

Aristotle is convinced that certain traits that today we assume to be essential for someone to be called a citizen of the state are not essential to citizenship. We assume for example, that in order to be a citizen of a State it is essential to be living in the territory of the state (the City for Aristotle) or to be descending from citizens, or even to have some legal rights. Aristotle declares these characteristics insufficient for someone to be a citizen: direct participation to the political administration of the government (creating laws, applying laws, administer justice, etc.) is the essential characteristic of citizenship.

Individuals are citizens only if they participate *directly* to the government of the City. Consequently, no settler nor foreigner could have ever been a citizen (unless he was granted the privilege of participating in political activities, which never happened in ancient Greece). Not even regular, natural born Greeks, workers could be real citizens: they were free men (they were not slaves, nor foreigner), but they did not have the *time* to dedicate to exercise the functions that are, according to Aristotle, essential to be called citizens; the workers are too busy working to really be citizens. Citizens, in this system, are few whereas all the other people living in the city end up being nothing but tools to satisfy the needs of the citizens proper. Worker and slave are different because the latter only tends to the needs of one man whereas the former tends to public needs, but both are just means, tools.

In Aristotle's mind, *citizens*, to summarize, are only the people that are *actively* involved in political activities; everyone else is only an instrument that provides to the material needs of the society. Only political beings, remember, can live a life worth living, a happy life, therefore, simple working-class people are always to be considered less than happy and living less than desirable lives. On one hand, this concept of the state leads to some sort of elitism that it is hard to conceive for us, and even more difficult to justify; on the other hand, Aristotle's view tells us something really important about the way in which we should organize our time. We don't have to agree with him in regards of the strict rules of citizenship, but we should admit that there is something to the idea that only through participation in political activities (activities that go beyond our immediate biological needs and beyond any sort of accumulation of goods), we can build some sort of legacy that will make our life meaningful. Carving time away from work is essential to live a happy life even in our era, otherwise we will end up living to work, rather work to live.

2.3 Different Constitutions, Polity, and the Golden Mean

The goal of the State is, in synthesis, to historically realize human moral perfection, and to let individuals live the good life. Aristotle establishes (as we just saw) also who can be *naturally* part of the category that we call citizens.

Now he turns his attention to the different forms that the State can take in its actualization; Aristotle examines different *Constitutions*:

> *Now a constitution is the ordering of a state in respect of its various magistracies, and especially the magistracy that is supreme over all matters. (Ibidem, A 6, 1278b 8–10.)*

It is clear to Aristotle that *Sovereign Authority* can be historically realized in different ways, and that depending on the specific forms that the constitution takes, power can be exercised by a single man, by few men, or by the majority of men. This is a way to distinguish between constitutions, but not the only one: each one of these three forms of government can be exercised either correctly or incorrectly. Aristotle says that when the one, or the few, or the many use their power for the *common interest*, then we experience good constitutions; instead, when the one, or the few, or the many use their power to advance their *private agenda*, we have corrupted constitutions. This way Aristotle identifies three kinds of constitutions that he calls good: *Monarchy, Aristocracy*, and *Polity*, to which correspond three forms of degenerated constitutions: *Tyranny, Oligarchy, and Democracy*.

> *Our customary designation for a monarchy that aims at the common advantage is 'kingship'; for a government of more than one yet only a few 'aristocracy' (either because the best men rule or because they rule with a view to what is best for the state and for its members); while when the multitude govern the state with a view to the common advantage, it is called by the name common to all the forms of constitution, 'Polity'. [. . .] Deviations from the constitutions mentioned are tyranny corresponding to kingship, oligarchy to aristocracy, and democracy to polity; for tyranny is monarchy ruling in the interest of the monarch, oligarchy government in the interest of the rich, democracy government in the interest of the poor, and none of these forms governs with regard to the profit of the community. (Ibidem, A 7, 1279a 32–b 10.)*

We have to be careful considering Aristotle's words here. Democracy is a form of corrupted constitution because it favors the good of a specific class (the poor) at the expenses of the common good; Aristotle thinks that the main error in democracy is to believe that because all are equally free, all should be equal in all things. In other words, Aristotle is warning us (like Plato before him) about the danger of demagogy, the form of government where whoever is in power uses buzz words such as "freedom" and "equality" just to advance a specific, private agenda.

Going back to the best forms of government, which one of the three is the best? Aristotle answer is not univocal. First of all, according to our philosopher, we have to understand that all three forms are correct, natural, and, therefore, good: the three constitutions aim solely to the common good. It is possible, though, to make some distinctions:

But if there is any one man so greatly distinguished in outstanding virtue, or more than one but not enough to be able to make up a complete state, so that the virtue of all the rest and their political ability is not comparable with that of the men mentioned, if they are several, or if one, with his alone, it is no longer proper to count these exceptional men a part of the state; for they will be treated unjustly if deemed worthy of equal status, being so widely unequal in virtue and in their political ability: since such a man will naturally be as a god among men. Hence it is clear that legislation also must necessarily be concerned with persons who are equal in birth and in ability, but there can be no law dealing with such men as those described, for they are themselves a law. (Ibidem, A 13, 1284a 3–14.)

Basically, Monarchy would be, ideally, the best form of government, if there was in the city an exceptional man; and Aristocracy, would be, if there was a small group of exceptional men in the city, very good. Unfortunately, these conditions appear rarely (the presence in the city of exceptional people), Aristotle thinks, that realistically we should consider Polity as the best form of government: even if there are no exceptional individuals, in a State we can find amongst the many some men that can alternate in positions of power, and that can exercise power according to the laws and regulations of the State. Polity is a middle ground between Oligarchy and Democracy: in Polity, a multitude is in power (like in democracy) and not a minority (like in oligarchy), but this multitude is not poor (differently from democracy), on the contrary is a wealthy enough multitude that is able to serve the state and to be part of the military. It is obvious, at this point, that Polity has a peculiar place in the political geography designed by Aristotle: this form of government is on a different plain compared to the other two perfect constitutions (monarchy and aristocracy); Polity seems to take away the flaws of the degenerated forms of government and captures whatever there is to save about those constitutions. Polity is the form of government that values the middle class and that, because this class is the one that stays in the middle—it does not identifies with the rich or the poor—it offers the better chances of stability:

surely the ideal of the state is to consist as much as possible of persons that are equal and alike, and this similarity is most found in the middle classes; therefore the middle-class state will necessarily be best constituted in respect of those elements of which we say that the state is by nature composed. And also this class of citizens have the greatest security in the states; for they do not themselves covet other men's goods as do the poor, nor do the other classes covet their substance as the poor covet that of the rich; and because they are neither plotted against nor plotting they live free from danger. Because of this it was a good prayer of Phocylides—"In many things the middle have the best; Be mine a middle station." It is clear therefore also that the political community administered by the middle class is the best, and that it is possible for those states to be well governed that are of the kind in which the middle class is numerous, and preferably stronger than both the other two classes, or at all events than one of them, for by throwing in its weight it sways the balance and prevents the opposite extremes from coming into existence. (Ibidem, A 11, 1295b 25–38.)

This concept of middle ground is not new for the Aristotelian system: already in ethics the philosopher had established that the virtues are nothing but the golden mean between two extremes. The fact that the best form of government seems to be the one that tempers the excesses of the others, it is, therefore, coherent within the Aristotelian canon.

2.4 The Ideal State and the Role of Education

Aristotle in the last two chapters (books) of his *Politics* focuses on the illustration of what he calls the ideal state. We have to be careful here: the philosopher is not painting for us a Utopia, just like Plato does in the republic; on the contrary, Aristotle, when he talks about the ideal state, has in mind actual practical rules to implement in order to make a real, historical State, functioning the best way possible.

We can divide the work of these last books in two different parts: a first one, where Aristotle delineates the goal of the State; and a second one where he gives us the "material condition" for the realization of a good State. Let's take a look, first, at the goal of the State.

In his *Nicomachean Ethics*, Aristotle makes it clear that there are different kinds of goods, three to be precise. He calls them *external* goods, *bodily* goods, and *spiritual* goods: external goods are, according to Aristotle, friends, offspring, a good family, etc.; bodily goods are physical pleasures such as good food, sex, sleep, but also good health; spiritual goods are what he calls the virtues of the soul, traits of character that lead us to happiness and to a life of philosophical contemplation.

Aristotle is convinced that external goods and bodily goods are not as important as spiritual goods to achieve *Eudaimonia* (good, happy life)—in fact he believes that only spiritual goods are proper of human beings and can make them happy—but he believes also that without the first two kinds of goods complete happiness is impossible:

Nevertheless it is manifest that happiness also requires external goods in addition, as we said; for it is impossible, or at least not easy, to play a noble part unless furnished with the necessary equipment. For many noble

actions require instruments for their performance, in the shape of friends or wealth or political power; also there are certain external advantages, the lack of which sullies supreme felicity, such as good birth, satisfactory children, and personal beauty: a man of very ugly appearance or low birth, or childless and alone in the world, is not our idea of a happy man, and still less so perhaps is one who has children or friends that are worthless, or who has had good ones but lost them by death. As we said therefore, happiness does seem to require the addition of external prosperity. [. . .]
(Aristotle, *Nicomachean Ethics*, A 8, 1099a 31b 7.)

External and bodily goods are just means to the complete realization of spiritual goods, which, again, are the only ones that can lead us to *Eudaimonia*. This is true, according to Aristotle, of the individual person, and of the State: The State also, in fact, must seek in a limited way external and bodily goods (and only in function of the spiritual ones), while pursuing vigorously the spiritual ones; this is the only way to achieve happiness.

For external goods have a limit, as has any instrument (and everything useful is useful for something), so an excessive amount of them must necessarily do harm, or do no good, to its possessor; whereas with any of the goods of the soul, the more abundant it is, the more useful it must be—if even to goods of the soul not only the term 'noble' but also the term 'useful' can be properly applied. And broadly, it is clear that we shall declare that the best condition of each particular thing, comparing things with one another, corresponds in point of superiority to the distance that subsists between the things of which we declare these conditions themselves to be conditions. Hence inasmuch as our soul is a more valuable thing both absolutely and relatively to ourselves than either our property or our body, the best conditions of these things must necessarily stand in the same relation to one another as the things themselves do. Moreover it is for the sake of the soul that these goods are in their nature desirable, and that all wise men must choose them, not the soul for the sake of those other things. Let us then take it as agreed between us that to each man there falls just so large a measure of happiness as he achieves of virtue and wisdom and of virtuous and wise action: in evidence of this we have the case of God, who is happy and blessed, but is so on account of no external goods, but on account of himself, and by being of a certain quality in his nature; since it is also for this reason that prosperity is necessarily different from happiness—for the cause of goods external to the soul is the spontaneous and fortune, but nobody is just or temperate as a result of or owing to the action of fortune. And connected is a truth requiring the same arguments to prove it, that it is also the best state, and the one that does well, that is happy. But to do well is impossible save for those who do good actions, and there is no good action either of a man or

of a state without virtue and wisdom; and courage, justice and wisdom
belonging to a state have the same meaning and form as have those virtues
whose possession bestows the titles of just and wise and temperate on an
individual human being. (Aristotle, *Politics*, H 1, 1323b 7–36.)

Now that we know that the goal of the State is to conduct us to happiness,
we can look at what Aristotle thinks are the necessary practical "applications" to achieve this goal. He says that there are various fields that need to
be regulated to arrive to *Eudaimonia*, if we want to have a functional State
we need to be concerned with: (a) *population*, (b) *territory*, (c) *quality of the
citizens*, (d) *essential work within the city*, (e) *education*.

A. Population is the first necessary condition for the existence of a State: without subjects to govern there is no government. Population cannot be too
small or too big, but it has to be just the right amount. A State that has too
little number of citizens, in fact, it will not be self-sufficient whereas a State
that is built to succeed needs to be self-reliant. On the other end of the spec-
trum, a State that has too many citizens will be difficult to govern: no one
can be in charge of an army that is too big, no news can be delivered coherently to all citizens, and, most importantly, the citizens will be strangers to
one another and will not create a real community where everyone tends to
his task. Aristotle thinks, in conclusion, that a State has to be, population
wise, moderate in order to favor the existence of a real community.
B. The territory of the State, similarly to its population, will be big enough
to fulfill the needs of people's lives, without producing anything superfluous. It should be defendable and in a favorable position when considering
its position in relation to the hinterland and the ocean.
C. The citizens will need to have certain qualities that make them superior
to all others (and, no surprises here, Aristotle think that the Greeks have
these qualities): they need to be rational, intelligent, but also spirited and
fierce, and, finally, they need to live in freedom.
D. There are some functions that within a State are considered essential. To
exist and prosper a State needs: *farmers* to produce food, *artisans* to build
tools and products, *warriors* to defend itself from internal and external
enemies, *businessmen* to produce wealth, *philosophers* to establish what
useful to the community and what rights and obligation citizens have to
each other, *priests* to administer religious cults. A good government will
not allow every citizen to partake in all of these activities: there should be
rules to regulate who does what and what kind of lifestyle citizens should
really live by. Citizens should not live the lifestyle of farmers or workers or
businessmen: these ways of living are unworthy of a virtuous life because
they don't live enough freedom or free time to the people. For this reason,
the farmers would be slaves, and the workers and the businessmen will not

be considered proper citizens. True citizens will only concern themselves with war, government and religion. The younger citizens will be appointed to take care of the "war affairs" because they are strong whereas the administration of politics, that requires wise people, will be left to the older. In time, the young (when they age) will eventual be part of the political decisions. True citizens will follow a common career path: they will be first warriors, then politicians, and finally priests. All of them will be relatively wealthy, and because farmers, workers and businessmen will take care of all material needs, citizens will have enough free time to dedicate their whole life to realization of *Eudaimonia*. In this system, obviously, only the citizens will enjoy a fully happy human life. All other groups (the majority of the people living within the State) will be condemned to live a subhuman life, where they are just tools, means, to the realization of other people *Eudaimonia*. Aristotle is implying that, by nature, the necessary condition for a small worthy group to achieve real happiness is the "subhuman condition" of the majority of the people.

E. Finally, the happiness of the city depends on the Virtue, that inhabits every citizen. Therefore, the State can become (and be) happy only if each citizen is virtuous. How can we make sure that single citizens can become virtuous? Aristotle says: first we need a natural disposition. Only if a man has in himself the ability to become virtuous, he will become virtuous. Aristotle here is saying something powerful and simple at the same time, he is saying that we cannot go against nature and that no matter what we do we cannot learn something that is not in our natural predisposition. An example to clarify: no matter what we do, or how hard we try, we can *never* learn to fly; we are lacking the main physical dispositions to do so (we don't have wings, our bones are too heavy, etc.). The same, for Aristotle, is true about virtues: if we don't have the right "spiritual" characteristics, we cannot acquire any virtue. Natural disposition is essential, but not sufficient to become virtuous; we also need to make it a habit of behaving virtuously aiding ourselves with reasoning and customs. This is, for the philosopher, the essence of education. All citizens should be educated in the same way because the virtue of a good citizen is the same as the more general virtue of a good man, and education should have as its goal to create good men.

A corresponding classification we shall also pronounce to hold among its activities: the activities of the part of the soul that is by nature superior must be preferable for those persons who are capable of attaining either all the soul's activities or two out of the three; since that thing is always most desirable for each person which is the highest to which it is possible for him to attain. Also life as a whole is divided into business and leisure, and war and peace, and our actions are aimed some of them at things necessary and useful, others at things noble. In these matters the same principle of preference that applies to the parts of the soul must apply also to the activities of those parts: war must be for the sake of peace, business for the sake of leisure, things necessary and useful for the purpose of things noble. The statesman therefore must legislate with all these considerations in view, both in respect of the parts of the soul and of their activities, and aiming more particularly at the greater goods and the ends. And the same principle applies in regard to modes of life and choices of conduct: a man should be capable of engaging in business and war, but still more capable of living in peace and leisure; and he should do what is necessary and useful, but still more should he do what is noble. (Ibidem, H 14, 1333a 26–b 3.)

For this reason, education should be administered by the state, and not by private institutions. At first the State will educate the body of the citizen, because bodies develop before reason; then it will educate instincts, appetites, and impulses; finally, it will train the intellect. A Greek traditional education (gymnastics and music) is deemed, by Aristotle, to be the best possible way of achieving these educational goals. It is worth mentioning that the only people participating in any sort of education are the *true* citizens: all other classes (farmers, worker, businessmen) are excluded. In fact, any sort of technical or professional education is absurd for Aristotle: a professional education is by definition an education that will benefit the things that are useful to men and not men themselves. In other words, Education should serve men to become fully men, and not to learn a practical skill or to make money. The real goal of education should be to form men and guide them toward *Eudaimonia*.

While this way of thinking about the State in general, and education in particular, seems noble and interesting, we cannot forget that at the foundation of this system Aristotle poses the condition that the majority of the people have to live a subhuman life, and that a considerable part of these people will be property of other people, will be slaves.

Toolbox

Language as a Mean of Discrimination

The Ancient Greeks, we have seen, thought of themselves as the depositary of the only real truth and perfect morals, and considered everyone else, whomever was not Greek, irrational, uncivilized, ignorant, and therefore, subhuman. All this should come as a surprise, considering that this population, was so advanced intellectually and scientifically, and these people were otherwise so curious and interested in different customs. How could have the Greeks, with their inquisitive and democratic minds, justified their belief that all Non-Greeks were so different from them that they could be utilized as tools, as slaves?

The answer to this question is obviously complex and multifaceted. One thing, though, seems clear: the material evidence on which the Greeks founded their racist claims was the inability of these strangers to speak proper Greek. Language was the basic element that proved, according to the Ancients, the intellectual inferiority of the strangers. *Barbarian*, after all, literally means non-speaking Greek. This idea of a "verbal" racism might seem bizarre to us, but, if we think about the whole intellectual system on which the Greeks founded their civilization, we will soon realize that it makes perfect sense.

The Greeks live in a "cultural world" where everything is objectively knowable and where everything has its natural place in the universe. Nothing happens by chance and everything is ordered according to immutable laws (think the world of forms by Plato or the natural world by Aristotle). They believed that thoughts were not just products of a physical brain, but rather that they were images of real objective things that existed on a rational plain, and that could be discovered thanks to our intellect if we follow specific rational rules. Words, and therefore, language in general, did not escape this general logic. When we talk, most of the time we describe reality (the world outside of us) or we express our thoughts (the world inside of us, based on the true reality that is out there). Language is, in summary, the representation of thought and it has to represent it faithfully by expressing rationality and harmony in all of its parts: the grammatical structure, the syntax, and even the sound. Now, if there is only *one* reality that can be discovered only by *one kind* of (rational) thought, it is only natural that there must be only *one* language that can rationally represent this reality, and that with this reality shares the quality that we can call *intelligibility*. Whomever is unable to speak this language, obviously, in the eyes of the ancient Greeks lacks the intellectual abilities to represent and fully grasp the true nature of reality, of morality, of democracy, etc. Therefore, he cannot be considered really human (rationality is a main characteristic of human beings) and he can be enslaved.

PART 2

THE MODERN CONCEPT OF SOCIETY AND POLITICS

Premise to Part 2

We have seen how Plato and Aristotle inscribe social and political activities within the realm of what they call the Good. For the Ancients, politics and ethics are inseparable: some of them might consider one subordinate to the other, but all of them connect the two. There is, at that time, the general belief that a government can be good or bad depending on the quality of life and the amount of freedom that it is able to produce for its citizens. At the same time, we have seen, there is the idea that whomever is going to be in charge of the *res publica* needs to have recognizable superior qualities that would make him (or more rarely her) the perfect individual (or group of individuals) to lead the population. All philosophies agree that a good leader will make a good state, and that a good state will produce the conditions of freedom and prosperity (not necessarily material prosperity) to let the citizens live a good life.

Governments exist, in the mind of the Ancients, simply to realize the raw (we would say biological) potential, that every human being possess, to live a good life. Governments are, in other words, the *humus* on which human excellence can grow. The political organization is seen as the natural way in which people come together, to the point that a "society" separated from its political context (an association of all people that is not political) is impossible even to think for the Ancient Greeks. It is within *human nature* the necessity to organize and participate directly to the political activities of the State. Human nature *is* to be political.

Rulers and Governors, at the same time, exist to fulfill their potential as human beings, and to lay and maintain the rules that will help the whole population to live the perfect human life. Doing the common good is the only way of doing *the good*. The only thing on the mind of the Ruler should be the happiness of his people and the greatness of his City (note that the two are exactly the same thing). If a Ruler is following his own interest, then he is either a tyrant or a non-virtuous man that needs to be educated or removed from power. The Ancients were very rigid about this point: some people will try to seize power just because they like it, or because they believe that power can help them achieve whatever egoist goal they want to achieve; therefore, we need to put some rules in place to prevent that, and if a tyrant "happens" we should always have a plan for how to remove this person from power or for changing this person mind. Good States and good Politicians, in a formula, are defined by their natural disposition toward the common good.

Things do radically change with the advent of what we can call the *modern concept of politics and society*. Toward the end of the fifteenth century, we see a shift in the concept of political organization, political power, and in general, in the idea of politics. For the first time, in fact, politics will be separated *officially* from ethics and *unofficially* from religion. Ethics will not be part of the political discussion anymore, and instead of discussions on the Good or Justice in ethical terms, we see an emphasis on security and economy that either did not exist before or that was explicitly considered out of the realm of politics. Religion and the laws of God will still nominally be present in the discussion of politics, but its role will be merely complementary if not formal. While we will often see mentioned God and God given rights, we will rarely see a political argument based on God's authority.

Governments, in this era of political thought, are not the natural entities fruit of the inescapable political nature of human beings. They are, rather, artificial being created to absolve specific functions: States are created to protect people from themselves, to protect their natural rights, to make the people wealthy, to do the will of the people that otherwise will remain undone etc. Human nature itself is not, anymore, the general *being political* described best by Aristotle, but becomes a series of traits that determine the natural disposition of humans to be good or bad. Depending on the author, we will see how human beings are represented in their pre-political natural state either as evil, violent and destructive or as good hearted, gentle beings. And this is probably one of the biggest differences between the way of thinking of the ancients and the way of thinking of the moderns: there is no pre-political stage in the evolution of human beings for the Greeks, humans exist naturally in political communities. For the Moderns, instead, the political stage comes after what they would call the state of nature.

Furthermore, the qualities of the Ruler change: he does not have to be necessarily morally virtuous or do what is best for his subjects in the traditional sense: keeping the power and its role might be *the* quality that makes him a good ruler. There no more connection between the good character of the politician and the goodness of the state. As long as certain goals are met (the goals will vary depending on the author of the philosophical theory) the Ruler must be considered a good ruler.

We will see how this way of intending Politics and Society will be much more familiar to us than the one described in the previous part of this volume.

Specifically, we will analyze in this part the philosophy of eight very different theorists covering a time frame of almost six hundred years. The first philosopher that we will study will be **N. Machiavelli**. He will be the one that more clearly than others will spell for us the complete separation between ethics and politics, he will tell us what the real goal of a good Ruler should be. After Machiavelli, we will describe the political thought of **T. Hobbes**. This British philosopher will help us understand the new idea of government as a contract between individuals, and the extent of the power of the ruler while providing us with a bleak description of human nature and the pre-political stage in which humans used to live. We will then turn our attention to **J. Locke**. He also gives us a description of Contractualism and of the pre-political stage in human development, but he also provides us with the idea that there are certain rights that are inalienable from us just because they are naturally connected with humanity. We will then meet the thought of **J-J. Rousseau**. Another Contractualist, Rousseau gives us an alternative take on pre-civilized life, natural rights and education. Toward the end this section, we will analyze a science born during the enlightenment, **Political Economy** and the critique of this science by **K. Marx and F. Engels**. The fathers of political economy describe the good of a nation and the well being of people in purely economic terms giving politics a dimension that will be very familiar to us. Marx, on the other hand, will provide us with the tools to radically criticize and analyze this new idea of State and the system that originates from it, Capitalism. Finally, we will take a look at **Philosophical Anthropology** in the works of **H. Plessner** and controversial historical and political figure **C. Schmitt**. The theoretical way inaugurated by philosophical anthropology will be very prominent during the first half of the twentieth century and it will influence one way or another, many contemporary philosophers.

Politics without Justice

3 Machiavelli on the Different Kinds of Principalities

Niccolò Machiavelli (1459–1527) participates to the history of political thought in a very different way compared to the ancient Greeks or even to his contemporaries. We will see throughout this chapter how he radically changes the debate over politics and how these changes have become, with time, permanent. We can say that politics, the way we intend it today, has more connections with the ideas expressed by Machiavelli than the ideas expressed by Plato or Aristotle. Machiavelli's book, *The Prince*, can be considered a practical guide to how to understand politics and the art of being a politician. The book has been described at the same time revolutionary and scandalous, immensely wise and terribly cynical. The truth is that this book is both famous and infamous and can be defined using any and all of those four adjectives. We will see, in details, in what consists the revolutionary nature of this book when compared with the tradition in political thought up to the time in which Machiavelli lives, and we will try to establish if the book is really as scandalous as tradition reports.

Machiavelli, wanting to make an analysis that is not just theoretical starts *The Prince* by introducing *principalities* (the form of government that he is using to describe political organization and the extent of political authority) to us stating that all of governments that have held power or that hold power over people are either principalities or republics, he then divides principalities in two different kinds: *hereditary* ones and *new* ones. These distinctions, between principalities and republics and, within principalities, in hereditary and new, are very significant. Let's analyze first the opposition between principalities and republic.

You might remember how for Plato and Aristotle there are different ways in which human beings can organize themselves politically. Traditionally, the Ancients mention at least six different forms of government, some good, some "degenerated," but still different one from the other. Machiavelli immediately distances himself from the political tradition by saying that there are only two kinds of real historical incarnation of political power: republics and principalities. He also does not distinguish between corrupted forms of government and good ones: we will see that Machiavelli does not make this distinction purposely, because he thinks that governments cannot be corrupted or honest: ethical adjectives do not apply to political power. The distinction the he makes, instead, is the one between hereditary principalities and new principalities. And after describing hereditary principalities as the ones where "the bloodline of their lord has been their prince for a long time" and telling us that he will not talk about republics because he has done so somewhere else (in reality he will talk about republics, just not at length), he immediately states that he wants to examine how these principalities (hereditary and new) should be governed and maintained. Again, Machiavelli here is not interested in describing how principalities should be in order to be good for their citizens, but rather in how, the *prince*, should govern and keep power. For this reason, Machiavelli's first point will be that between hereditary and new principalities the first ones are easier to keep and maintain, while the second ones are more challenging when it comes to maintain power.

New principalities are difficult to maintain especially if they are *mixed*: added to another through conquest to one already in place. This is, according to Machiavelli, because the new prince will never be able to quite the discontent that arises with the conquest. The reasons for these difficulties are two: firstly, Machiavelli thinks that when a conquest takes place there is always a degree of complicity from the inside of the new province, where there is some sort of discontent within the population against the power in place. For this reason, when a new prince comes in place, it will be difficult for him to live up to the expectations of the conquered population, because when a population rebels it does so hoping that the change will benefit them, but, usually, it is soon discovered that the change did not bring the benefits hoped for. The second issue with mixed principalities is that when conquering a new "province," one always has to *offend* (to do something wrong to) the people living in the newly conquered territory to impose order. This brings some unwanted consequences: the people who were the Prince's friends, who "opened the gate" for the him, because they soon realize that he is not necessarily the agent of change that have expected turn on him; the people that did not push for the change because they still perceive the prince as an invading force and remain against him. At this point, in a classic (ancient or medieval) treatise of politics the author would explain how a prince can be considered good, soon after the conquest, by showing that he is Just or by putting in place laws that are in agreement with the ideal Justice, or with the laws of nature or of God. Machiavelli, instead, goes in a different, completely new, direction: he does not tell us about abstract principles or the good character of the prince or how to have the population benefit from the new *regime*; on the contrary, he tries to show us what kind of *strategies* and, in general, what can *benefit* someone who wants to keep the newly conquered principality. Machiavelli says, for example, that it is easier to maintain control over new states acquired when they share the same customs and language as the occupying force: when the main customs remain the same, even if other things change, men tend to live quietly. But when the new acquisition is not of the same language, customs and order it is difficult to keep the people under the same government: *great luck and industry is needed*. In other words, when occupying a new place, the prince should choose carefully: it is better to expand in territories where the population has, more or less, the same habits as the one of the occupying force. If that is not the case, there will be the need for the prince to be lucky, to spend a lot of resources and to be very cunning in order to keep the new conquest. One way of keeping this new conquest, according to Machiavelli, is for the prince to go and live in the new territory. This way one can avoid several problems: the abuse from his own officials of the new population, the possibilities of complains and conspiracies against the prince and the new order, and the lack of real contact with the new subjects. In fact, being in the new principality will be good for the ones that need the prince's help because if he is readily available, they will love him more; but it will also be good for the ones that would like to conspire against him, because if he is present they will be more fearful. Also, if a new occupying force would want to take the newly acquired principality, they will hesitate, because a prince loses the province where he lives with great difficulty.

There is also another way of keeping the new province (that does not imply for the prince to change his residence), which is to send there either *colonies* or a lot of *men at arms*; Machiavelli believes that it is better to send colonies. They are cheaper and give the prince few powerless enemies: the only people that will be "offended", in fact, will be the ones that are dispossessed of their houses and their fields (which will be a small part of the population), but these people will be left poor and dispersed so they can never harm him. *Men should be either caressed or eliminated, because they avenge themselves for slight offenses but cannot do so for grave ones.* Keeping men at arm, instead, produces more discontent and enemies that can come and seek revenge because the entire population suffers when there is a military occupation, and the entire population keeps its means of subsistence and can organize and conspire against the prince; and when everyone is against the prince, he will soon be in ruin. Notice here the radical departure from a classical view of power and politics: the advice for a wise prince is not to make friends or to be just with the new subjects, the suggestion is, rather, to make sure that the new subjects, that will not like him regardless, are made power-less. This could be achieved either by giving them something that they like, which is not always possible, or by taking them out of contention with every mean possible. This is why it is best to send colonies; the moment a prince sends his people to live in the new principality, he is achieving two goals: (1) He is putting in the new territory someone that is faithful to him and that will love him because the prince is giving them a house and land. (2) The prince will "offend" only a small portion of the population that will not be able to rebel because they would have lost everything and will not have the power (physical, political, and financial) to strike back at the prince. In addition, the rest of the population will not partake in any rebellions because they got to keep their keep. The assumption here is that the prince must do whatever it takes to keep his principality, even at the expenses of whomever, no matter how innocent they could be. All wise princes, in fact, should:

> not only have to have regard for the present troubles but also for future ones, and they have to avoid these with all their industry because, when one foresees from afar, one can easily find a remedy from them but when you wait until they come close to you, the medicine is not in time because the disease has become incurable. (Machiavelli, *The Prince*, Ch. III p. 12.)

We can already see here how concepts typical of the previous views of political organization are not taken in consideration here: it is obvious that the concept of Justice, fundamental in Plato, or the concept of Natural Order, or Natural Law, one of the pillars of Aristotle's philosophy is, if not absent, at least reinterpreted. We will see soon, in what this reinterpretation consists. Let's go back, for now, to the necessary means to keep new principalities.

Machiavelli continues his analysis of historical principalities by making another fundamental distinction. He says that principalities have been governed either by one prince, which means that all other people that are part of the government are servants who administer and help govern the kingdom by his favor and appointment; or by a prince and by barons who hold that rank not by favor of the lord, but because their forefathers held their position before them. According to our author, it is more difficult to conquer the first kind, but it is easier to keep it, once conquered. While it is easier to conquer the second kind, it is more difficult to keep it. This is because, when servants and administrators are appointed by obligations to the prince they are less likely to betray him, but once the prince is gone, the new conqueror will be regarded in the same way. In the second case, instead, it is easy to find some baron that for malcontent, want of change, or ambition, will open the gate for the new prince; but it is also difficult to prevent that one (or the very same) of the barons will open the gate to someone else. Once more, when making the distinction between principalities, Machiavelli is not interested in describing which kind will represent the better form of government for the citizens of that state. He is interested in establishing which kind of principalities are easier to conquer and to maintain. The object of the analysis is not the common good, but the security of the prince. This is why, in *The Prince* we find clearly stated, for example, that when acquiring states that are accustomed to living by their own laws and in liberty, one can hold them in three different ways: ruin them, go there to live personally, or let them live by their laws, while taking tribute from them and establish a local oligarchical government faithful to the prince. No mention about the best way to make the principality prosper or to make the citizens happy, actually, quite the opposite, if there is a risk for the prince extreme measures should be taken:

> *In truth there is no secure mode to possess them* [states that are accustomed to live free] *other than ruin them. and whoever becomes patron of a city accustomed to living free and does not destroy it, should expect to be destroyed by it.* [. . .] *In free cities the memory of the freedom and liberty are hard to dissipate.* (*Ibidem*, Ch. V p. 20.)

3.1   The Prince Gains Power in Different ways

Different kind of principalities, we have seen, can make it more or less difficult for a prince to get or to maintain himself in a position of power. The type of principality, though, is just one of the factors in play when it comes to governing a State. The means through which a prince gains power will be also crucial in his success or his ruin.

Machiavelli, like he will do throughout the entire book, looks at history and declares that one can obtain and keep a principality by virtue or fortune, but who has relied less on fortune has maintained himself in power longer. Opportunity and fortune, though, need to be both present even when we talk about the greatest princes. This means that one's rise to power is determined by his character or ability (virtue) and by a certain dose of luck (fortune). Some people have found themselves is position of power, but just by pure luck, and these people, according to Machiavelli, historically have been in power much less than the people that have obtained power mainly based on their virtue. In fact, men that become princes by the path of virtue acquire the principalities with difficulty but keep it with ease. The difficulties arise from the fact that they have to introduce new laws and customs to build their state and their security on solid foundations. It is particularly important to understand that nothing is more difficult to handle (more dangerous) than introducing new laws: the innovator is surrounded by enemies that benefited from the old laws, the citizens who were satisfied with the old regime; and he has *lukewarm* defenders in all those who might benefit from the new law. This *lukewarm-ness* comes partially from the fear that the friends of the new prince might have of the adversaries (they have the current law on their side), and partially from the natural skepticism of men when it comes to new things. The successful innovators are, usually, the ones that after they have convinced the people of the rightness of their cause are able to keep them convinced. To this end, the use of fear or of the military force (or of force in general) is what makes the difference between successful innovators and the ones that are instead unsuccessful. The use of military force is key in keeping consent and build strength to succeed when it comes to start a principality. Notice, once more, how the successful prince does not convince his subjects to accept the innovations thanks to rightness of the policies or the goodness of the laws; he convinces them of the rightness and the goodness of the laws thanks to fear and force. Again, the object of Machiavelli is not to depict a wise prince as a prince that has ideas that would benefit his subject, but rather as someone who knows how to keep power.

We cannot forget about fortune (luck), though, when we talk about gaining power: even the most virtuous of the princes will be ruined if he did not have some luck on his side. But there is an important difference, as Machiavelli noted before, between someone who has some fortune on his side as a complement to his virtue, and someone who acquires power just through fortune. Individuals that become princes solely because of fortune can rarely hold on to power. In fact, these individuals end up in a position of power only when a State is given to them either for money or by the favor of whoever gives it to them. These individuals' position of power rest simply on the fortune or good will of other individuals (let's call them the "donors"), and both of these things are unstable.

> They do not know how to hold and they cannot hold that rank: they do not know how, because if one is not a man of great ingenuity and virtue, it is not reasonable, that having always lived in private fortune, he should know how to command; they cannot hold rank because they do not have forces that can be friendly and faithful to them. (*Ibidem*, Ch. VII p. 26.)

It is interesting to notice how, for Machiavelli, people coming from the private sector that have not previously concerned themselves with politics, and see it just as a mean to acquire more power (this is why they "buy it" with money in the first place, or why they accept it as a mean of payment!), unless they are exceptional, are doomed to be puppets in the hands of more skilled individual and they will, eventually, be eliminated. The odds of political (and in Machiavelli's time physical) survival for an "amateur" prince are very low. This does not mean that all private individuals will end up ruined or will be at the mercy of someone else: all new princes are coming from the private sector, after all. The object of this discussion is, rather, the prince who is not virtuous at all, in fact, in the long run, the prince that acquires power *only* through fortune will not succeed and will be, eventually, out of luck and power.

There are certain means to obtain power, Machiavelli claims, that some people believe would not be correct to attribute completely to fortune or virtue. Two examples of such ways are: political power obtained through *crime*, and political power obtained by *acclamation by the fellow citizens*. As for acquisition through crime, Machiavelli is conscious of the fact that someone might question how anyone can like someone that has acquired power through crime and how is it possible that such individual can hold it for a long time. At this point, Machiavelli introduces to us a concept that is completely alien to the political tradition that comes before him and that still makes some of us cringe. He says, in fact, that we should distinguish between *well used cruelties* that are done at a stroke, out of the necessity to secure oneself, and then are not persisted in, but turned to as much utility for the subjects as one can. On the other hand, there are the *badly used cruelties* that are few in the beginning but grow with time instead of being eliminated.

> [. . .] *it should be noted that in taking hold of a state one who seizes it should review all the offences necessary for him to commit, and do them all at a stroke, so not to have to renew them everyday and, by not renewing them, to secure men and gain them to himself with benefits. Whoever does otherwise, either through timidity or through bad counsel, is always under necessity to hold a knife in his hands; [. . .] injuries must be done all together so that being tasted less they offend less; and benefits should be done little by little so that they may be tasted better.* (*Ibidem*, Ch. VIII p. 38.)

Machiavelli's thought here goes in two different directions: on one side he is telling us that there are *cruelties* that can be considered well used and others that are ill used. Basically, there are no such things as cruelties, but rather that there are certain behaviors that can be considered cruelties when they do not achieve the goal that were supposed to achieve. A crime, when it comes to seizing power, is not really a crime unless it fails to aid the prince to keep his power. When it comes to keeping power there is a list of behaviors that Machiavelli believes are legitimate, here is an example:

> *So whoever judges it necessary in his new principality to secure himself against enemies, to gain friends to himself, to conquer either by force or fraud, to make himself loved and fear by the people, and followed and revered by the soldiers, to eliminate those who can or might offend you, to renew old orders through new modes, to be severe and pleasant, magnanimous and liberal, to eliminate unfaithful military, to create a new one, to maintain friendships with kings and princes so that they must either benefit you with favor or be hesitant to offend you. [. . .]* (*Ibidem*, Ch. VII p. 33.)

All these behaviors are not only *criminal*, they should be used not just by the individuals that want to obtain their principality through crime, but also by the "regular" prince. Acquiring power through crime, properly speaking, is not possible: when one acquires and keeps power for a long time shows that, regardless of the initial means, he is a skillful prince that has used all the means possible to acquire and maintain power.

The other direction of Machiavelli's thought, here, regards when and how to be violent: it is impossible, as we will see in more details later, to seize power without any sort of violence and *cruelty*. Therefore, the important thing, for the prince, should be to understand when and how to use this violence; hence the invitation to be swift and final when it comes to it. Violence and cruelty, to be valuable tools in the hands of the prince, need to be not dictated by passion or irrational urges, but calculated and premeditated. How much violence to use, who exactly to kill, how cruel to be, are all calculations that a prince needs to make before he strikes to take power.

Regarding the people that acquire power through acclamation by fellow citizens, Machiavelli notices how even they should take precautions when it comes to maintaining power. Specifically, he says, what counts is *who* is making you prince by acclamation: it is better to be made prince by people that are inferior to you by rank than by people of your same status. In fact, it is very difficult to rule among equals, while it is easier to lead among people that are already willing to obey. It is easy to satisfy common people whereas it is difficult to satisfy the higher ranks without offending someone: there is always some sort of admiration and acceptance that common people have for someone that they have elected to power, while there is always some sort of resentment amongst peers when one of them is elevated to a position of power. And having a certain degree of favor within the people that are ruled by him it is, for the prince, necessary; to have the people friendly is key, otherwise the prince has no remedy in adversity. At the same time, however, a prince should not base his power on how the people respond to him in times peace

> [the prince should not believe what he sees] *when citizens have the need of the state, because then everyone runs, everyone promises, and each wants to die for him when death is at a distance; but in adverse times, when the state has needed of citizens, then few of them are to be found.* (*Ibidem*, Ch. IX p. 42.)

The goal of a prince, then, it should be to make the state and himself always needed by the people: in war and peace, in times of abundance and in times of scarcity; only then he could be sure of the faithfulness of his subjects. A prince, someone who acquires power, according to Machiavelli, should have as one of his goals to find ways in which his subject will need him. We will see, though, that being needed does not equate with the need of order and safety, or with the need of good guidance that a multitude of people might have in different times; rather this "need of the prince" is functional to the prince himself to keep his position of power.

3.2 Avoiding Ruin and the Art of War

Up to here, Machiavelli has been discussing the quality of all principalities and the way to obtain and keep them. He now turns his attention to the means necessary to build a good foundation to avoid the prince's ruin: how can a prince avoid revolts and revolutions that might dispossess him or be fatal to him? The main way that all states have to avoid ruin are good laws and good military. Moreover, Machiavelli says, because there cannot be good laws where there are not good military, and where there are good arms there are good laws, he will leave out the reasoning on laws and speak of arms. It is important to notice how good laws here does not mean laws that are good for the citizens; if the laws were intended to be good for the citizens, it would not make sense that they are connected with the military strength of the state. It is evident that the premise on which Machiavelli's reasoning rests is that the laws have to be good to keep the prince in power. Proof of this reasoning is the analysis of the different kind of military that the philosopher makes right after. He identifies four kinds of military that one can have defending the principality: *Mercenary, Auxiliary, Own, and Mixed*. Immediately, Machiavelli deems mercenary and auxiliary arms useless and dangerous; and, he adds, if one keeps his state founded on mercenary arms one will never be secure: they are disloyal, without discipline, and have no love nor cause to keep other than the stipend which is never sufficient to make them to want to die for the prince. They want to be soldiers of the state while there is no war, but when war comes they either leave or flee. During Machiavelli's time, mercenary arms were also infamous for looting and robbing their own people and being resilient to respecting the law. It is significant that, while analyzing mercenary arms, there is no mention of these issues, no talks of oppression of good people, or taxes and expenses that have to be paid by the people to maintain the mercenary: the only important issue is the opportunity for the prince to thrive and keep his power. There is more. Let's take this in consideration, Machiavelli says: Mercenary Captains are either excellent men at arms or they are not; if they are, they cannot be trusted because they will always aspire to their own greatness, in contrast with the greatness of the prince, either by oppressing the prince or by oppressing people that the prince has no intention to oppress; but if the captain is not virtuous then he ruins the prince the ordinary way, by not providing the service that he is paid for: defending the prince in times of peril. A prince should always be the captain of his army, and in a republic only the best men should represent the people as a captain, so the soldiers will obey one of their own rather than someone from the outside. No moral judgments about mercenaries here, just opportunity. The essential problem with the *virtuous* mercenary is not his moral character when he pursues his own agenda while he swore to pursue the agenda of the prince. The problem is, to be more precise, that he might be a danger for the prince. The skilled mercenary captain is not wrong to try to achieve greatness at the expenses of the prince (he might very well be a future new prince!); it is the new prince, if he wants to be great and avoid ruin, which has to be careful with the mercenaries. Recapitulating, mercenary armies are useless and dangerous, not for the people but for the prince, because either they don't perform their duty (they flee in time of war) or because they are some sort of enemy force, fed by the state, captained by a man that might want to take the place of the present prince.

Auxiliary arms are defined as the arms of a power that is called to come to help and defend the prince. They also are useless and dangerous. Even if they are great by themselves, when they come to aid the prince they are almost always harmful: if they lose the prince is undone, and if they win then the prince is their "prisoner." Often the winning troops end up looting the city or they never leave and become, de facto, an occupying force. Auxiliary arms are, in Machiavelli's opinion, more dangerous than mercenary ones: they are united under the command of a well-organized principality and can really become a new enemy that seizes power from the prince to give it to the state that they are faithfully serving. A wise prince always prefers to lose with his own arms than to win with someone else's.

> *Without its own arms no principality is secure; indeed, is wholly obliged to fortune since it does not have virtue to defend itself in adversity. [. . .] And one's own arms are those which are those which are composed of either subjects or citizens or your creatures; all others are either mercenary or auxiliary. (Ibidem, Ch. XIII p. 57.)*

Why is it so important, to Machiavelli that the prince has his own army and that he acts as the captain of his army? The answer is given at the beginning of chapter XIV of *The Prince*: a prince should be mainly concerned with the *art of war*: actually, the art of war should be the only art studied by who is in command. This art is so important that not only keeps in power those who has it already, but it also enables men that want to be in power to rise to the rank they want to rise to. On the contrary, the absence of this art is a clear sign of imminent ruin for the powerful. In fact, there is no reason why someone who is armed should willingly obey someone who is unarmed, and that someone who is unarmed will be secure amongst armed servants. Since there is no moral principle to rest on, obedience has to be based on force or fear: this is why having an army is fundamental for the prince to keep his power. In addition, war is inevitable when everyone in power is not after the good of his subject, but his own greatness and rank. Therefore,

A prince should never lift his thought from the exercise of war, and in peace he should exercise it more than in war. (Ibidem, Ch. XIV p. 59.)

The prince can do this in two ways: by practicing and by studying. Practically by keeping his army well-ordered and ready, and by going hunting and exploring his own territory in order to know whatever it is useful to plan defenses of the principality in case of an attack by the enemies, and also to build knowledge that is applicable to similar new terrains. This way when war really comes he will be able to lead his soldiers, taking in consideration the surrounding environment. As for the studying, a prince should study history and analyze the causes of victories and losses in previous wars in order to imitate the winners and avoid the tactics used by the losers. Everything that the prince does should prepare him for the coming adversity: if he wants to avoid ruin, he needs to resist the inevitable changes in fortune and try to hold his rank; this is why studying and practicing offensive and defensive strategies of war is so important.

Machiavelli, we can see it clearly, believes that virtue in a state equals military strength or, at the very least, the ability to defend the principality. Virtue, in the system described in *The Prince*, then is something very different from what is described by Aristotle or Plato; we will see what this means in the next sections.

3.3   The Lion and the Fox

Plato and Aristotle built their political philosophy around two ideal concepts that were kept in high regard by the ancients and that we still consider important today: justice and virtue. Their philosophies aim to show us how we can build an ideal state that would really benefit the citizens of that nation; they say, basically, that the goal of the state should be to enable citizens to be virtuous and to develop their natural potential. They go in details explaining to us how who is in charge (a group of people or even one man) should govern to achieve this goal, and how all aspects of the life of the individuals living in the state should be involved in the process of betterment of life: the structure of the family, the role of education, the involvement of the private citizens in the legislative process and so on.

Machiavelli, on the other hand, does not attempt to formulate such general theory, in fact, he is chiefly interested in

writing something useful to whoever understands it [. . .] many have imagined republics and principalities that have never been seen or known to exist in truth. (Ibidem, Ch. XV p. 61.)

Our philosopher, then, wants simply to describe the best way to govern, without indulging in idealized general principle to build a *Just* or *Virtuous* society. In reality, he seems to believe that not only Just or Virtuous societies and governments do not really exist, but also that *Justice* and *Virtue* in general are not objective concepts to which people have to conform. We have already seen this, partially, when Machiavelli declares that there are no such things as princes that acquire and maintain power through crime, but that there are rather successful princes (that we call legitimate) and unsuccessful ones that we sometimes call criminal. If that is true, the very concept of *criminality* (and conversely the very concept of *Justice*) assumes in Machiavelli's point of view a whole different meaning.

A successful prince, thinks Machiavelli, cannot behave according to lofty ideal—like justice—and disregard reality: a prince should do what needs to be done to seize and keep power and not what *should* be done according to a hypothetical perfect moral world. There is more: the prince that prefers to live according to these "fantasies" ends up experiencing his ruin rather than keeping is power. In addition, if the prince is good natured, he needs to learn how *not* to be good. Therefore, the ideal descriptions of government are useless, especially because they describe false realities where everyone is good, and because they are concerned with the "ideal" good that the prince should achieve. Machiavelli, on the contrary, believes that being good has to be a matter of opportunity, because in world where the majority is not good, the good prince meets his ruin all the times. This way of thinking can be considered an assault on all the traditional views of morality and political science; before Machiavelli, morality was considered the ideal goal of all governments and all governments were supposed to approximate as much as possible the ideal republic or principality. Laws and regulations were considered to be grounded in objective principles towards which society was supposed to move: Justice, Goodness, and, in general, Virtues were the inspiration for the legislator. When Machiavelli denies the existence (and the possibility of existence) of these imagined governments, he also implying, that there are no such things as ideal moral rules that are the "spirit" of the legislations. The rules or laws that exist are the ones made by governments or other powers; these structures of power made these laws by necessity, to keep the power that they have acquired, and people obey them also by necessity, to avoid punishment and ruin. All that these government deem necessary, then, might be called "just" or "reasonable":the concept of Justice ends up simply describing the prudence to do what one must to acquire what he wants and to live safely. Men, Machiavelli thinks, cannot afford Justice in any sense that is detached from their preservation, and princes especially, cannot afford this kind of justice, because it will lead them to ruin.

Machiavellian

The adjective Machiavellian is used today to describe some sort of cunning twisted plan or idea. It is interesting to notice that, while the ideas expressed by Machiavelli in "The Prince" definitely separate the realm of politics and morality, ultimately, commentators have described his philosophy more as a political realism (some sort of science of politics) than a pure teaching of evil. It is true that Machiavelli counsels the prince to avoid values like Justice, wisdom, mercy, and temperance, but it is also true that politics at the time of his life (and still today) seems to have been an especially dirty game. The general consent is that Machiavelli theoretical view of politics is extremely pragmatic and descriptive of what politics really is; all of this in contrast with the almost romantic and utopian view of politics and power expressed by the works of Plato and Aristotle. At first sight, this view seems correct: isn't politics, still today, a game where everything is allowed in order to maintain power? Don't we still think today that compromise and a certain moral "malleability" are necessary characteristics of politicians? The issue is, though, another one. Is it possible that the political reality described by Machiavelli was just an accident in history, and that because he crystallized in a theory, we now consider it normal? In other words, what if the cruelty, the duplicity, the amorality of the politicians at the time of Machiavelli was just a way of intending political activity that flourished under specific circumstances in Tuscany and had nothing to do with the way politics is by nature? There have been other times in history when politics or other human activities have taken a malignant turn, but not always we have normalized them. Nazism and Fascism were endemic ways of intending not just politics, but life, and yet, we do not believe that it was normal. The same thing can be said about racism or slavery, for example. So why have we decided that, in the case of Machiavelli's description of politics and power, instead, we are dealing with the normal way in which we do things? It seems that we believe, almost, that politics has a specific immutable nature, evil in itself. What if, though, politics has crystallized this way because of Machiavelli normalization of it? What if Machiavelli had despised this way of doing politics and described it as a perversion of politics? Would we still believe that politics is a dirty game? Would our political practices be any different? It is hard to say. We know, though, how influential ideas can be and how deeply they can inform our practices; so we should at least take in consideration the possibility that Machiavelli and his Prince might be responsible for some of the bad politics with which we deal today.

Machiavelli, in summary, is convinced that justice does not exists by nature or by God, but that it is merely a tool that the government can use to keep power. At this point it should be clear that the goal of *The Prince* is to show the ruling class that one should govern knowing that there is no natural justice, and that one should act like there was such thing only out of convenience, only because men like to think that it exists.

We need to be, in one word, cynical not just about justice, but also about all virtues intended in the classical way. Therefore, even though it would be "nice" that the princes should have virtues and be exempt from vices, we have to realize that this is impossible; And actually, if one looks at history, one will find that something that appear to be a virtue, if pursued, would be the ruin of the prince, and something else that appears to be a vice, if pursued, would results in the prince security and well-being. Being virtuous is not synonymous of being a good, or morally sound, prince, and if we really want to see the truth we will realize that sometimes being vicious might be better for the prince. Considering that, as we have seen right before, morality is a matter of opportunity, and that what is important is to be perceived in a favorable way, it is licit to wonder how one should behave in order to gain the favor of the people.

> [. . .] *I say that all men, whenever one speaks of them, and especially princes, since they are placed higher, are noted for some qualities that bring them either blame or praise. And this is why someone is considered liberal, someone parsimonious* [. . .]; *someone is considered a giver, someone rapacious; someone cruel, someone merciful; the one a breaker of faith, the other faithful; the one effeminate and pusillanimous, the other fierce and spirited; the one humane, the other proud; the one lascivious, the other chaste; the one honest, the other astute; the one hard, the other agreeable; the one grave, the other light; the one religious, the other unbelieving; and the like.* (*Ibidem*, Ch. XII.)

While it is natural that we would say that the best prince would be the one that, among the qualities mention above, has all the ones that are considered good, the truth is that a good prince would be the one that behaves according to opportunity. Machiavelli shows us what he means, exactly, through an analysis of the pairs of qualities mentioned. He starts by asking if it is better to be liberal and parsimonious and by assuming that people would think that it would be better for the prince to be liberal, so people would love him. Our philosopher believes the opposite: between being liberal or parsimonious a prince should choose to be the latter because liberality will be in time be perceived as stinginess; the prince not to be in financial ruins, in fact, will need to be rigorous with taxes (for example) which it will lead the people to believe that he is not capable to manage his resources. On the contrary, parsimony will eventually lead to the belief that the prince knows what he is doing financially and that he is not as financially demanding of his subjects.

Between being considered merciful or cruel, the Prince should not fear to be called cruel. Cruelty is sometimes more merciful than being merciful. Machiavelli has already made this point: new princes have to kill and offend a lot of people in the very beginning, and if one is merciful and spares some, he will end up killing more people over a longer period of time. Machiavelli is saying here something interesting: in order to appear to possess the good quality of the two taken in consideration, one needs to appear to possess the bad one at the beginning. This does mean that the good quality are the ones to favor, but not because they are objectively good or better than the other ones: these qualities are good because the system of morality put in place by the government deems them good. And it is opportune for the prince to display these qualities.

One of the most important choices that a prince has to take, one that is almost inevitable, is if he wants to be loved or feared. When possible (rarely), a prince should be both, but if he has to lack one, it is better to be feared than loved.

> *For one can generally say of men: that they are ungrateful, fickle, pretenders and dissemblers, evaders of danger, eager for gain. [. . .] And men have less hesitation to offend one who makes himself loved than one who makes himself feared; for love is held by a chain of obligation, which, because men are wicked, is broken at every opportunity for their own utility, but fear is held by a dread of punishment that never forsakes you.* (*Ibidem*, Ch. XII p. 66–67.)

It is better to be feared because human beings are wicked beings. This is a consideration that will go a long way in the modern understanding of politics and society, and that was absent in the ancients; for Aristotle, for example, the *nature* of humans was not something that should have been taken in consideration when talking about politics: all human beings tend by nature to the good, and education is the tool to steer them in the right direction. For Plato, through education we will find the right "placement" for each individual and he will be good just by performing the job (the duty) that he is supposed to perform. Human nature in the sense of the way humans are *Naturally*, outside of government, is not a concern for the Greeks because men almost do not exist outside of the *polis*. Machiavelli, instead, clearly declares that humans are terrible beings, that cannot be trusted and that will obey only because of fear. This way of thinking, and its polar opposite (the idea that men are good by nature), will be the centerpiece of many of the political philosophies that we will study in the next chapters.

Being feared, though, could be also dangerous, therefore, the prince should make himself feared in a way that, if he is not loved, he at least escapes hatred, because *being feared and not being hatred go together very well*. A prince can escape hatred, according to Machiavelli, if he does not interfere with his subjects' property and women. And if, in the event that he has to take someone's life, does so only when there is a good justification and an evident cause for it. But it is more important to stay away from the property of others than from the life of someone, because

> *men forget the death of a father more quickly than they forget the loss of a patrimony.* (*Ibidem*, Ch. XVII p. 67.)

Not taking properties away from the people, then, seems to be the main way of avoiding hatred (one should notice also the fact that women are grouped with properties: misogyny, after all was not a distinctive feature of Aristotle only): even killing seems to be more forgivable than taking someone's wealth away.

Another very important issue regards the alternative between being honest (keeping the faith, in Machiavelli's language) and being dishonest (being astute and disregard his faith, in Machiavelli's language). It is evident, if one looks at history, that the princes that have been *astute* have outlasted, and often defeated, the ones who have been honest. This has happened primarily because in the fight for power there are two kinds of combat: one that occurs through laws and one that is fought with force. The first one, Machiavelli says, is typical of men, the second one of beasts; often, though, the fight through laws is not enough to win and acquire or maintain power, therefore, one must resort to use the beastly one.

> *Therefore, it is necessary for a prince to know well how to use the beast and the man. [. . .] Thus, since a prince is compelled of necessity to know well how to use the beast, he should pick the fox and the lion, because the lion does not defend itself from snares and the fox does not defend itself from wolves. So, one needs to be fox to recognize snares and lion to frighten the wolves. [. . .] A prudent lord, therefore, cannot observe faith, nor should he, when such observance turns against him and the causes that made him promise have been eliminated. (Ibidem, Ch. XVIII p. 69.)*

This is probably the most famous quote from Machiavelli's prince and the meaning of it should be clear: one needs to be astute and display strength like the fox and the lion. Being strong and not astute is not enough, in fact, like a lion is strong but subject to traps that will find him unprepared, a prince that is only displaying strength might find himself caught in someone else's trap. Being astute but not displaying force it is also not good enough because the enemies (the wolves) will never be afraid to try to dispossess whoever is not feared. The combination of the two beasts is, instead, the winning tools for a prince: displaying force scares away the ambitious enemies and being astute prevents the prince from being taken advantage by someone else. For this reason, concludes Machiavelli, the prince should not be honest, and actually seek dishonesty anytime it is convenient for him.

Machiavelli, judging from the previous paragraphs, seems to suggest that the prince is supposed to have all sorts of "qualities" that are necessary to survive in the wicked world that men have created. In reality, he is suggesting something slightly different: it is not necessary for a prince to *possess* all the above-mentioned qualities, but it is indeed necessary that he does *appear* to have them. This should not come as a surprise: Machiavelli has told us already that *displaying* certain quality is necessary for the success of the prince, which is different than saying that is good to have these qualities. Having them and always observing them, in fact, might be harmful, while appearing to have them, might be useful: coherence could be equated to predictability and might harm the prince rather than aid him.

Men in general judge more by their eyes than by their hands, because seeing is given to everyone, touching to few. Everyone sees how you appear, few touch what you are. (Ibidem, Ch. XVIII p. 70–71.)

Appearing to have certain qualities is better than having them because, if you are just "faking it," you are not bound by any principle and will do what is needed without having any sort of remorse, or internal conflict. In addition, few end up really knowing you whereas many will see how you appear, so it is more important, Machiavelli argues, the way you are perceived than the way you really are.

3.4 The Role of Fortune in Human Affairs

Perception is everything for the prince, but why? What is at stake here? The reason why someone has to appear to have certain qualities is to avoid hatred by the people, which is of the highest importance for the prince. Avoiding hatred, it is obvious at this point, is necessary not because the prince should care about his subjects, but because having the people by his side is necessary to keep power for a long time. Specifically, the prince has to avoid hatred, so he can be safe against outside forces and against internal conspirators.

In the effort to avoid hatred a prince should follow some rules: one of them is that whatever subject he feels it might be controversial and cause hatred by the people, he should have it administered by someone else that can be eventually blamed for the decision made: scapegoating it is not only acceptable but encouraged by Machiavelli. Moreover, princes should never disarm their subjects, otherwise they will think that he is afraid of them, and this will bring hatred, or they will think that he distrusts them, and this also brings hatred. There is an exception to this rule and it regards the acquisition of a State that was part of an old one: then the prince needs to disarm the people, even the ones that are evidently on his side. Because, as we have seen, they might eventually revolt against the prince.

Avoiding hatred is of supreme importance but achieving the appearance of *greatness* it is also necessary for the stability of the principality. Therefore, a prince should "nourish" some enemy so that when he defeats them he can claim greatness from the battle. An astute prince will always nurture some enemy that he can defeat. Cultivating some enemies to defeat is important because, according to Machiavelli, military power is chiefly important for the prince: showing off some power is always important to be feared and to reinvigorate the army, the lion has to be seen from time to time. Still for the sake of greatness, the prince should, from time to time, try to win over someone that was previously his enemy: this way the fox can be seen at work and people will consider him a great politician. In conclusion, Machiavelli says that nothing makes a prince more esteemed than leading great enterprises and making himself an example to follow. In addition, a prince is esteemed when he has true friends and true enemies (once again, friends and enemies are here to be intended has allies and enemies, friendship, as an abstract virtue does not exist or does not matter). This means that when two powers close to the principality clash in war it is always better for the prince to *declare* himself and to choose publicly a side rather than to stay neutral. If the prince stays neutral, in fact, he will always be in danger of being dispossessed of his power by the winner: a wise prince will not sacrifice on the altar of the present peace the future existence of the principality and his power.

But even with all the advices and the precautions that a prince might take to try to be great and stay in power, there might be something that it is out of his control. There are some elements within human existence that cannot be foreseen, and that are absolutely casual. The totality of these unpredictable events is called by Machiavelli *Fortuna* (fortune or luck in English). He thinks that we can estimate that fifty per cent of what happens in the world can be considered to be under the influence of luck, while the other fifty percent can be considered to be controlled by men. If this is true, though, even if the prince follows all the rules that Machiavelli lays for him, there is still a great chance that he might not be successful. Well, fortune plays a big role in human affairs, but men can do something to mitigate the consequences of bad luck.

> *I liken her* [fortune] *to one of these violent rivers which, when they become enraged, flood the plains, ruin the trees and the buildings, lift earth from this part, drop in another; each person flees before them, everyone yields to their impetus without being able to hinder them in any regard. And although they are like this, it is not as for men, when times are quite, could not provide for them with dikes and dams so that when they rise later, either they go by a canal or their impetus is neither so wanton nor so damaging. (Ibidem, Ch. XXV p. 98.)*

Fortune can and must be accounted for in human affairs and not doing so is a mistake that humans can blame on themselves. When it comes to princes, especially, it is necessary that they are able to prepare for times in which fortune will not be on their side: leaning completely on fortune means ruin as soon as the fortune varies. But how should a prince (or a man in general) be prepared for the times where lady luck is not on his side? What causes princes not to prepare for such times? The main issue detected by Machiavelli is the inability that men have to change. People get stuck in their ways and follow principles that have served them good in the past. What they fail to understand is that one should never be fixed in his ways and he should always go with the flow of the times: if one tries to go against the current, he will be ruined. A man should not let a quality become his nature. One needs to adapt to change, and this ability to develop flexibility according to the times and situations can be considered, probably, the new meaning that Machiavelli gives to politics.

Toolbox

Aristotelian Virtues vs Machiavellian Virtues

Aristotle idea of virtue is fairly simple. Human beings have different traits of character, but these qualities will be virtuous only if who possesses them exercise them in the "right" amount. For example, being courageous means not to be a coward (a coward is defective of courage) nor to be foolhardy (that would be an excess of courage). The Virtue, in a formula, is a mean between two extremes. Human beings have to learn to be virtuous in order to achieve happiness. Also, virtuous men, in Aristotle's system, are the preferable ones to be in charge of the government: virtuous people make virtuous cities.

Machiavelli, on the other hand, wishes to set himself apart from the Aristotelian tradition (as well as from the Christian tradition). His idea of virtue runs parallel to Aristotle's one (the number of virtues mentioned by Machiavelli is the same—eleven—as Aristotle's): For Machiavelli, in fact, the importance to posses certain virtues is relative: *virtuous* for the prince are those characteristics that help him to stay in power. Just like in Aristotle the virtues need to be learned, better, a prince needs to learn how to *show*, how to *appear*, virtuous without necessarily be it. The virtues are "virtuous" only if they effectively bring an advantage to the prince. In other words, virtues are not *good feelings* or *ideal* traits of character, they are effective means to gain and/or acquire power.

CHAPTER 4

The State of Nature

4 Hobbes and the Natural Equality Amongst Men

Thomas Hobbes (1588–1679) is regarded as one of the founders of modern political thought and his contributions are pivotal for the continuation of our philosophical journey. In his book *Leviathan*, in fact, he elaborates a coherent modern version of the *social contract theory* that is considered highly influential for many of the political theories (not all of them agreeing with Hobbes' version of the *contract*) that come after the book was published.

Hobbes understanding of politics, and human association in general, is particularly original because it starts not with examination of the already associated people (like it was custom for the ancient thinkers, for example, where political activities were considered already part of human nature and therefore, inalienable from the people living in the City), but with the analysis of the condition in which humans lived *before* they associated themselves together to form a political community. Specifically, Hobbes starts with an exposition of the nature of human beings in an almost *biological* sense considering first the way human beings think, feel, and communicate, defining them as rational and passional animals, we could say. Human beings, in fact, are naturally rational, but are also driven by very strong urges that are difficult to keep under control. The reasons why Hobbes starts his analysis in such a peculiar way are at least two: firstly, he needs to establish, as a foundation of his political thought, that human beings are capable of reason, but that they are also, like other animals, driven by passions that are strong and difficult to control in a natural setting. Secondly, he needs to go in details when explaining how we work as individuals because, as we will see, he will compare the State to a well-formed man with all the "biological" characteristics that such men should have.

Hobbes, after more than ten chapters of meticulous analysis of thoughts and passions (and the systems that govern and regulate them, like science and "discourse"), moves to the analysis of men considered not anymore in their *singularity*, but rather as in *relation* to each other. The first observation that he makes regards the way in which men are born in *nature*; he says, in fact, that nature has made humans equal both in body and mind. All human beings come into existence with the same abilities, mentally and physically. Regarding men's physical abilities, we should not be deceived by the fact that someone might appear obviously stronger than someone else; the difference between the strongest and the weakest is, nonetheless, very limited: the weakest of men can always kill the strongest (through conspiracies or alliances or by building a weapon). Regarding men's mental capacities, Hobbes says, there is no more obvious example of equality than the fact that everyone is convinced to be wiser than all others, even though there is no true way of establishing if someone is wiser or smarter than someone else. This equalities in abilities lead to another kind of sameness: all humans, in fact, equally hope to achieve their goals. But if people are all equal in strength and smarts and if they all hope to get what they want, it is easy to see how if two men want the same thing, but cannot both have it, they will try to destroy each other or to dominate each other in order to achieve what they want. It is also reasonable, then, to think that when someone possesses something (land, a house, etc.) others might arm themselves and try to come and take it from her, and maybe, also, take her life. But, if this is true, then the aggressor should also be aware that the same can happen to him.

This is how men become *diffident*: diffidence is the sentiment that motivates men to not to trust each other and that leads men to always be vigilant or to try to anticipate whatever evil can come from someone else's conduct. For this reason, Hobbes notes, there is nothing more *natural* than to act preemptively and to try to dominate (through violence or dishonesty) as many men as one can until there is no one that has enough power to threaten his well-being. This is perfectly permissible, in nature, because this is the only way to conserve one's own life, and men have the *right* to try to defend themselves to keep alive.

Because of this natural distrust among themselves, men do not like to live in groups. But diffidence is not the only issue here: everyone, in fact, also wishes to be appreciated by the others in the same way in which one appreciate himself. And at any sign of disrespect the individual, naturally, will try to get more respect by the others by damaging them, in order to show the others what happens when someone disapproves of him. So, Hobbes says, from what we have observed regarding the relationships among men, it is evident that in human nature we can find three causes of contest: *Competition* (when two or more men want the same things), *Diffidence* (when two or more men do not trust each other), and *Glory* (when two or more men want to be respected by the same people). The first brings men to attack to gain an advantage, the second to gain security, and the third one for reputation. In the case of competition, men result to violence to become masters of other people and things; in the case of diffidence to defend people and things that they already possess; in the case of glory for every sign of disrespect to them, to their things, to their opinion or to their friends. From this description one can clearly see that, when men are not subject to a common power that they fear, they find themselves in that specific condition that we call *war*: war of every men against every men.

> For WARRE, *consisteth not in Battellonely, or the act of fighting; but in a tract of time, wherein the Will to contend by Battell is sufficiently known: and therefore the notion of Time, is to be considered in the nature of Warre; as it is in the nature of Weather. For as the nature of Foule weather, lyeth not in a showre or two of rain; but in an inclination thereto of many dayes together: So the nature of War, consisteth not in actuall fighting; but in the known disposition thereto, during all the time there is no assurance to the contrary. All other time is* PEACE. (Hobbes, *Leviathan*, Book XIII.)

Hobbes is giving us a definition of war that will go a long way in history: war does not consist only in battle or in the act to face each other in battle, but in a *time* in which the will to fight each other in battle is sufficiently clear. This means that, until there presents some condition of enmity that can concretely bring a real violent battle, people are in a state of war. In history, such condition has been evident more than once: think, for example, of the entire period of the so-called *Cold War*. Throughout that era, people were well aware of the concrete possibility of an armed conflict, for this reason the entire period is called cold *war*, which would be the equivalent to what Hobbes had called, simply, war. It is important to understand, though, that when Hobbes is referring to war, in this part of the *Leviathan*, he is evidently talking about the war of *every man against every man* the way it is set to happen *in nature*. It is also true, however, that by equating governments to men Hobbes is foreshadowing a world order of constant war of nations against nations: if governments are like men (we will see how Hobbes makes this point later), then naturally they will fight for their survival in the same way and for the same reason in which men do. Wars among States will be *natural* and cannot be considered bad or evil because they are fought following a natural survival instinct proper of all government (and men). But let's go back, for now, to Hobbes' analysis of the state of war.

The consequence of this constant war, according to our philosopher, is the absence of any kind of interest that is not directly connected to immediate survival: in a state of war there is no technology, no art, no society, and no improvement at all, because people's mind will be preoccupied only with the possibility of their violent death.

> *In such condition, there is no place for Industry; because the fruit thereof is uncertain; and consequently no Culture of the Earth; no Navigation, nor use of the commodities that may be imported by Sea; no commodious Building; no Instruments of moving, and removing such things as require much force; no Knowledge of the face of the Earth; no account of Time; no Arts; no Letters; no Society; and which is worst of all, continuall feare, and danger of violent death; And the life of man, solitary, poore, nasty, brutish, and short. (Ibidem, Thomas Hobbes, 1651.)*

The evidence of this natural condition is given by the habits that we still keep today: locking our doors at night, keeping our stuff close to us, rarely travelling alone, possessing weapons, or insurances. Hobbes clearly says that none of these actions (or the ones that these actions want to prevent) are unnatural or evil, this is, on the contrary, simply *human nature*. What can make these actions (the violent ones) wrong is *only the existence of laws that forbid them*; In the *State of Nature* nothing is unjust. Where there are no laws, there is no notion of just and unjust, or wrong and right. Where there is no common power, where there is no State, there is no law. If we think about it, for example, in war, violence and fraud are virtues because they are conducive to the only thing that is important in that context, which is winning. Justice, for Hobbes, is not a virtue of an isolated man, it is a virtue of a man that lives in society: Justice, and the parameters that one should follow to be considered *Just*, do not exist in nature, but are established by a state. For the same reason, Hobbes continues, one can say that there are no properties nor dominion: everyone possesses something until he can hold it because private property or dominion over something need to be regulated to exist. Without a State regulation, property is not guaranteed and one's possessions are his only until someone does not designs a way to take it from him.

This is the picture that Hobbes presents about the people that live in what he calls the *State of Nature*: a condition where humans live just by following the laws of their nature, their instincts, their passions, and their needs. The State of Nature is also a state of constant war, as we have seen, in which men live in constant misery due to their natural equality (of strength and needs) and selfishness. Life in the state of nature is horrible, but there is hope; we need to remember, in fact, that men do also have another characteristic: they are rational being. Now, the combination of reason and passions, elements that are natural in men, will lead people to make some sort of agreement that could benefit all, according to Hobbes.

> *The Passions that encline men to Peace, are Feare of Death; Desire of such things as are necessary to commodious living; and a Hope by their*

Industry to obtain them. And Reason suggesteth convenient Articles of Peace, upon which men may be drawn to agreement. These Articles, are they, which otherwise are called the Lawes of Nature: whereof I shall speak more particularly, in the two following Chapters. (Ibidem.)

4.1 Jus Naturale vs Lex Naturalis

Considering the premises stated before, Hobbes wants to detail how men arrive to the rational conclusion that it is better to reach an agreement that can bring them peace than living in the state of nature. To do so, he starts with the distinction between *Natural Right* and *Natural Law*.

Natural Right (*Jus Naturale*) is the freedom that everyone has to use his power to conserve his life and, in doing so, the right to use whatever mean it takes, according to each person own judgment and reasoning to accomplish this goal. The only natural right (a right that people are born with) that Hobbes recognize is the freedom to do whatever it takes to survive. This means that there is nothing that is forbidden to a man; when it comes to his self-preservation, a man is absolutely free. A Natural Law (*Lex Naturalis*), on the other hand, is a rule discovered by reason that prohibits men to do something that would destroy their lives or that would take away from them the means to conserve it. A Natural law, we can say, is a law that is consistent with our biological nature, with the way in which we act in the most animalistic sense of our existence, and that, even though is not written anywhere, it can be retrieved by simple reasoning. A sign of such law, and also an example of how this law is not codified but almost intuited by all human being, could be the *stigma* that we put on behaviors like self-mutilation or masochism. Of course, there are some people that engage in such activities, and even when we try to *normalize* these behaviors, we still feel that there is something wrong with them. Why do we feel this way? Hobbes would say that it is because we understand through our reason that who performs these acts is infringing upon the natural law that forbids any act that goes against self-preservation. Even if *Jus* and *Lex* are connected we need to distinguish, clearly, between them, between rights and laws. *Rights* consist in the freedom to do or to abstain from doing something, while *laws* determine and oblige someone to do one of the two things. Rights are expressions of freedom, laws expressions of obligations.

Consequently, we can say that human beings have the *natural right* to do whatever it takes to survive in the state of war against everyone in which every man naturally lives: they can kill, rape, enslave, oppress, cheat, and so on. Given these circumstances, it is obvious that nobody can live safely, no matter how wise or how strong one is, and there are good chances that every man will live less that what nature would have allowed him; he would probably be killed by another human being. If this is the case, though, we can consider *reasonable* that everyone should seek peace in order to maximize their chances of survival, at least as long as he has hope to find it (at the same time if there is no chance to obtain peace it is understandable that everyone should try and utilize all means and advantages of war).

> And consequently it is a precept, or generall rule of Reason, "That every man, ought to endeavour Peace, as farre as he has hope of obtaining it; and when he cannot obtain it, that he may seek, and use, all helps, and advantages of Warre." The first branch, of which Rule, containeth the first, and Fundamentall Law of Nature; which is, "To seek Peace, and follow it." The Second, the summe of the Right of Nature; which is, "By all means we can, to defend our selves." (Ibidem, Book XIV.)

According to Hobbes, a second Natural Law can be derived from this first one: men should renounce, when others would also be in such disposition, to the natural claim that they have on everything and should also be satisfied to have as much freedom regarding the others as they are willing to grant others over themselves. They should do this to truly pursue peace. What is at stake here is the removal of all obstacles to the possibility of a true peace among men: *naturally* all men have a right over everything that exists and that can be used by them to survive; we have seen that this means that they have the right to dispose of others pretty much like they want to because other people might be in the way of their self-preservation. But we have also seen that it is logical, if men want to increase their odds of survival, to seek peace. How can we seek peace, if anyone has such selfish right? Hobbes says that the road to peace passes by giving up the right over everything and by reserving for one-self as much freedom as one would like others to have. In other words, people should concede themselves as much power over other people as they are willing to concede to other people over them. The act of abdicating their right absolute power it has to be, for men, voluntarily, and it needs to be justified by some reciprocal transfer of rights or by something more important that can be gained soon after they abandon their right. For a right to be truly abdicated, there is the need for this right to be genuinely forfeited voluntarily: there is no abandonment of rights under coercion. At the same time, when someone does abandon a right, he does it to gain something is return. In the case of human beings, in the state of nature they should give up voluntarily the right to do whatever they want to gain, in return, safety. The fact that people are willing to part from their rights only under the condition of being *compensated* by some other sort of gain makes plain that there are some rights that are not *alienable*: men cannot abdicate the right to resist to whom assaults them violently to take their life, because this act will not bring them anything in return. The same can be said about being wounded or imprisoned. In the state of nature, therefore, the only reason why a human being would give up a right or would transfer a right is to acquire *personal security regarding his own life, and the means to conserve it*. The reciprocal transfer of a right is called, by Hobbes, *Contract*. A contract is an agreement where the parts declare that they willingly concede rights to each other; just like when we sign a loan we agree to exchange money to gain whatever object we are buying, in the state of nature men willingly transfer their right to absolute freedom in order to receive safety in return.

This is already a big step toward peace, but another law is necessary if we really want to achieve peace among men: *all men have to keep the agreements that they have subscribed to*. Without this law, all agreements and contracts are useless, and we still are in a condition of war. If no one is keeping in word any promise (which is what a contract is in the end), any agreement has no value, according to Hobbes. This law can be considered the origin of justice; without agreement or transfer of rights there is no justice or injustice. But when there is an agreement to break the agreement is *unjust*: *injustice* is the non-compliance of the agreement. *Just* is whatever is not unjust. Justice and injustice are not natural entities but come into existence when men enter in relation with each other. The way in which justice and injustice are born, Hobbes writes, is through the birth of a power that can be trusted by all actors in a contract and that can enforce the terms of the contract.

> *Therefore before the names of Just, and Unjust can have place, there must be some coercive Power, to compell men equally to the performance of their Covenants, by the terrour of some punishment, greater than the benefit they expect by the breach of their Covenant; and to make good that Propriety, which by mutuall Contract men acquire, in recompence of the universall Right they abandon: and such power there is none before the erection of a Common-wealth. And this is also to be gathered out of the ordinary definition of Justice in the Schooles: For they say, that "Justice is the constant Will of giving to every man his own." And therefore where there is no Own, that is, no Propriety, there is no Injustice; and where there is no coerceive Power erected, that is, where there is no Common-wealth, there is no Propriety; all men having Right to all things: Therefore where there is no Common-wealth, there nothing is Unjust. So that the nature of Justice, consisteth in keeping of valid Covenants: but the Validity of Covenants begins not but with the Constitution of a Civill Power, sufficient to compell men to keep them: And then it is also that Propriety begins. (Ibidem, Book XV.)*

The existence, not only of justice, but also of property is directly connected with the existence of the *Commonwealth*, of the State: only when there is a State that can establish the rules regarding who can have what, and therefore, men have given up their right to all things and have submitted to the authority of the State, there could be true property. In the state of nature, in fact, there are no *properties*, there is nothing that one can call *his*. The only things that exist in the state of nature are *possessions*: things that one has until he can keep them, but over which he is no real right.

4.2 Commonwealth and the Rights of the Sovereign

It is easy to see how, in Hobbes' philosophy, the State will play the role of the entity that can coerce people into respect the agreement to renounce to their right to absolute freedom. At the same time, we have seen that the State is the necessary entity that makes possible the existence of concepts like Justice and Injustice and the transformation of possessions into properties. Therefore, the goal of men when they introduce limitations on themselves, as we see when they live under a State (a government), is to live in safe and a satisfying way. Men, thus, want to get out of the condition that we called state of nature, where following their natural inclination they live an unhappy fearful life. In fact, the natural laws that are supposed to regulate the state of nature, by themselves, without the terror of some power there to enforce them, are rational but against men's passions.

> And Covenants, without the Sword, are but Words, and of no strength to secure a man at all. (*Ibidem*, Book XVII.)

If there is no State to enforce the laws, people will do—legitimately— what they can to protect themselves against the others. Only a well-organized state can guarantee the safety needed to get out the state of nature: no small groups or families nor a multitude can do so. Small groups because they cannot deter enemies to try to harm them; multitudes because they are lacking the unifying will of a State, because they are ineffective against the enemy, and because men in it fight each other according to their own interest in time of peace. Having a large group of men that live in peace and that are devoted to justice is impossible, without a submission to a superior power that must be continuous and not limited to times of war and danger. A State provides just that. Hobbes throughout this description is laying a fundamental rule about the constitution of the state: states have to be in existence not only when there is an immediate danger or *actual* war coming, but also in times that might be perceived as peaceful. The reason why it needs to be like this is that without the State people will be back in the constant state of war (intended as a *possibility*). It is also worth noticing that *fear* and *power* are the only reason humans can enjoy such things such as justice, properties and so forth: without coercion there is only the state of total war.

It might seem bizarre, writes Hobbes, that men (whose are rational beings) cannot live peacefully in nature whereas other living creatures, like bees or ants, can somehow live socially without intimidating powers. Well, men are different than these creatures in that: (1) as we have mentioned before, men fight because of glory, or in other words, they are always competing with each other for their honor and their dignity whereas these creatures don't; therefore, between men envy and hate and war come as a consequence, while among these creatures nothing like this happens; (2) among beasts the private good is the same as the public good, therefore, by doing their private business they do the good of the colony whereas for men this is not true. This is because every ant or bee in the colony, for example, has a specific mansion that it will maintain throughout its life, and the *goal* programmed in every individual associate with the colony is the well-being of the group itself. This is obviously not true when it comes to men: one's personal interest can be in evident opposition to the well-being of humanity. Let's make an example: a man that wants to become as rich as possible and that has no offspring can easily decide to pursue this dream of wealth by poisoning the planet without any worries; at the end of his life, he would not care about the state of the planet, and if his conduct should lead to the extinction of humanity he might very well not care. It is obvious, in this extreme example, how the goals and the wants of a man, can be in evident opposition to the goals and the wants of the rest of the group; (3) animals don't have intellect; therefore, they don't see any shortcomings in the administration of the public affairs. Men, on the other hand, believe that they can always do better than others when it comes to govern society: they innovate and change and reform until they bring society to a civil war. This is why they need rigid laws to prevent such changes dictated by their presumption to know better; (4) animals cannot speak like humans, therefore, cannot lie by representing what is good as bad, and what is bad as good; they cannot exaggerate or diminish the appearance of what is good and bad making the other unrestful; (5) irrational creatures don't make the distinction between injustice and harm; therefore, until they are at ease they are not offended by their fellow beasts whereas men when they are comfortable, will still complain and criticize the actions of the others. This means that men are capable of understanding that there might be things that are unjust, but not harmful and vice versa; and (6) the agreement among these creatures is natural whereas for men is artificial and derived solely from the social contract. If there is nothing else besides words, if there is no common power to keep men fearful and that directs their actions toward the common good, the agreement will be broken. This is probably the most important difference between men and beasts: animals that live in groups do so by nature, men, on the other hand, are capable of living in organized groups just because there is an artificial power that coerces them to do so. Aristotle thought that humans were political animals by nature, Hobbes believes that they are so by necessity and that if it was not for their desire to live of longer better lives, coupled with the fear of the organization that they create to achieve this goal, they would never be able to peacefully create a community.

The only way to create a common power to defend men from foreign forces or from reciprocal harm is, therefore, to transfer all their power and strength to *one man* or *one assembly of men* (from now on I will refer to this alternatively as "a single man," "one man," or "an assembly") that will have power of life and death over them. This means that the single men in charge will constitute a *new body* of their person and therefore, that they submit to whoever gives body to their person; and that they submit their will and their judgments to the will and the judgments of this man. This would be more than a consent or an arrangement, it would be a real unity under one person that can be realized thanks to the agreement of everyone with everyone else. It would be just like everyone saying to everyone else:

> *"I Authorise and give up my Right of Governing my selfe, to this Man, or to this Assembly of men, on this condition, that thou give up thy Right to him, and Authorise all his Actions in like manner."* (*Ibidem.*)

This way the multitude will be united in one person that is called State or, in Latin, *Civitas*. This is the generation of that Leviathan, or mortal god, to which we owe our peace and security.

This is a section of the *Leviathan* that is worth analyzing more in detail. Hobbes, in fact, is laying down the foundation of his idea of State. People that enter the social contract acquire a new body, which is represented by the Sovereign power (a single man or an assembly) and a new will, also represented by the Sovereign. And just like they would do with their physical body and their will, they are in need to submit to what the body does and agree with their will, otherwise they will appear crazy: a man that fights his own will and body cannot be sane. The agreement, obviously, presupposes that everyone else involved would submit the same way to the sovereign power, so that the *political body* can transform a multitude in one person. This new powerful body will be called a State (or a Commonwealth).

> *And in him consisteth the Essence of the Common-wealth; which (to define it,) is "One Person, of whose Acts a great Multitude, by mutuall Covenants one with another, have made themselves every one the Author, to the end he may use the strength and means of them all, as he shall think expedient, for their Peace and Common Defence.". And he that carryeth this Person, as called SOVERAIGNE, and said to have Soveraigne Power; and every one besides, his SUBJECT.* (Ibidem.)

Hobbes makes a distinction though: not all states are born the same. Depending on how the Sovereign acquires his power, we can be staring at very different kinds of organizations. The acquisition of sovereign power, it is written in the *Leviathan*, can happen in two different ways: through natural force or through Agreement. A Sovereign acquired to natural force is the one acquired through *conquest*: one becomes a subject to the Sovereign because he is forced to do so. Hobbes makes the examples of man that in war submits his enemies trading their lives with their submission (the concept of bending the knee as a mean to have their lives spared). The kind of State that results from this submission, is called *Commonwealth by Acquisition*. A Sovereign power acquired by agreement, instead, is the one proper of the original social contract where a group of people organize and submit, voluntarily, to a man or an assembly of men trusting that this will guarantee their protection from everyone else. This kind of State, that results from this submission, is called *Commonwealth by Institution* or *Political Commonwealth*.

We call a State "political", then, when men of a multitude agree that a man or an assembly of men will have the right to embody their will, or, in other words, to represent them. This means that, independently from their ideas (for or against the will of the Sovereign) on singular specific cases, they will authorize all the actions and the judgements of that man just as they were their own. The institution of such State has, according to Hobbes, implicit consequences: when men voluntarily agree to transfer their power to a single man, or an assembly of men, to gain protection and safety, they are signing away more than just their freedom to do whatever they want. Better, when entering in this association they are implicitly agreeing to a series of regulations that are *necessary* to keep this agreement in place. Here are some of the implicit consequences of the social contract:

1. Because it has stipulated an agreement, the multitude is forbidden do anything incompatible with the agreement. Therefore, it cannot, without the permission of the authority, change the form of government. Once the multitude has decided to transfer its power to a king, for example, it cannot decide, without the authorization of the king himself, to move to another form of government. Changing the terms of the contract *at will* would mean that the agreement can be broken at any time, resulting in the agreement in itself to be nullified. Think of it as if a bank could change the terms of a loan at any point in time, would it make sense to sign any sort of agreement?

2. Because the power to the Sovereign is given by an agreement *among* the multitude and not by an agreement *between* the Sovereign and the Multitude, there is nothing that the Ruler can do that justifies one or more of his subjects to feel free from his authority. The only obligations present in the agreement are between people in the multitude: the Sovereign represents the multitude, he is not in any agreement with it, therefore it

cannot breach the contract or don't respect its terms. Therefore, nothing of what the Sovereign does can be used to avoid his authority.

3. Nobody can protest, without being unjust, about the proclamation of the Sovereign proclaimed by the majority. If someone does not submit to it, he has to be destroyed. In other words, if the majority, within the multitude, has decided to transfer power to a *specific*, let's say king, all others have to agree, and if they don't, because they are betraying the original contract, they need to be killed or imprisoned by the rest of the multitude. Once a man consents to unite and vote on a specific *ruler*, this man cannot protest if who is elected does not encounter his favor. It would be like if, in a democracy, someone that does not like a law decides to disobey it, even if the majority agrees with this law. In a democracy, *that* someone would also be "destroyed" (his punishment will vary accordingly with his offense: he might be fined, imprisoned, or even executed).

4. The actions of the Sovereign cannot be considered against his subjects and cannot be called unjust. The Sovereign, in fact, represents the will of his subjects, which means that they are acting *within* him. Therefore, it would be illogical to complain or to call unjust something that we do to ourselves by blaming who represents us. If a lawyer, for example, represents someone in agreement with the line of defense concorded it would be absurd to call the lawyer unjust or to say that he is acting against his defendant.

5. No man that has sovereign power can be killed or punished by his subjects: it would be like killing or punishing oneself. Killing or punishing the man in power would be unjust, in fact, he is merely representing the multitude.

6. The Sovereign is the judge of what is necessary for the peace or the defense of his subjects, and he is the judge of what doctrines can be accepted and taught to his subjects and which ones have to be banned. Although this principle sound harsh, in Western democracies, it is always been in place: there are numerous state entities that decide what has to be done to keep peace, avoid war, and that regulate what should and should not be taught is schools. This for of censorship, today, it is actually more endemic that Hobbes ever wished: we regulate not only academic material, but also the entertaining industry by indicating what is appropriate to whom and, is some cases, what is not appropriate at all.

7. The Sovereign establishes the rules of properties: he decides which things can be called properties and which ones are to be considered common goods. This is another simple, but very important principle: What can be owned by private citizens and what it has to be *public* it is a prerogative of the State, of every state. In some nations, private entities can own things such as cars, houses, or natural resources like oil and water but

cannot own parks or state lands whereas in other nations, for example, oil and water are considered public goods and cannot be owned private individuals whereas every single speck of land can be privatized.

8. The Sovereign has also the right to settle all controversies, which may arise concerning law, either civil or natural, or concerning facts. No private citizen can be judge of any sort of controversy and assign legal punishment. Only the people that are designated by the ruler to do so, or the ruler himself can legally judge and punish someone.

9. The Sovereign has the right to declare war or make peace accordingly with what he believes to be the best way possible.

10. The Sovereign has the right to pick and choose all ministers, secretaries in war time and in time of peace. It is a prerogative of the State to appoint people to specific offices.

11. The Sovereign has the right to punish or reward his subject according to a law previously established or according to what he believes to be the right thing to do. Punishment and rewards can be conferred at the discretion of the ruler: he can pardon someone or declare someone an enemy of the state if he thinks that it is fit to do so.

12. The Sovereign has the right to create a public rate of worth to reward the people and to honor them when they deserve it. It is the Sovereign that decides, in the name of the multitude, what kind of behavior or moral conducts are worthy of praise and reward. All these rights are inalienable unless the Sovereign Power decides to cease and desist. Even the right to give up these rights resides in the Sovereign power: only the ruler can decide to alienate himself for some of these prerogatives.

It is evident from what we have said above that the powers of the Sovereign (the ruler) are incommensurable with the ones of the multitude: once the multitude transfers its original power to the ruler this one is powerful in a way that no single individual can be; in fact, the Sovereign power can be calculated as the sum of the powers present in the multitude. The multitude, however, cannot achieve such power because, in it, the powers of the single individuals are never converging and acting as one, they are always a disorganized blob.

It is also evident (number 4 above) that Hobbes thinks that the power and the decisions made by the ruler can never be harmful to his subjects, and the reason for this line of thought is easily understood. When the conditions of the subjects are miserable, and their life is in the hands of such power-hungry man (or group of men) that possess such unlimited power, people blame specific forms of government: who lives under a monarch believes that the miserable condition that they are in is determined by that specific form of government; while the people living in democracy believe the same of their government. The truth is that the amount of power that the Sovereign has on his subjects is the same in any form, and that the inconveniences that provokes to the subjects is the same regardless of the form of government. But no matter how terrible of a life one might have under a ruler, that individual is still living a better life than he would be living without it, in the State of Nature. Actually, Hobbes notes, most of the harm that comes to us under a ruler comes to us because we don't understand immediately that living in a civilized society, independently of specific conditions, is the lesser of two evils. Here is the famous (or maybe infamous) conclusion to which Hobbes arrives: it is better to live an entire life of serfdom under the dominion of an evil power-hungry ruler, than a brief period of time in complete freedom in the State of Nature. Nothing can be worse than living in that constant state of war of everyone against everyone else that exists beyond the borders of a civilized state.

4.3 Different Forms of Government

Established the general conditions of the relationship between the Multitude and the Sovereign authority, Hobbes is interested, now, in determining what form of government is preferable to build a society that can guarantee safety and stability to its people. In doing so, he begins an analysis that is molded on the classical description of the possible forms of government like the ones that we have seen in Plato and Aristotle. But at the very beginning of his description, Hobbes distances himself from the ancients: while Plato and Aristotle describe the different forms of government to establish which one of them is more beneficial to the citizens in terms of participation to that government and freedom, Hobbes says that the only true difference between governments is given by the number of people that rule. This is an important difference between the idea that the ancients have of the government and the one that is presented in the *Leviathan*. In fact, for the ancients there are real dissimilarities between forms of government, and there is, objectively, a better form of government in terms of the quality of life for the people; also, for Plato and Aristotle, it is possible to identify some forms of government that can be considered a degeneration, or a corruption, of good forms of governments: Tyranny or Anarchy, are simple degenerations of the acceptable forms of government Monarchy and Democracy. On the other hand, we have seen how in Hobbes' opinion all forms of government have the same amount of power and can create the same "inconveniences" for their subjects. This is why he will say that the difference between States is given by the difference that there is between rulers in the sense that Sovereignty can either reside in one person, or in many people; and when it resides in many people it will be residing either in all the people or in some of them. This means that there are only three kinds of States: Monarchy, Democracy, or Aristocracy. The so-called degenerations of the states, Tyranny, Oligarchy, and Anarchy are nothing but names that describe Monarchy, Democracy, and Oligarchy, when someone is unhappy with them. One has to understand, Hobbes continues, that the difference between the three kinds of Government does not consist in a difference in power, but in a difference in the advantages or disadvantages that they present when it comes to produce the safety of the population, which was the reason why they were instituted. The issue is not Power, because all of them have absolute power; but rather which one of them can do a better job at protecting the citizens from each other or from someone else. For this reason, when trying to establish which one is the *best* for of government, what it needs to be considered is not the abstract elements of *freedom* or *justice*, but the efficacy in protecting the people.

Given these premises, in the *Leviathan*, we find clearly expressed that monarchy is the best form of government possible. Now, it is not necessarily original for political theorists of the time to favor Monarchy (even Plato and Aristotle were fascinated with the possibility of a *philosopher king*), what is original, though, is the reasoning behind this choice: Monarchy is better than any other form of government because who embodies the interest of the multitude (The King) embodies also his interest. Considering that when there is a conflict between the private interest and the public interest, men, in general, will tend to choose the private one, it is easily understood that the best way to do the public interest is to strongly tie it with the private interest. It is evident, Hobbes thinks, that there is complete communion between the public interest and the private interest of the Monarch: the wealth, the power and the honor of the monarchy is nothing but the wealth, the strength, and the reputation of its subjects; if the subjects are poor, too weak, or in constant disagreement they will be unable to fight in case of war and the monarchy itself will be destroyed. In a democracy or in an aristocracy, on the other hand, the private interest of some of the representatives might not be in line with the public interest: a civil war, or a bad political decision might bring them private fortune while being disastrous for the people living in the State. For example, if the private fortune of a group of people that have Sovereign power derives from producing weapons, they might think that it is advantageous to have a war, so they can make a profit. This private interest it might clearly be in contrast with what is good for the subjects. This way of reasoning regarding Monarchy and Sovereign Assemblies is an obvious reversal of the common way of understanding both entities: when people think of monarchy, they think of a form of government where the only interest that is done is the one of the king; at the same time, when people think of democracy (to mention one specific form of sovereign assembly), they think of a system when the public interest is done by representatives of the people. Hobbes inverts these views and says that in Monarchy the king will always do the interest of his subjects because it coincides with his own interest: the safety of the king depends largely on the safety (or perceived safety, Machiavelli would say) of its subjects. In democracy, instead, a group of people that are part of the government can try to pass laws that are not in the interest of the citizens, but only in their own interest: the glory and safety of the assembly (or of part of it) does not always overlap with the one of the people.

The alignment between private and public interest is not the only reason why Monarchy is better suited to work better than assemblies as a form of government. In another reversal of common sense, in fact, Hobbes declares that the Monarch is more *liberal* when it comes to take advices: a king can take advice from whoever and whenever he wants, so he can talk to the experts in the fields on which he has to make a decision as soon as a problem presents itself. In an assembly, conversely, only the people that are part of it since the beginning can speak and express their suggestions: no experts are admitted to the assembly to make a better decision, or, at best, they are summon after precious time is wasted in deciding if the opinion of someone that is not part of the assembly is really needed.

Hobbes enumerates a series of other reasons why Monarchy is preferable to any other form of government. The reasons that he proposes at number three and four (the previous two are the ones that we have just discussed) are classic arguments in favor of Monarchy, the same kind of arguments that were put forward by many that considered monarchy a legitimate form of government that had some advantages to it. The reasons are: (3) the decisions of the monarch are not subject to any inconsistency other that the ones typical of human nature whereas in an assembly there are inconsistencies due to numbers; and (4) a monarch cannot be in disagreement with himself because of envy or interest. In an assembly, instead, there can be such kind of disagreement. Both of these reasons why monarchy is preferable to other forms of government are based on the advantages that having *one* single person in charge of the State can give. If one person is in charge, aside from the normal flaws that all men have (human nature), there will be two major advantages when compared with Assembly-ruled governments: The decision-making will always be coherent, and the reasoning behind the decisions will be based solely on the calculation of one man. These characteristics are very important, in fact, in assembly-ruled government it is not uncommon for the people in charge to constantly revert or undo previously passed laws because of a change of opinion within the assembly, once new people participate. In addition, it is not uncommon, in an assembly, that some decision making can be driven by envy or personal hostility without any regards for the public good.

The fifth reason why we should prefer monarchy over assembly-ruled governments it is (just like the first two that we analyzed) counterintuitive. Hobbes writes, that there are some people that rightly think that in monarchy it might happen that a subject, because of the power of a single men (the king), can be targeted by the Sovereign Authority and lose everything he has, to favor someone that the monarch wants to reward. This serious *inconvenience*, as Hobbes calls it, it is really present in monarchy: it can really happen that a man is dispossessed just because the king wants to favor someone. But the same can happen in democracy (for example), and, if the matter is truly analyzed with unbiased eyes, one will arrive to the conclusion that in a democracy it is even worse: the amount of people in power in a democracy is larger, while the amount of power in the hands of the people in power is the same as the one in the hands of the monarch. Therefore, there are more "favorites" in a democracy that can potentially benefit from the dispossession of a man than there are in a monarchy.

Finally, Hobbes identifies a common complaint when it comes to monarchies: there are times in which who becomes king is a minor or someone that is not able to distinguish good from evil. This issue with monarchy, though, is not a flaw of the system in itself, he writes, it is rather a flaw of the multitude that did not establish better and/or clearer guidelines for the succession process. Blaming monarchy as a system of government based on this issue is unfair, and if truth be told, assembly-based systems might not be safe either: if the guidelines for who can be in the assembly are not clear or good, one can easily and up with an assembly full of incompetent people. In addition, let's not forget, warns Hobbes, an incompetent rule is better than the State of nature and civil war, which we have seen is more easily brought by assembly-based governments than monarchies.

Monarchy, in summary, is a better suited form of government because it conveys more functionally the kind of power that a government (of any kind) needs to have in order to maintain the safety of its subjects.

> *So it appeareth plainly, to my understanding, both from Reason, and Scripture, that the Soveraign Power, whether placed in One Man, as in Monarchy, or in one Assembly of men, as in Popular, and Aristocraticall Common-wealths, is as great, as possibly men can be imagined to make it. And though of so unlimited a Power, men may fancy many evill consequences, yet the consequences of the want of it, which is perpetuallwarre of every man against his neighbour, are much worse. The condition of man in this life shall never be without Inconveniences; but there happeneth in no Common-wealth any great Inconvenience, but what proceeds from the Subjects disobedience, and breach of those Covenants, from which the Common-wealth had its being. And whosoever thinking Soveraign Power too great, will seek to make it lesse; must subject himselfe, to the Power, that can limit it; that is to say, to a greater.* (*Ibidem*, Book XX.)

The power of the Commonwealth has to be absolute, if it is not, there are good chances to go back to the state of nature. Therefore, even if there are bad consequences to this absolute power in the hands of a man (or assembly of men), any of these consequences are still better that the constant state of war and misery that is proper of the uncivilized societies.

4.4 The Hazards of Liberty

The most visible problem in the system presented by Hobbes so far is probably the limited amount of freedom with which the individual subject is left once entered the social contract. This loss of freedom can be intended in three ways: firstly as a loss of *rights*, in the sense that, by subjecting voluntarily to a sovereign power, the men of a multitude give up the right to freely do whatever they want. Once the power is constituted in the political body they have just to follow the direction that this body indicates them; secondly as a submission to *fear*, in the sense that, because men in order to be faithful to the social contract have to be terrorized by the Sovereign authority, they will do anything that they have to just because they are scared into doing it and not because of their free will; thirdly, as a partial *lack of free will*, in the sense that the actions of men seem to follow chains of events that are independent from their will, like when there are "subjugated" by their passions. Now, the evident downsizing of freedom in Hobbes system is not a problem just for the people reading his works today, it was a problem already during Hobbes' times. The issue was so problematic, in fact, that our philosopher decides to assign himself the task of solving such problem. We can call it the problem of the compatibility between liberty and the absolute power of the government.

One might think that the road toward the bridge between liberty and absolute government might pass by some sort of limitation of the sovereign power: nothing can be farther from the truth. The tactic used by Hobbes to bridge the gap between freedom and authority is to show how the former is absolutely compatible with the latter, and that the term freedom really needs to be redefined to avoid costly (in terms of human lives) mistakes. Hobbes writes, in fact, that firstly we need to see what *Liberty* really means: liberty means absence of opposition and is not proper of just human beings, it can pertain all living beings, even irrational ones. When something is physically closed up and cannot go anywhere because of other *bodies* blocking the way, we say that it is not free. *A man is therefore free when, regarding the things that he is capable of doing with his strength and with his ingenuity, he is not impeded from doing what he wants to.* This is the only correct definition of liberty, anytime we refer as "freedom" to something that is not a body free from material impediments we are abusing the word: when we say, for example, that the road is free or that we speak freely, it should be obvious that it is not the road or the speech to be free but whoever is passing by the road or is giving a speech.

Given this definition of liberty, Hobbes proceeds to show us how freedom is compatible with fear and necessity. He writes, in fact, that fear and liberty are compatible because all actions performed by men because of fear are voluntary and therefore, free. Fear, for Hobbes, is not coercive, it is just something that men take in consideration when deciding how to act. Technically, we are free to go against our fears: when someone, for example, installs an alarm in his home because he is afraid to be robbed, he does so freely, of his own free will; the same can be said of someone who obeys a law of the State because he is afraid. Fear is a deterrent, but technically does not mandate any sort of behavior. By showing how fear and liberty are compatible Hobbes is able to refute one of the reasons why people think that freedom is irreconcilable with the system exposed in the *Leviathan*.

Moreover, liberty and necessity are compatible. Human actions are always free, in the sense that they are dictated by human's will, but they are necessary in the sense that they are following a chain of causes that are determining what will happen. This is a powerful argument: what Hobbes is saying here is that we have free will to do whatever we want, but the things that we can do are necessarily determined by some conditions that are proper of the universe where humans live. Humans are free within the realm of will, but there are some necessary limits to what they can or cannot do, for example, no matter how much they want to, they cannot defeat the law that says that we can't live without breathing; there are certain objective condition that limit what we can or what we cannot do. So, Hobbes seems to say, are we *completely* free? No, there are objective limitations to what we can or cannot do. Are we free, within the limitations set by nature? Yes, we are free to do whatever we want in the context of a limited set of choices. This means for Hobbes, that one can be free, also, in the context of a limited set of choices that we call "State".

> But as men, for the atteyning of peace, and conservation of themselves thereby, have made an Artificiall Man, which we call a Common-wealth; so also have they made Artificiall Chains, called Civill Lawes, which they themselves, by mutuall covenants, have fastned at one end, to the lips of that Man, or Assembly, to whom they have given the Soveraigne Power; and at the other end to their own Ears. These Bonds in their own nature but weak, may neverthelesse be made to hold, by the danger, though not by the difficulty of breaking them. (*Ibidem*, Book XXI.)

The moment people create the Commonwealth, and they give it a body in what is the Sovereign authority they have created a new set of circumstances that are the limits of their freedom. The new body, of which they are part, has to answer to a new set of natural rules that from the outside might look like limitations on someone's freedom (like the need of constant breathing in men can look like a limitation from the perspective of an external observer, like an alien or a god), but that can be natural and necessary to guarantee its normal functioning. Within these ties, it is possible to talk about the freedom of the subjects in a state. Considering that there are no states where there are sufficient laws to sanction every action or word of people, men are free to do whatever is more advantageous for them in *all matters not sanctioned by law*. Therefore, men have freedom of buying and selling, to make among them other contracts, to choose their place to live, their diet, their occupation, and to educate their kids the way the want to, etc. Note how there is no contradiction between these freedoms and the fact that the Sovereign authority has absolute power (power of life and death) over his subjects. Hobbes thinks that there are certain things that are outside the realm of legislation, and that out of that realm a man can truly do what he wants. Again, to make an analogy with nature, we can say that biologically human beings can make a specific set of sounds, we can say that nature has legislated that they can only produce these sounds and that do not have the freedom to produce sounds that are different from those assigned to them. At the same time, nature has not legislated on the way in which we can articulate, and order these sounds, hence the freedom that human beings have enjoyed creating any language that they want. Freedom and necessity coexist in nature therefore, they can coexist also within the social contract. Hobbes, at this point, has refuted the argument that men are not free in the Commonwealth because they have to necessarily follow the rules of the government. But there is still a problem, in his eyes: there is a long tradition of studies that refer back to the Greek and Roman thinkers and that seem to affirm that the main goal of a State should be to give its subjects as much freedom as possible. These understanding of freedom, Hobbes says is misleading: the freedom described by the Greek and Roman authors is not the freedom of the single individuals, but the freedom of the States, which is identical to the one that men would have if they would live without civil laws nor State. And identical are the effects of such freedom: men without a Sovereign live in a state of constant war of everyone against everyone else, have no properties, and have no security, but have plenty of freedom; in the same way States, which do not depend on each other, have the absolute freedom to do what they judge to be more beneficial to their own interest. At the same time, States live in a condition of perpetual war, on the verge of conflict, with fortified frontiers, and weapons pointed at each other.

The Athenians, and Romanes, were free; that is, free Commonwealths: not that any particular men had the Libertie to resist their own Representative; but that their Representative had the Libertie to resist, or invade other people. There is written on the Turrets of the city of Luca in great characters at this day, the word LIBERTAS; yet no man can thence

*inferre, that a particular man has more Libertie, or Immunitie from the
service of the Commonwealth there, than in Constantinople. (Ibidem.)*

Greeks and Romans were free. It means that their States were free but
their subjects needed still to be subjected to their Sovereigns, and they would
be harshly punished if they would not do so. Because people misunderstand
Aristotle and Cicero, they acquire the mental habit to disobey to the State in
the name of this so-called freedom, with the effect to produce such a bloodbath that makes Hobbes write

*there was never any thing so deerly bought, as these Western parts have
bought the learning of the Greek and Latine tongues. (Ibidem.)*

Instead of dwelling in such misunderstanding of the word freedom, Hobbes
thinks, we need to analyze in what it consists the *true* freedom of the subjects,
or rather which things that they might be commanded to do by the Sovereign
they can refuse to do without incurring in any injustice, without breaking the
natural limits of their freedom. It is, in fact, on submission by law (contract)
that rests men's obligation and men's freedom. The possibility of being truly
free resides in our voluntary subjection to the sovereign power that is born
when we enter the social contract, therefore, one can refuse anything that is excluded in principle by the original agreement: a subject can legitimately refuse
to comply with an order when the Sovereign authority commands a man to kill
himself, to mutilate himself or to wound himself, or to not to resist to whom
tries to hurt him, or when the authority commands him to abstain from food,
air, medicine, or any other thing without which he cannot survive. Also if the
subject is interrogated about a crime he cannot be obligated to confess, because
no agreement can subscribe that. It is interesting to notice how the body of the
subject and his speech (accusation) are the two things that cannot be included
in the contract, so it might seem, at first sight, that the Sovereign authority has
no power over the *naked life* of its subjects. The truth is, though, that this limitation is valid only when the damage to the body or the limitation of speech is
self-imposed: the sovereign *can kill* the subject, but he cannot ask him to kill
himself; the Sovereign *can accuse* a subject of a crime that he has not committed, but he cannot ask the subject to accuse himself.

So, in what does it *really* consists the freedom of a subject? The freedom
of the subject depends on the *silence of the law*. If something is regulated,
then people have to follow the law, and there is no freedom to transgress; if
something is not regulated, then people are free to act in their best interest.
For this reason, the freedom of the Subjects varies from state to state and
from time to time. Freedom, in other words, is relative to the regulations and
the laws of every state: in some places people might have the freedom to buy
and sell whatever they want, in others this freedom limited by some laws that
say, for example, that nothing that is alive can be sold and bought; in some

places on might have the freedom to eat whatever he wants, in others there might be a certain limitations about what one can eat (think cannibalism) etc.

There are also some special limitations when it comes to the power that a Sovereign has over its subjects that have to do with the contract in itself: the obligation of the subjects toward the sovereign is intended to last as long as it lasts the power that the Sovereign has to protect them. The goal of absolute obedience is protection, and if protection is not possible anymore, there is no more obligation. In addition, if a Sovereign renounce to his power for himself and his heirs, the subjects are not bound to him anymore and they go back to their original natural freedom. Finally, if a man is exiled, for the time of the banishment, he is not a subject anymore and he is not required to obey anymore. There is one more case that Hobbes points out, the case of a Sovereign that loses a war and that becomes subject to another sovereign. In this case the Subjects of the loser automatically become the subjects of the winner, because this last one now guarantees their protection. The subjects have an obligation only toward whom is in effect protecting them currently, no other loyalty is expected or required.

4.5 Dura Lex, Sed Lex

Hobbes has analyzed a series of relationships within the social contract: he has analyzed the relationship between the people in the multitude (exemplified by voluntary exiting the state of nature), the relationship between the Sovereign and the people (when it studies the different forms of government and the rights that the State has over the people), and the relationship between the people and the laws (by delineating the scope of people's freedom). What is still unclear, at this point, is what laws are and how are they made, and the relationship between the sovereign and these laws. It is obvious that different laws exist in different states (this is why Hobbes told us that in different States there might be different kinds of freedom), but laws are present in every state and do play the same role in all states, *Civil Laws*, in general, are the laws that men have to observe not because they are part of a particular state, but because they are part of *a* State. The interest of general political theory, like the Hobbesian one, is not to explain the particular law of this or that State, but to explain what *the Law* is: Hobbes wants to put himself in the same tradition as Plato and Aristotle and speak of laws is general, like a philosopher, and not of specific laws like a lawyer would do.

The definition of civil law is therefore

> *I define Civill Law in this Manner.* "CIVILL LAW, *Is to every Subject, those Rules, which the Common-wealth hath Commanded him, by Word, Writing, or other sufficient Sign of the Will, to make use of, for the Distinction of Right, and Wrong; that is to say, of what is contrary, and what is not contrary to the Rule.*" (Ibidem, Book XXVI.)

It is easily recognizable here the purely *formal* nature of this definition: no content is provided, just a formula that describes what all civil laws are. Two general observations can be done here: (1) civil laws are unequivocally defined as the determining factor of morality. Right and wrong are, in Hobbes system, synonymous of legal and illegal: what is contrary to the rule of law (illegal) is what is wrong, and what is in agreement with the rule of law (legal) is what is right. Morality is a legislative matter, and not a matter of abstract principles. (2) As civil laws are commanded to the subject by the Commonwealth, it is obvious that nobody can make laws except for the Sovereign: we have seen how the subjects owe to him, and only to him, their obedience. Aside from these general observations, Hobbes believes that it is possible to deduct, from the definitions of civil laws provided above, many principles and rules.

The first of these principles asserts that in all States only the legislator is the Sovereign. Either one person (Monarch) or an assembly (democracy and aristocracy) can make civil laws: the state can make laws, and the state makes laws only through the Sovereign. At the same time, the right to abrogate a law resides only in the Sovereign, because abrogating a law means to make a law to annul another law. This principle is self-evident, in fact, in a political state only the legislator can make or repeal laws: if making laws (and abrogate them) was not a prerogative of the legislator, and anyone in the common-wealth could make or repeal laws at will, the state would be dismantled in a very short period of time. Imagine a citizen that feels that a law is impeding him and has the power to repeal it whenever he wants or another citizen that keeps on changing the rules regarding his property making constantly new rules to annex more and more of his neighbor yard, while this neighbor does the same thing. If there was no clear rule about who can and cannot make the rules (or modify them), the State would be in chaos, and it would not dif-fer much from the state of nature.

A second principle that can be deducted from the general definition of civil laws can be expressed as follows: The Sovereign of a commonwealth *is not subject to its laws* (no matter if he is a monarch or an assembly). Not only that, if he wants he can repeal any law that impedes him because he is absolutely free to do what he wants. This principle is a very important one: Hobbes is stating that the authority is above the law, that the sovereign is not obliged to follow the same rules that the subjects are supposed to abide by. This is necessary because the Sovereign needs to be free from every impedi-ment when it comes to do his will in order to protect the subjects from each other, from a foreign force, or from the ever-present fear to fall back to the state of nature. This last danger, in particular, justifies the special status of the sovereign: if the authority can be brought to court, judged and sentenced just like any other subject, then he will be scared to take some unpopular measure to protect the subjects, and this will bring back the state of nature. In addition, if he is sentenced, let's say to jail, then the people will be without a sovereign authority, and will revert to the state of nature. It is in the nature of the Sovereign authority to be absolutely free: States and Sovereign authorities live according to the rules of the state of nature.

Another principle deducted directly from the definition of civil law expresses the status of customs and their relationships with the laws. There are customs that have been in place in societies for a long time and do acquire the authority of law. When this happens, it does so not because the custom has been there for a long time, but because of the will of the Sovereign manifested by his silence. In other words, only because the Sovereign has allowed this practice to survive, the custom has had the opportunity to crystallize itself as some sort of unwritten law, and it stays an unwritten law only until the Sovereign keeps quite about it. The Sovereign, in fact, has the authority to abrogate the custom at any time, and to make a law that is in line with his own will. This idea reaffirms the principle that nobody and nothing is above the will of the Sovereign, not even age long customs.

Considered this way, civil laws are pervasive and powerful tools in the hands of the sovereign. Are there any limitations to them, aside from the will of the legislator? We might be tempted to think that a limitation to the civil laws must be something *natural*, something that it is not created within the social contract; we might think that the so-called *natural laws* must be the limits of the civil laws. The truth is, according to Hobbes, that the Laws of Nature and the Civil Laws contain each other and are of equal extent. In fact, the Laws of Nature, which consist of *equity, justice, gratitude and other moral virtues*, in the state of nature are *not properly laws*, but individual qualities that make men inclined to peace and obedience. These qualities become real laws only when the state is instituted, when they become commands of the state and therefore civil laws; it is the Sovereign power that obliges men to respect them. In fact, considering the general disagreement between individuals regarding the definition of such moral virtues, and the disagreement regarding the procedures devised to make these virtues universally accepted, it is easy to understand why there is a need for the prescription of a Sovereign power. In all Commonwealths of the world the Natural Law *is* part of the civil laws, and reciprocally the civil laws are part of nature. When natural laws and civil laws are considered as one to be part of the other, or as one implying the other, disobeying the laws of the laws of State equates with disobeying the laws of nature: doing something illegal, then, means to do something that is immoral and unnatural; legality, morality and nature are clumped all together in the Hobbesian view, and a criminal is, at the same time, immoral and against nature.

Nature, intended as a series of natural dispositions, is not the limit of civil laws. Maybe, then, some human characteristic might play the role of limit of the laws. Hobbes seems to go toward this direction when he declares that the law is a command and the manifestation of this command (meaning that the law has to be not just a thought in the head of the sovereign, but something that is known and intelligible to others). When someone is commanding something to someone else, there is the necessity of two things: that the commander expresses his request in an intelligible way, using a language that is understood by the "commandee"; and that the receiver of the command is able to understand the said command. Therefore, it is obvious that the command of the commonwealth is law only for the people that have the *means* to understand it.

> *Over naturall fooles, children, or mad-men there is no Law, no more than over brute beasts; nor are they capable of the title of just, or unjust; because they had never power to make any covenant, or to understand the consequences thereof; and consequently never took upon them to authorise the actions of any Sovereign, as they must do that make to themselves a Common-wealth. (Ibidem.)*

Hobbes is clearly tying laws to rationality: only rational men can decide to enter the social contract; therefore, only rational men can be required to follow the law that the sovereign power produces as a direct consequence of that contract. In the Hobbesian civil society, something like an insanity plea in court is a non-issue: these people are by nature out of the law and cannot be judged by it.

Rationality is then a limit when it comes to the extent of the law. Another limit tied to rationality is the communicability and knowledge of the laws: all laws need to be brought to the knowledge of the people that have to follow them. Orally or in writing, or through any other mean that would help the subjects to receive it clearly. If the laws are not public, there is nothing that obliges the subjects to follow them. We must be careful here, Hobbes is not saying that if one subjects is ignorant about a specific law, then he is not punishable; he is saying that if a law has not been made public, then nobody is obliged to follow it, and nobody can be considered culpable to have not followed it. In addition, Hobbes adds, there is the need that in the law we can recognize, clearly, the will of the Sovereign: some people might pose as the sovereign and end up publishing laws that are the opposite of the Sovereign will. The sovereign must be identifiable with his laws, his will needs to transpire from the laws: if it does not, this can be considered the equivalent of a law not being written in an intelligible language for the people, and therefore, authorizes the people to disobey it.

Civil laws, in conclusions, are rules that emanate exclusively from the Sovereign authority that must be followed by all subjects all the times because they are natural and are the necessary condition for a state to exist. The only exceptions to this rule come in play when the subjects are unable to understand the laws either because they are unable to—the subjects in question lack rationality—or because the laws are not made public, clearly stated or do not evidently reflect the will of the Sovereign—the authority has failed to communicate the laws effectively.

4.6 The Illnesses of the State

Hobbes has described all that is needed to build a long-lasting state that can protect his subjects from themselves and from others. Yet, nations rise and fall, sometimes because they are conquered by other nations, but more often because they crumble from the inside. Why does that happen? What are the reasons of these collapses? As we have seen before, Hobbes has established an equivalence between human beings and states: the state acquires a body and a will when it is constituted by the people in the multitude. He thinks that what happens when States are destroyed or collapse can be equated, once more, with what happens to when a person dies; there are different reasons for people' deaths, some people are killed by external agents—another person, a foreign object—while others die because of internal issues like congenital illnesses or contracted illnesses. In the same way, some States are destroyed by external factors like natural disasters, famine or the conquering force of an enemy, while others disappear because of congenital or acquired diseases proper of States.

Hobbes seems to be sure, the dissolution of the States derives mainly from the imperfect organization of them. If men would build a State with a solid foundation the state would live as long as there are humans around. When states are ruined by forces that are not external (conquered or dismantled by the enemy), men are culpable not because they ruined the state, but rather because they built the state in a way that allowed for its ruin. The culpable individuals are not the ones assisting to the fall of the state, rather the ones who established the state on such shaky grounds. This is the first cause of *infirmity* when we talk about states: States well-built should last forever, therefore, when States dissolve they do so because they were born *defective*. Hobbes proceeds to enumerate several kinds of congenital infirmity that can afflict a state. We will see that, aside from the acuity with which He identifies these diseases, what it is of interest here is how throughout the description of the illnesses Hobbes will find a way to reinforce the general principles of his doctrine.

The first congenital *infirmity* consists in the fact that a man to obtain power, sometimes, will be satisfied with an amount of power that is not sufficient (it is not absolute) to keep the peace and the defense of the state. This happens because the mentioned man wants to appeal to the people of the multitude by presenting himself as more liberal and therefore more respectful of the freedom of his future subjects. When this happens, however, the Sovereign will eventually try to acquire the missing power *after* the constitution of the state, which will be perceived as an unjust request and will lead men to revolt. It is necessary, then, for the Sovereign to have absolute power from the beginning of the social contract, otherwise men will perceive the change in power as illegitimate. Therefore, a State that is well instituted will immediately give absolute power to whoever is in charge.

At the second place among the illnesses of a State, Hobbes writes, there are the ones that derive from the poison of the *seditious doctrines*. One of these doctrines is the one that maintains that every private citizen has the right to judge what actions are right or wrong. Although it is true that morality is an individual enterprise in the state of nature, where there are no civil laws, and it is true also under a civil government with regards of cases that are not regulated by law, it is obvious, as showed before, that in all other cases the rightness and wrongness of actions is determined by the civil law. Therefore, the supreme judge of morality is the legislator appointed by the commonwealth. Because of this false doctrine, though men believe that they can decide to obey or not obey to a law based on what they think is right. This confusion weakens the State. So, although there is a specific right and wrong in the state of nature (specifically what is right is what benefits *the individual* and what keeps him alive) and it is obvious that a man should be judge of what he deems right or wrong, one cannot refuse to follow a law because he thinks that the law is wrong. There are no wrong laws, who established the *morality* of the law is in fact the civil law itself.

Connected to the previous illness there is the doctrine that one is committing a sin if he does something against his conscience. This, again, depends of the presumption that men can be judges of what is right and wrong. Moreover, again, while this is true in the state of nature, it is false when we live in a civil state where the law is the *public conscience*. In a civil society, in fact, the one who sins is the one who goes against this conscience that he agreed to follow. So, not only personal beliefs are to be subordinated to the law of the State, but also questions of conscience that might be tied to religion are subordinated to the law: the law, in fact, is the conscience of the state, the public conscience that is the fruit of the "mind" of the person that embodies the multitude (the Sovereign).

Another important doctrine that is incompatible with the nature of the state is the belief that who has the sovereign power is subjected to the civil laws. This is, according to Hobbes (we have seen this), plainly wrong: the sovereign cannot be under the rule of any law, because he is the law and the supreme judge. Therefore, he cannot be punished because that would mean that there must be a power higher than his own, which in turn, if it has to be subjected to the laws, will need a third power to be judged and so on to infinite, which will lead to confusion and ultimately to the dissolution of the state. Once more Hobbes wants to make clear that the sovereign authority is above the law: if the supreme judge can be judged, then he is not supreme, and if we pose that every judge has to be judged, then we will be stuck in an infinite regress toward an ultimate sentencing that cannot be found.

There are other smaller illnesses that can make the government weaker: the impossibility to get enough money to sustain the State, especially during war time (this usually derives from the wrong idea that the subjects can refuse to give to the State whatever the state needs); the excessive wealth that a single or few men can accumulate; the popularity of a powerful subject (people will tend to follow him even though they have no clue about his real motives); the excessive size of a city and/or of associations; the freedom to disagree with the sovereign power; the lethargy of the subjects given by excessive wealth. If we pay attention, all these small *ailments* of the state cited by Hobbes are examples of situations where the state is not being considered, for a reason or another, the supreme authority by its subjects. Ultimately this is the major concern for Hobbes: the state needs to hold supreme power over the individuals, if this does not happen society will disappear, and men will return to their solitary warlike life of the social contract. The function of the Sovereign is to guarantee the security of the people. Security does not merely mean survival, but life with all the satisfactions that one can procure for himself legally and without endangering the State. This has to be actuated not just by taking care of the single individuals, but also by a general care visible in the institution of public education and in the actuation and creation of laws to which individuals can refer to when they need. Therefore,

> To the care of the Soveraign, belongeth the making of Good Lawes. But what is a good Law? By a Good Law, I mean not a Just Law: for no Law can be Unjust. The Law is made by the Soveraign Power, and all that is done by such Power, is warranted, and owned by every one of the people; and that which every man will have so, no man can say is unjust. It is in the Lawes of a Common-wealth, as in the Lawes of Gaming: whatsoever the Gamesters all agree on, is Injustice to none of them. A good Law is that, which is Needfull, for the Good Of The People, and with all Perspicuous. For the use of Lawes, (which are but Rules Authorised) is not to bind the People from all Voluntary actions; but to direct and keep them in such a motion, as not to hurt themselves by their own impetuous desires, rashnesse, or indiscretion, as Hedges are set, not to stop Travellers, but to keep them in the way. And therefore a Law that is not Needfull, having not the true End of a Law, is not Good. A Law may be conceived to be Good, when it is for the benefit of the Sovereign; though it be not Necessary for the People; but it is not so. For the good of the Soveraign and People, cannot be separated. It is a weak Soveraign, that has weak Subjects; and a weak People, whose Soveraign wanteth Power to rule them at his will. Unnecessary Lawes are not good Lawes; but trapps for Mony: which

where the right of Soveraign Power is acknowledged, are superfluous; and where it is not acknowledged, unsufficient to defend the People. (Ibidem, Book XXX.)

Good laws are, in the end, the real goal of the government, they illustrate the purpose of it and express its spirit: good laws, though, are not good because they adhere to some immaterial principle of justice, but they are good because they are the truthful expression of the will of the sovereign and are a guidance for the people that want to live a satisfying life. The same can be said of a good government: a government is good not because it appeals to an idea of justice and freedom that can be imagined and wandered by some people; a government is good if it helps people to live safely. Therefore, the sovereign power, which is the body of the state, has to exercise absolute power on his subjects, and his subjects need to peacefully obey all the laws promulgated by the Sovereign: the good of the people always equal the good of the Sovereign; there are no unjust laws, there is no tyrannical Sovereign. The perceived tyranny of a civil society is still better than the effective freedom of the state of nature.

Toolbox

Few Words about the Commonwealth

It is important to understand the concept of commonwealth and the difference that there is between it and the one of government. Commonwealth, in fact, refers to the entity that precedes the formation of a government. The commonwealth can be understood as the moment in which the people agree on the necessity of the social contract and actively put power in the hands of the sovereign. At that moment, the association among people is still free and all individual in the commonwealth are equal. On the contrary, in an organized government, according to Hobbes, people are obligated to follow the laws promulgated by the sovereign, and perfect equality is not present nor desirable. In an organized government, in fact, the sovereign is, by definition, above the law and more powerful than everyone else; also, people cannot "opt out" of the laws of the government unless they move away. The obedience to the laws, from the people living in the territory ruled by the sovereign, is mandatory and whoever disobeys is punished accordingly. In few words, from a chronological perspective the commonwealth comes after the state of nature, but before the organized government; from an ontological perspective, the commonwealth embodies the power and the will of the people that it is transferred to the Sovereign.

Natural Rights

5 Locke: The State of Nature vs the State of War

John Locke (1632–1704) is also considered one of the masters when it comes to modern political thought: his contributions to Contractualism, and in general to political philosophy are considered the centerpiece of liberalism and his *Second Treatise of Government* is regarded as one of the most influential woks in Western political theory. We will see that, although the theoretical field that he explores is the same as Hobbes', he has a very different understanding of the way and the reason why people unite under a contract, and, probably more importantly he has a different idea regarding the relation of power present in the contract and outside of it.

Locke, at the beginning of *The Second Treatise of Government*, sets the stage for the main differences between his take on Contractualism and the take of other thinkers like Hobbes: the origin of politics, in fact, is not the product of violence and force, and of the fact that men live together by no other rules that of beasts. Political power has to be distinguished from the power of a father over his children, of a master over his servant, a husband over a wife, and a lord over his slave.

> *Political power I take it to be a right of making laws, with penalties of death, and consequentially all less penalties for the regulating and preserving of property, and employing the force of the community in execution of such laws, and in defense of the commonwealth from foreign injury, and all this only for the public good.* (Locke, *Second Treatise of Government*, Ch. 1 p. 2.)

Locke's definition of political power is interesting, and we will analyze it more in details below, but it is also interesting to notice that he distinguishes different kinds of authorities and power present in human relationships: all relationships seems to be guided by different *powers* that regulate them. In all relationships, there seems to be one of the people involved that is naturally in charged whereas there is another (or others) that suffers the power, that has to endure it. This idea, that in Locke is mentioned almost a-critically, will be analyzed and expanded later in history by philosophers that will concern themselves with the effects and the origin that this power has, and that will understand it as a different kind of political power. For now, let's go back to Locke's concept of political power.

To understand political power, Locke writes, we need to start by considering men in their original state (State of Nature): that is a state of perfect *freedom* where people order their actions and dispose of their possessions and persons as they think fit, within the bounds of the Law of Nature, without asking leave or depending upon the will of any other man. Also, in the State of nature, we have absolute *equality* where the power and jurisdiction that men have are reciprocal, meaning that everyone has the same power and authority to do to others what others can do to him. If we look at the state of nature, we will see only creatures of the same species and rank, and with the same potential abilities. Naturally, they will be equal amongst another unless they decide to give themselves a lord or a master to be the authority to be above them. The State of Nature is, therefore, the place of liberty and equality where everyone can do whatever he considers fit to his needs, and where everyone has an equal claim of power and authority, but also where everyone knows that the others are entitled to the same claims. We have to be careful, though, *the state of Nature is a state of liberty, but not of license.* Men have the freedom to do what they want with their person or possessions, yet they have not the liberty to destroy themselves, or any creature in their possession, except if a virtuous use demands it: nobody should kill an animal—for example—unless this kill is directed to noble uses like eating or, in modern terms, to experimentations that can increase the quality of life of many people. The State of Nature is governed by a law of nature, which obliges everyone: Reason. This law teaches all mankind *that being all equal and independent, no one ought to harm another in his life, health, liberty, or possessions.* Life, health, liberty, and possessions are what Locke calls *Natural Rights* and he considers them God-given; therefore, no human organization can legitimately authorize men to destroy one another or to take stuff form one another. And unless people self-preservation is in competition with the one of others we should help the others to preserve the rest of mankind by preserving *the life, the liberty, health, limb, or goods of another.* In other words, in the state of nature men are free to do whatever they want until they infringe on someone else natural rights. Natural rights are given to them by God and they are, therefore, inalienable, to the point that when possible we should do everything that we can to help others keep theirs. It is easy to see that the state of nature that

Locke is shaping is radically different from Hobbes' one: in the *Leviathan*, the only natural right is the right to preserve one's life at any cost. Hobbes even says explicitly that no one is entitled to any sort of private goods in the state of Nature because property is defined within the social contract and cannot exist outside of it. Although both Hobbes and Locke seem to agree on the absolute freedom and equality of men in the state of nature, they disagree on the fact that there are some basic principles, the natural rights, that are the *de facto* natural limits of this freedom. Infringing on someone else natural rights is not just wrong, according to Locke, it is also against nature and against the divinity. All men, then, should restrain from invading others' rights, and from harming one another: this way the law of nature will be observed, and men will live in peace and prosperity. Again, a great difference between this view of the State of Nature and the Hobbesian view of a life that in the state of nature can only be miserable and brutish: according to Locke, if men observe the law of Nature, if they use reason, life in the state of nature can be prosperous and peaceful.

A law, though, even the law of nature, needs to be enforced. If every man is equal, who has the prerogative to execute the law? The execution of the law of nature is a prerogative of all men, writes Locke, anyone can punish everyone in the state of nature if he or she transgresses the natural law. The punishment, however, should always be proportionated to the harm done, and its aim should always be to retribute the wrong done. There are various reasons why people in the state of nature would be punished and should be punished, even harshly. For example, everyone in the State of Nature has the power and the right to kill a murderer. This sort of punishment can be enforced to prevent the same kind crime to be perpetrated by the same person, to make of the punishment an example, and to reestablish the common idea that if you hurt mankind you will be disposed of just like people do with any dangerous disease that might endanger humanity. Every offense should be punished enough so to make it not convenient for the offender to try to commit that crime. It is worth it to notice how Locke is putting this idea of crime and punishment almost in economic terms. Committing crimes, in this system, is against the natural law, but there is really no mention about the "badness" of the crime: crimes are going to be committed and we should make it anti-economical for the offender, so we can deter others from doing the same thing. What really justifies all punishment is not only the removal of the *bad* individual from society, so we can live without being worried about this individual committing the same crime again; mainly what men want to achieve is to deter all other *potential* criminals by making an example of the one that was caught. In a sense, Locke here is establishing that the state of fear present, to a certain extent, in the State of Nature is not derived, Like Hobbes wanted, from the anarchy present in this state, but rather form the collective enforcement of the natural law.

Many people at the time of Locke's life (and even today) were skeptic about the whole premise of Contractualism. In fact, this doctrine assumes the existence of an entity—the State of Nature—that many people consider the fruit of someone imagination. Locke, being a Contractualist, defends the existence of the state of nature and declares that not only the state of nature existed before, but also it exists still now: we encounter it every time two man from two different countries, and therefore, from two different law systems, trust each other when they bargain or exchange goods, when they believe that the information given to them by the other person is true, etc. There are certain interactions between humans that are not regulated by law, either because these people do not follow the same positive law, and/or because the "transaction" outside of regulated places, and that therefore, these interactions are the embodiment of the State of Nature. In terms that might be more familiar to us, we can say that to a certain extent all sorts of transactions that are not happening in a store, like goods bought and sold in a yard sale or from a private individual, and/or exchanges that are not regulated by laws, like information, opinion knowledge (in a broad sense), are expression of the state of nature where people interact with each other not as citizens but as human beings.

It is clear at this point that this way of looking at the State of Nature in incompatible with the view previously presented by thinkers like Hobbes: that version of the state of nature was defined as a state of constant war of everyone against everyone else, while this version of it seems to be attuned with peaceful living. The State of Nature and the State of War are different: the first one is a *state of peace, goodwill, mutual assistance, and preservation where men live together according to reason without a common superior on earth with authority to judge them.* The second one is a *state of enmity, malice, violence, and mutual destruction where force or declared design of force upon the person of another, and where there is no common superior on Earth to appeal for relief.*

> *Want of a common Judge with authority puts all men in a state of nature; force without right upon man's person makes a state of war both where there is and is not, a common judge.* (*Ibidem*, Ch. 3 p. 12.)

State of Nature and State of war are, obviously, not compatible. But there is more. The possibility of politics is given by the restauration of the state of nature: the use of reason and the existence of a common judge to appeal to are signs of the state of nature and presuppositions of politics whereas violence, in general, is the sign of the state of war. The state of nature is peaceful and rational because men understand that they are all equal and free. While in the state of war people try to use their power to infringe on other people rights. Therefore, in such a state, the existence of a common judge (a king for example),would not make a difference: politics cannot be seen as the direct result of a state of war, rather, it can be seen as the restauration of the original moral state that was the state of nature where all men respected each other Natural Rights. One might ask, then, if there are any differences regarding the state of nature and the political state. The difference that Locke finds is the *quality* of the freedom that people enjoy in them. The *natural liberty* of a man is to be free from any higher power, and not to be under the will or authority of anyone, having only the law of nature as his rule. The *liberty of a man in society*, instead, consists in being under no other legislative power except for the one established consensually in the original agreement among men. *Freedom is not a liberty for everyone to do what he likes, to live has he pleases, and not to be tied by any law*; freedom of men under a government is to have a set of rules to live by that is common to everyone in that particular society and that it is made by the legislative power that was elected. Locke is also convinced that, in every state, freedom from absolute, arbitrary, power is necessary as it is the preservation of life: in fact, when someone is under the rule of thumb of someone else (like a slave) he is not able to decide of his own preservation, because a master can always decide of the life and death of his slaves. We see here hinted a couple of basic principles of Locke's theory of government: the power of a State, or the power of whoever is in charge, cannot be absolute and/or arbitrary; laws must be erected to establish a rule to live by and have to be equal for everyone and have to come from the legislative power elected within that society. Liberty is a natural right: without freedom one cannot be in complete control of his life, in the sense that he cannot fully preserve it. For this reason, total institutions, where one is not fully in control of his life and possessions—like Slavery—should not exist because they are against nature and infringe on men natural rights.

5.1 Property as a Natural Right

It is evident that the concept of Natural Right plays a central role in Locke's system, and although it might seem a fairly intuitive concept, it is exempt from difficulties. For example, we might be inclined to believe that life or freedom are *natural* rights, that are proper of human beings just because they are born. The simple fact of existence, we might say, entitles humans to preserve their life and to be free. But what about property? Is that a natural right? From the simple fact that human beings exist, can they deduct the right to own something? This issue, already complex from our point of view, was even more complicated at the time of Locke's publication. Religion, in fact, was much more prominent in people's life back then, and it was common knowledge at the time that God gave men the world to support them and for their convenience. Now, if God gave the world to all men, as a community, how can someone claim something in this world as his exclusive property?

The argument in favor of private property as a natural right, exposed in *The Second Treatise of Government*, is considered a classic of political theory and can be considered a pillar of liberalism. Locke argues, as we said, that Men are born with the right of preservation, to eat and to drink and such other things, and that God has given them the world to support them and for their convenience. It has given it to them as a group, in common. Everything that exists in nature is given in common to people, so when we look at fruits that *spontaneously* grow on trees and animals that *walk around* we correctly say that they are *common property of humanity*. But, the fruit or venison that nourishes the man who hunted or gathered, can we call *that* his? There must be a way, our philosopher writes, to establish that something belongs to a specific individual: in nature, everything exists on earth for the sustenance of men as a group, so how can we establish that something can be someone's fruit or meat? At the end of the day, it is him that is nourished by it. The idea that it is hinted, here is that until we talk about goods the way in which they exist in nature, in their natural state, a fruit on the tree or an animal that pastures around, we correctly identify them as *in common*. But when we talk about them in relation to a hunter or a gatherer that has taken them out of their natural state, he has picked the fruit and killed (and maybe cooked) the animal, things start changing.

If we think about it, there is at least a natural property, in fact, every man has a "property" is his own *person*. Nobody has any right to it but himself. And also, the labor of his body and the work of his hands are his property, in fact they are an extension of his being.

Whatsoever, then, he removes out of the state of nature hath provided and left in it, he hath mixed his labor with, and joined to it something that is his own, and thereby makes it his property. (Ibidem, Ch. 5 p. 16.)

Removing something from its state of nature, through labor, annexes to the *natural* object an *element* that makes it private, that removes it from commonality. In other terms, because everyone has ownership of his own body, and labor and work are natural extensions of this body, we can consider everything that one mixes his work as property. Anything that is removed from the state of nature, because it has been removed through work (the specific work of *a* specific individual), becomes unquestionable property of the laborer, and no one has the right to take it away from him. To Locke, it is obvious that it is labor the decisive factor in adjudicating property: it is not the act of eating or the act of bringing something home that makes something property of a man, it is when the man first picked up the object of nourishment—an acorn under an oak tree, for example—that it became his, because he added something to it, something that nature had not provided for, the strength necessary to pick it. Some people might say,

Locke continues, that he had no right to the acorn because nobody consented to him to take it: they believe that it is robbery to claim to oneself what belongs to all in common. But, if such consent was really necessary, man would have starved to death independently from the plenty God had given him. Just like a roast on a table is everyone's and when is cut and portioned and distributed in different plates each slice becomes of the person that is going to eat it, everything that exists in the world is in common until someone claims it through his labor. If we really think about it, this law regarding property the way is in nature, which is what it has been described up to now, it is also in place in civilized places: when people go hunting or fishing they make *theirs* some of the things that are still in common, like the animals in the woods and the fish in the ocean; in a sense, the origin of property is still honored in today's societies.

Intended this way, it seems that private property can be claimed as a natural right. But does that mean that everyone is entitled to everything he can put his hands on? Is really everything in nature subject to become property of a man? Are there any limitations on the appropriation on natural goods? Locke believes that there are *natural limitations* to the appropriation of natural resource, in fact, the same law of nature that gives men right to property also limits the amount of property that they can amass. God has given men plenty to enjoy:

> *as much as anyone can use of any advantage of life before it spoils, so much he may by his labor fix a property in. whatever is beyond this is more than his share and belongs to others. (Ibidem, p. 18.)*

If these are the rules, then there could be little room for a mistake when it comes to the right to property: there is a limitation to property as a natural right: one can accumulate as much as he wants but cannot accumulate more than he can use before it spoils, and he cannot accumulate just to destroy it. This is a general rule that can be applied even to "assets" that might look as perishable, and therefore, spoilable; land, for example, follows the same principle: if someone ploughs it, plants something, improves and encloses a plot of land from the commons can declare it his. When talking about land, though, Locke adds that someone has the right to enclose a piece of land, and can call it his, also because there is enough land left for everyone. Here, we can foresee another limitation to private property as a natural right: enough of that same good as to be left for others; no monopolies are permitted.

Labor seems to be the absolute measure that is used in establishing property, to the point that, in this system, laziness becomes absolutely not acceptable and trying to get something without working is deemed wrong: God gives the world to the people that want to work it and not to the people that want just to argue and do nothing; and he who wants to appropriate of something that is not fruit of his labor, would have no right to it, especially because if enough is left for him to use his ingenuity to gain the same thing. This idea rests on the principle that in the state of nature

> *No man's labor could subdue or appropriate all, nor could his enjoyment consume more than a small part; so that it was impossible for any man, this way, to entrench upon the right of another to acquire to himself a property to the prejudice of his neighbor, who would still have room for as good and as large a possession (after the other had taken out his) as before it was appropriated.* (Ibidem, p. 20.)

It is clear that the principle made explicit here is that enough land and as good as land (and property in general) is always left for others: in the state of nature there is enough land, and resources in general, that we can imagine that whenever someone is enclosing the *just amount* of land there is enough of the same quality left for everyone else. Regarding this principle, we can make two observations. First, it is evident that the state of nature hypothesized by Locke is very different from the one described by Hobbes: the latter saw the state of nature as an arid place where resources where scarce and the struggle to find enough to live was real; the former, on the other hand, imagines the state of nature as a place of abundance where there are more resources than the entire humanity can consume, and where there is no need to fight for the same piece of land because there is always another plot with the exact same characteristics. The second observation that can be made has to do with the conditions in which we are today: when it comes to land, things have changed radically. If we think about overpopulated areas where there is no room to subdivide land to everyone, or where the space is limited, we can see how finding a place with the same characteristics is almost impossible. To be honest, the condition in which we are today is not what Locke is describing here and, actually, he makes a clear distinction when it comes to land in a civil society: the moment people invented money and added other sorts of value to land, the entire system of subdivision of property described for the state of nature changes.

In the State of Nature, before the desire of having more than a men needed had altered the intrinsic value of things; before the invention of money or the use of gold as currency, if a man had more than he can consume or enjoy he would be offending the law of nature and would punished: he had implicitly invaded his neighbor share by taking more than he could consume; in nature property has limits, and taking more is a wrongdoing to the community. The same could have been said about land: one would claim as his just a plot of land that he could work and/or use. Obviously, then, the amount of land that one could legitimately possess increased with the number of family members present in the household: more people are able to work more land. Once again, labor is what gives someone the right of ownership over something. This becomes obvious, Locke says, when we consider the difference in value between an acre of cultivated land and an acre of abandoned land without any husbandry upon it. It is also clear that most of the things useful to men are made *useful through labor*. Labor is what really gives value to things because when we find them in nature they are not ready to be used by men but need the refinement that only men can give them: this is why refined products are more valuable than their rough materials (bread is more valuable than grains, wine than water and so on).

Because of what we have said about the transformative force of labor, it is implicit that things that do not spoil can be accumulated more and for longer periods of time. Locke says, for example, that someone can keep more sheep or cattle for longer than he can keep plums and nuts without being deemed doing something wrong. This is the reason why money was invented: it gave people the possibility to keep something without spoiling it and over which there was agreement to use to exchange it. So, we can deduct that there are, in general, some "societal" things that can be accumulated without spoilage: money would be such thing. Opposite of Aristotle (as you might remember), then, Locke believes that the accumulation of money is permitted and, actually, encouraged. Accumulating money, or gold and silver, is permitted in because there is no risk of spoilage and money is, theoretically, infinite. While in Nature Labor is the dividing factor when it comes to the ability of acquiring and keeping property (and the laws of nature limit the amount of property that might have),when money is invented men agree that someone can accumulate much more than another by keeping unspooling things like gold and silver to buy more than he needs. In a Government, laws regulate how and what a man can acquire, but there are actually no natural limits to the amount of property that one can have.

To summarize, then: labor, as an extension of our body, gives us the right to property. We can amass as much property as we want as long as we enjoy it, not spoil it, not destroy it and do leave enough to others. This also applies to land. Money, and the invention of currency (gold and silver and diamonds or whatever men agree upon to use as currency) blurred the boundaries of properties acquisition to the point that one can accumulate these things as much as he wants because they don't spoil and there is always enough left for others.

5.2 Different Powers and Different Societies

We have seen at the beginning of this chapter that Locke believes that humans can enter in contact through different relations of power. These different powers lead to different kinds of organization among people and need to be carefully distinguished, if we don't want to be grossly mistaken about the origin and the nature of societies. The first distinction to be made is the one between the power of the parents and the power of the government. To make this distinction, we need to establish, firstly, what is the role of the parents in the life of their kids and where the authority that the parents exercise over their kids comes from.

What is the main role of parent when it comes to his or her kids? It is to take care of their offspring during the imperfect state of childhood to inform their minds and govern their actions till reason shall take its place and ease them from that trouble. Kids are by nature not rational and need adults to guide them until they are finally able to make their own rational decisions and be free. Freedom and the ability to make decisions are strictly connected, in fact, people that cannot reason are not, and cannot, be free: *children, lunatics, idiots,* and *madmen.* People that cannot make rational decisions need a guardian and are not even considered responsible for their own action: this is why we would never put in jail a two-year-old, if he or she shoots someone; when something like that happens, we call it an accident. There is, then, a necessity for the parents to be in charge of the kids, there is a need for the children to have a guardian; but the power that the parents have over the children in not given to them by any sort of natural right: they are the guardians of the children, their authority is temporary and ceases as soon as the kids reach the age of reason. When the children finally get free (acquire reason) they are equal to the parents, and the parents have no more authority over them. Just from this, we should be able to understand how the power exercised by the parent, the so-called *paternal power,* is different from the political power. In a state, there is never a point in which the citizens become "adults" and are not obligated anymore to be under the rule of law: paternal power and political power are perfectly distinct and separate and are built upon different foundations and to achieve different goals. This does not mean that the power expressed in a family is not conducive to the birth of any sort of society, quite the opposite: men are by nature sociable and have the necessity to seek the company of others. It is reasonable to believe, then, that the first societies were the ones between men and wife and, subsequently, the society made by master and servants. These Societies, though, are not to be considered political societies because of their ends and relations of power. in other words, there are social unions that are not political and that are antecedent to the political societies: Marriage and Servitude are two of those.

> *Conjugal society is made by a voluntary compact between a man and a woman, and though it consist chiefly in such a communion and right in one another's bodies as is necessary to its chief end, procreation, yet it draws with mutual support and assistance, and a communion of interest too, as necessary not only to unite their care and affection, but also to their common offspring who have the right to be nourished and maintained by them until they are able to provide for themselves.* (Ibidem, Ch. 7 pp. 42–43.)

In Nature, the reason for the birth of the institution "family" is obvious: men are nidicolous animals and there is the need to take care of an offspring. Locke here defines the natural family as the necessary, but voluntary, union of men and women that has the goal to give guidance and protection to the children. This natural origin of the family is also evident when we look at the way in which we deal with it in civil societies: the *natural society of marriage* is regulated in civil societies only regarding eventual controversies that might arise between men and wife and does not interferes with the goal and internal rules of the society itself; in a court of law, for example, nobody can impose to a family rules regarding the times in which every member has to go to bed or regarding who has to wash dishes or clean the floors of the house. The law will just try to remove obstacles regarding a controversy regarding the legal agreement that men and wife have: distribution of property when the union is declared broken (divorce), retribution in case of abuse of power within the union (domestic abuse), etc. This care in not interfering in family affairs is, according to Locke, one more proof of the nonpolitical nature of *conjugal societies*. Even when a family resembles a State (for number of people in it, let's say) it is still very different form it regarding its constitution, power, and goals; the master of this family, also, will be very different from a king or a sovereign authority: he has in fact very distinct and limited power, both in time and extent, over the people that are part of the family. Mainly, he is lacking the power of life and death over any of them that is instead typical of political authorities.

The absolute right of life and death, in fact, is the distinctive trait of political societies. In fact, men are born free and in control of all the rights and privileges of the law of nature. Therefore, men, in the state of nature, have the right to punish whomever tries to do harm to them, and these punishments can go to the extent of the killing the offender, for crimes that the offended deems terrible enough. But because no political society can exist without having in itself the power to preserve the property and to punish the offenses of those whom in the society transgress, we can say that there is a political society only

> [. . .] *where everyone of the members hath quitted this natural power, resigned it up into the hands of the community in all cases that exclude him not from appealing for protection to the law established by it. and thus all private judgement of every particular member being excluded, the community comes to be umpire, and by understanding indifferent rules and men authorized by the community for their execution, decides all the differences that may happen between any members of that society concerning any matter of right and punishes those offenses which any member hath committed against the society with such penalties as the laws has established. (Ibidem, pp. 46–47.)*

It will be easy at this point to understand what a political society is. The people that are united into one body and have a common established law and arbiter to appeal to, with authority to decide controversies between them and punish offenders, are in a civil society; the ones that have no such communion are still in the state of nature. Locke implies that the political society exists because people give away the freedom to make justice by themselves when it comes to protect their properties and establish punishment. Aside from this, a political society exists when people are united under a common body of law and can appeal for defense to a common judicial system that has the authority to decide any controversies that are *public* controversies. The *Commonwealth*, which is the name that Locke uses to designate the State in general (without any specific designation—i.e., monarchy, democracy, aristocracy etc.), expresses its power by deciding what punishment belongs to the several transgressions committed amongst the members of the society (which is defined as *the power of making laws*), as well as by punish any injury that comes from outside the commonwealth (which is the *power of war and peace*); the commonwealth does all of this for the preservation of the property of all the members of the society, as far as possible.

> *The original of the legislative and executive power of civil society, which is to judge by standing laws how far offenses are punished when committed within the commonwealth. (Ibidem.)*

Locke clearly says that the fundamental powers of the government are the power to create laws and to decide about war and peace, all justified by the protection of power property: it is evident here how these prerogatives are very different from the ones proper of the conjugal society that gain their power through paternal power.

In other words, whenever a number of people unite in a society by giving up the private executive power that they have in nature and give it to the public, *there and only there* we have a political or civil society. When one enters (or creates with others) such a society, he agrees that others can make laws for him according to what the public good of the society requires. This is the fundamental change that puts men out of the state of nature into that of a commonwealth. Therefore, any absolute form of government, (and especially monarchy) as intended for example, by Hobbes, is inconsistent with a civil society and cannot be a form of civil government at all. Because the goal of civil society is to create a common body of laws that *everyone in the society must obey to* and to which anyone can appeal for a fair and independent judgment. Moreover, when there is someone that is not subject to these laws within the society, people are still in the state of nature. Everyone has to be subject to the laws established for the common good of the society: any society where there is an absolute prince that is, by definition, above the law is not, according to Locke, a civil society. We are now at the point, in the evolution of the discourse presented by Locke, where people have exited the state of nature and are entering a civil society. We need to analyze more in details how civil societies begin and what are the goals of such societies.

5.3   Political Society and Its Goals

According to Locke, civil societies begin when a group of free men decide to unite in a group where the majority will rule. This is the necessary condition of existence of a civil society.

> *What begins any political society is any number of freemen capable of majority to unite and incorporate into such a society. (Ibidem, Ch. 8 pp. 53–54.)*

Entering in a civil society mean, indeed, to agree to rules and regulations and to the judgments that are emanated by such society. This includes the rule that majority will decide what the entire group will do. What Locke means is that there is no need for unanimity to make decisions in a society—there can be disagreement within the group—and that the majority of the people have to decide in which direction society needs to move. It is interesting to notice how the issue here is not that people need to follow the majority because of some sort of moral characteristic that is inherit to the greater number of people over the lesser number of people, but simply that we need to do what the majority wants, in order to keep the society united and functional: "majority rules" is a foundational rule of society, but it is still a made up rule. There is no particular moral reason that makes this rule basic for societies, there is only a rational reason for it. Locke believes that it is more functional for a society to follow this rule rather than another one. He believes that where the majority rules we have more cohesive and stable societies.

When we look back at the beginning of civil societies, an interesting characteristic seems to be the fact that most of those societies were governed by one man only. But we will also notice, look at that period, that these monarchies were radically different from the ones that we have in the modern era: they were pretty much extensions of the rule and power that fathers had in their families and were usually *elective*. The "father" would usually rule to achieve or maintain the political happiness of the community; the affection and love of those under him were usually enough satisfaction for him. Monarchy was the most intuitive form of government derived by extension from the nonpolitical society that was the family. Monarchy was also suited for the needs of primitive societies where the main need was a war chief that would defend the society from external attacks on their property and lives, more than a legislator that would make laws to regulate the internal relationships of the society. Locke has an obvious problem when he looks back at the beginning of government: he despises monarchy, but he needs to admit that they were the primitive form of government and that, at the time, they were functioning properly and apt to the task. He needs, therefore, to justify the existence of these ancient monarchies against his previous comments that no civil society can exist if it is ruled by an absolute power—like monarchy. He does so by showing the different nature of that monarchy and of the needs of the people of the time. In other words, monarchy at the beginning of the social contract where a completely different species compared to the modern ones. They are elective, ruled for and by love, and very simple when it comes to the task that they have to perform. The king is, basically, a war chief that is in charge of defending his people like a father and that does not enjoy any special status amongst his people except for the time of war. It is easy to see the difference, here between such monarchies and the ones existing when Locke was alive. The golden age (the age were monarchies were not really absolute and the needs of the people were simpler) had more virtue than the modern age, and therefore, had better governments and less malicious subjects. In his age, Locke believes, ambition and greed have corrupted people's minds into a mistake of power and honor, people believe that they have to seize as much as they can of both. For this reason, starting with the modern age, there is the need of more regulations and monarchy is not suited anymore as a civil form of government.

Locke's other issue when describing the beginning of the civil societies is the possibility to enter of exit such societies. When we look at our world today (and the same was for Locke in his times), it seems almost impossible to believe that someone can decide not to partake in society. But if this is true, then the original contract is just a fictious tale that has no weight whatsoever in the evolution of our societies. Locke argues that that is not true, and that the contract is real and that there are ways to exit it (like there were ways to enter it at the beginning of it). In fact, one can be part of a government either by explicitly consent or by implicitly consenting to the rules of the government. Enjoying the possessions that are part of a territory under a government demands obedience the laws of that government until the subject in question wants to possess these lands. But as soon as he gets rid of such properties (by selling them or abandon them, for example), he is not bound by the rules of the government. Possessions, when it comes to implicit consent, are the ticket to get in and out of a society. The idea expressed by Locke here is pretty simple. One enters a society either by explicitly "signing" the contract, or implicitly by owning land, and wealth in general, within the borders of that society. Let's make an example of both cases like they present themselves in our society. One is explicitly consenting to be part of a society when *applies* for citizenship in a country where she is not born. Everywhere in the world, in order to become a citizen of a country, people need to pass a test that proves their knowledge of the laws and regulations of that country; Citizenship seekers, also, need to pledge loyalty to the new country and its laws and values. This example makes self-evident the case for explicit consent: one explicitly consents to be part of a country, when physically "asks" (orally or in writing) to be part of a society. As for implicit consent, we can look at the peculiar example of the authorization to work in the United States. Anyone who wants to work in the United States, and is not a citizen, needs to apply to obtain a special status—Work Visa—in the country that will allow him or her to work and make money. Why do people need this special authorization? Because if someone works in the United States that someone needs also to conform to the rules of the United States: he or she needs to pay taxes according to US tax code, he or she has to follow the rules of what kind of work is legal or illegal in the United States, and more importantly, he or she will need to accept the civic rules and laws of the United States. To receive a Work Visa, in the United States, there is no special test that helps establishing if one has knowledge of the United States. laws, but it is *implicit* that until, one works in the United States, he or she will need to follow the laws of the land. The moment the Visa holder leaves the United States or renounces his or her ability to work and gain wealth there, and has no property there, then he or she is not part of the US society anymore and can disregard the laws of the United States. To enter implicitly, all that one needs to do is to enjoy the opportunity offered by that society. If one does so, then he or she is obliged to follow the rule of that society as well. The same thing goes for exiting a society: to get out of a *contract*, one has to renounce to his or her possessions and possibility of building wealth within the borders of that society.

Locke has now justified the existence of a real contract that he considers the foundation of all civil society. He is still left with a problem, though. Since he believes, contrary to Hobbes, that the State of nature is not that bad (he calls it often the golden age), it is legitimate to ask, "if a man in the state of nature is so free as we have said, why should he subject himself to the control of any other power?". Because, Locke responds, in the state of nature men have all the natural rights that described (life, liberty, health, possessions, etc.), but the *enjoyment* of these rights is very uncertain and exposed to the vexation of others; because all men have absolute power and every man is equal, and most of them do not observe equity and justice the enjoyment of property is absolutely unsafe. This makes men willing to give up the condition of freedom and to join a society where they would be under certain restrictions in order to enjoy a mutual preservation of *lives, liberties and estates, which I call by the general name—property*. Locke, just like Hobbes, motivates the exit of human beings from the state of nature with the will to acquire safety, but a different kind of safety. In Hobbes, we see that the government has, as its main goal, to ensure the physical safety of its subjects whereas in Locke, we see that the main goal of the government is to provide a safe space where everyone one can enjoy the full potential of the natural rights. Specifically, Locke believes that the main goal of men uniting in civil societies (even before real governments are created) and eventually putting themselves under a government is the preservation of *their property*. This preservation in the state of nature is difficult because it lacks, essentially, three things: (1) established, settled, known *laws* that is agreed by all and that it is considered the standard of right and wrong and the measure through which people decide all controversies between them. (2) An *Impartial Judge* that can determine punishments and praises according to the established law. In the state of nature, this is impossible because everyone is his own judge and men are partial to themselves to the point that they will carry punishment too far if they want revenge. (3) The power to back and support the *execution of a sentence* when right. This is also impossible (or very dangerous) in the state of nature because everyone will try to defend himself making dangerous for the executioners to carry on the due sentences. Basically, Locke is laying down the main duties of a simple government: establishing laws, impartially decide controversies, and carry out the right amount of punishment for those who transgress either the laws or the impartial judgment. Again, there is a similitude to what Hobbes believed (Government is in charge of all three of these things, also for the author of the *Leviathan*), but he believed that the same person (or group of people) could be in charge of all three of these things necessary to a civil life amongst men whereas Locke thinks that we need different *branches* of government to take care of different functions necessary to preserve civil society. This and the one noted before are an enormous difference, and, we will see later in the chapter, they will lead to an opposite view regarding the extent of the power of a government.

In conclusion, regarding the goals of political societies in Locke, we can affirm that men give up their *equality, liberty, and executive power* (that they had in the state of nature) only because they think that they can gain back a better version of their natural rights, a more *secure* version of it. For this reason, the power of political societies cannot extend further than the common good. In fact, such societies exist only to correct the imperfections of the state of nature to give peace, safety, and public good to the people.

5.4   Different Forms of Government and the Separation of Powers

Locke, like his predecessors, writes of the different ways in which people can organize themselves. He writes that when men organize in a society and *all of them* keep their power to make laws for the community and appoint officers to execute those laws then the form of government is called *perfect democracy*. When the power is put in the hands of *few selected men and their successors*, it is called an *oligarchy*; if the power is in the hands of just *one man* we call it *monarchy*; if the man and his heirs are invested with power we have a *hereditary* monarchy, if the power is given to him only we call it *elective* monarchy. When the form of government is elective (and all forms are, but oligarchy and hereditary monarchy) once the governing cycle is over the power goes back to the commonwealth (the people) and they can decide if they want to keep or change form of government that they have experimented with; this change, in fact, can only be made by a power superior to the government and the only power superior to that that (we could call it the supreme power) belongs to the commonwealth. Locke gives us a classic distinction of forms of government with a special emphasis on elective forms of government. But the most important description here regards the distinction between Commonwealth and Government and the relation between the two. Commonwealth, in fact is not a form of Government, but the "assembly" of all people under the social contract. It is not some elaborate form of direct democracy but derives its meaning from the Latin word *Civitas* which denotes an association of people that a common goal. For this reason, the Commonwealth is *pre-government* and it is the source of power for the government. The people of the commonwealth have the supreme power when it comes to making decisions regarding the directing toward which the community of people under the social contract want to go.

Once more Locke is writing is direct opposition to Hobbes. As you might remember, Hobbes clearly states that the supreme power, once a social contract is established, resides in the newly created body that he calls the sovereign; He also clearly states that once the Commonwealth (intended in Hobbes language simply as group of people that are in the process of putting together a Government, and eventually used as synonymous of Government) gives mandate to the Sovereign, it has no power to revert back to simple Commonwealth and change the rules of government. It is evident, then, that the idea that the Commonwealth can change the form of government when it sees fit because it detains the supreme power is absolutely contrary to Hobbes' principles, and that Locke is distancing himself from Hobbes as much as possible by giving the people (the commonwealth) the last say when it comes to instituting laws and regulations, but also when it comes to supreme power. Again, if you remember, Hobbes declares that one of the reasons why the Sovereign cannot be judged according to its own laws is that a government at that point will need a power and superior to it, which would be impossible because the Sovereign has to have absolute power. Locke response is interesting. We can say that he agrees with Hobbes in that while the Sovereign is in charge, while serving its term (we could say), it does have absolute power. This power, though, is limited in time; the moment the cycle ends, and it is time to elect a new sovereign the power goes back to the Commonwealth which detains the real supreme power. These opposite views of power will also determine a different outcome, in the two thinkers, when it comes to the legitimacy of a government and its laws. Hobbes writes that all Governments and laws are legitimate, because they are the absolute authority. Locke maintains that all governments and laws are legitimate only until they express the true will of the commonwealth. Once more, important consequences can be deducted from this fundamental difference, and we will analyze these consequences toward the end of the chapter.

Considering, then, that the Commonwealth has the supreme power, it should not come as a surprise that Locke believes that the Commonwealth itself has the right (and the duty) to establish the most general laws regarding government and the administration of the civil society. Firstly, Locke theorizes that we need a separation of power: we need to separate the *legislative* power from the *executive* power and both need to be separated from what is called *federative* power. It is important to understand in detail what Locke means by that and what are the characteristics of each of these powers. Let's go in order.

Locke believes that the Commonwealth needs to establish some ground rules that will govern the general administration of political power. The first positive law that he believes is necessary for the commonwealth to establish is to put in place a legislative assembly that detains the power to govern everything (even the legislative itself) according to a general fundamental rule: *to preserve society* (as far as it consists with the public good) *and every person in it*. The legislative is the supreme power of the commonwealth and it needs to be obeyed once it is deposited in the hands of whoever has been appointed with it. Locke, like Hobbes, gives supreme power of legislation (power to make laws) to the government, but with some limitations. One of these limitations is that the legislative is sacred only as long as it acts in conformity with the common good. More specifically, the legislative cannot take away the natural rights of the people and it is limited to the public good of society, that is, it needs to act in conformity with the law of nature.

A second law that the commonwealth needs to establish is that *laws have to be stable and cannot consist of arbitrary decrees*; also, judges need to be known and authorized, the people that are in charge of applying the law need to be publicly appointed. This is, according to Locke, the only way to honor the reason why men entered in a commonwealth to begin with. Men abandon the state of nature and agree to submit themselves to rules that limit their power only to have clear guidelines and to preserve their property from arbitrary power. Therefore, the ruling class has to govern by declared and received laws and not by the caprice of a man that constantly changes him mind. In other words, people enter a commonwealth, so they can understand with clarity which are the laws to follow and what it is considered right or wrong. These things cannot change with the mood of a man and they need to be codified and received by the people, otherwise we are in presence of a capricious arbitrary legislative power, which is contrary to the spirit of the commonwealth.

The third law that the Commonwealth needs to lay has to do with the extent of power that a government can have over its subjects. The government cannot take from a man any part, or the whole, of his property without his consent. *The preservation of property is the main goal of the government* and it would be absurd for the government to take it away from any man. The fact that the government has absolute power over its subjects cannot be used as an excuse to take the property of a man. Locke here is telling us that although the government might dispose of the life and death of a subject, it cannot take away the property of his subjects. To justify this point, the British philosopher make the example of the military where absolute obedience to a superior officer is necessary, and where a soldier has to obey even to orders that can mean is almost sure death. But even in this extreme case, Locke says, the superior officer cannot take a penny from the soldier. What about taxes then? Shouldn't a government collect taxes from its subjects in order to maintain itself? It sure has to, but the government cannot lay or levy taxes without the consent of the people. The government, evidently, has power of life and death over its citizens by necessity (because it needs to be able to force them to put themselves at risk—e.g., military campaigns), but it absolutely *does not* have the power to take anything—any property—from its people unless there is consent from them. Taxes are no exception, and they have to be previously agreed upon by the commonwealth.

Other laws that the commonwealth needs to establish have to do with the limits of the power of the legislative. For example, the legislative cannot transfer the power of making laws to anyone else. That is a prerogative of the commonwealth: only the commonwealth can decide who makes the laws, not the government. The idea is that only the commonwealth can change what we could call the constitution. The government can only deal with the laws that are dealt to it by the commonwealth.

In summary, these are the limits that are put by society on those who are entrusted with the administration of the legislative power of any form of government: (1) they have to govern by established laws that do not vary from case to case and are the same for everyone; (2) these laws also have to be designed for no other end but the good of the people; (3) whoever is in charge cannot raise taxes on the properties of the people without the consent of the people; and (4) the legislative cannot transfer the power of making laws to anybody else or place it anywhere but where the people have established to be. It is now time, in Locke's view, to analyze more in depth the three branches of government (legislative, executive, and federative) and the relation that they have with each other.

The legislative power has as its goals to create the laws that have to be executed to direct the commonwealth. In commonwealths where the good of the people is really the center of political activity, this power should be separated by the executive power because people might be tempted to keep on making laws to exempt themselves to obey the same laws as the regular citizens. In addition, considering the nature of the legislative power, there is no need for it to be constantly present after the laws are made. In fact, after the institution of the laws the legislative power can be dissolved, and its members can return to be private citizens. The legislative power is the supreme power within an organized state, but the people can dissolve it, or alter it, if it is going against the reason why people came together as a community (self-preservation), or it goes against the common good. The *supreme* power that belong to the people, the one that has really no superiors, exists only *outside* the established state, just as an abstract force that exists when the state is dissolved. In other words, the legislative power is chief, and not subordinate to any power within an organized state, but it is always subject to the ultimate power of the people, considered as force that exists beyond the scope of a state.

The executive power, instead, is subordinate to the legislative: people in this branch derive their authority from the specific task that was to them assigned by the legislative. Therefore, if the executive does a bad job, the legislative can strip it from its authority and punish it. The executive power is made of people that have specific "technical" tasks to perform, and that are invested with the authority to execute that task. For this reason, when the legislative is made by representatives (so, in any form of government except direct democracy) and choosing the representatives is a prerogative of the people either through regular or extraordinary elections; If the executive is used by the legislator in power to hinder the ability of the people to have elections and replace the legislators, then the people have the right to remove them by force. In other words, the executive power is always subordinate to the legislative power, so when the Legislative asks something of the Executive, the latter usually obeys (it is in its nature to do so). But this is not an excuse when it comes to infringe on the right that the people have to choose their own representative. "Just following orders" is not an excuse for the executive, therefore, we can say that one motto of the people could be "free elections or rebellion!". Once again Locke goes directly against Hobbes by theorizing the possibility of a just rebellion against any form of government that just takes from the people away the possibility of changing their representative or even the form of government. We can say, then, that according to Locke, the executive has to always obey to the legislative and it is subordinate to the legislative except for those cases where is evident that the legislative is going against the common good of the people. Also in certain cases, and specifically to avoid that the legislative stays in session when there is no need and becomes a burden to the people, the executive is given the power to schedule the meetings (and the duration of them) of the legislative. This means that the executive can establish how often people have to meet and for how long they have to meet to revise or abolish older laws, or to promulgate new laws, but only if the legislative had previously established so. The executive, even in this case, is subordinate to the legislative. There seems to be an area where the executive has more freedom with respect to the legislative: all the legislative unregulated matters. Matters that are not regulated by the legislator, in fact, should be left to the executive at least until they are not legislated upon. In addition, the executive, being in more direct contact with the people and the true application of the laws, should have the power to mitigate the law or to pardon some offenders for the public good. Now, this discretion regarding non-legislated matter and this flexibility in the application of certain laws is called, by Locke, *Prerogative*. It is understood that prerogative can be exercised when it has as its goal the good of the people. Moreover, the good of the people should be the meter according to which we evaluate if keeping the matter unregulated or not if there are disputes in that sense.

Prerogative is nothing but the power of doing public good without a rule. (*Ibidem*, Ch. 14 p. 94.)

Prerogative is a very important aspect of governing, according to Locke, especially at the beginning of organized societies. As a matter of fact, it is easy to imagine how at the infancy of government, when commonwealths were very similar to families, the ruler would govern like a father would: with few laws and a lot of prerogative. Moreover, it worked well because the rulers governed truly under the guidance of the love for their people. But then, when corrupted princes that cared more about their private interest than the good of their people took power, the people demanded more specific laws to limit the abuse of power. They did this by limiting or revoking the privilege of prerogative. Locke also observes that the reigns of good princes have been always the most dangerous to the liberties of their people. This is because people would let the good prince govern by prerogative, with very few fixed real laws in consideration of how good the prince was. But when the enlightened prince died, and a not so enlightened one comes to power, then the people can lose their liberties very easily because the new prince will use the prerogative of the old one to justify his acts. Therefore, prerogative is important and can be good, but it can also be easily abused.

Finally, Locke briefly defines *the federative power*: the federative power is the power that governs the relationship that a political body has as a whole with another political body. It contains the power of war and peace, the power to make alliances and all transactions that have to do with whoever is *not* part of the commonwealth. This power is often united with the executive power, but it is more dangerous than this last one. The federative power, in fact, operates like a man would operate in the state of nature. And just like for a man it is dangerous to make decisions in the state of nature, so it is dangerous for the State to make decisions regarding foreign affairs. The federative power is what Hobbes called *natural power* because it resembles the one that men have in the state of nature. And just like

Hobbes, Locke believes that States operate like people in the state of nature with the same level of danger involved in the process of making decisions when it comes to enter in a relationship with foreign powers. The main difference between the two views of this power (between the Lockean and the Hobbesian version of it) is that once again Locke puts limits on the extent of this power. the federative power is limited by and it is subordinate to the legislative power. Which in turn is limited by the supreme power of the common wealth. Always, where Hobbes saw unlimited power of the Sovereign, Locke saw a power that needs balance in order to avoid the loss of any natural right.

5.5 Conquest, Usurpation, and Tyranny: Illegitimate Governments

Locke, still in classic fashion, after the analysis of the legitimate form of government and of the legitimate extent of different powers decides to analyze what form of government, or better, what ways to obtain power cannot be considered legitimate. To do so, he starts with the analysis of *conquest* intended as annexation of populations or land to a preexisting state.

> *Here it is in brief: if the conqueror has a just cause, he gets ·through his conquest· a despotic right over the persons of all those who actually aided and supported the war against him, and a right to use their labour and estates to make up for the damages he has suffered and the costs he has incurred (so long as he doesn't infringe anyone else's rights). He has no power over such of the people as didn't consent to the war, or over the children of the captives themselves, and no power over the possessions of either group. So his conquest does not entitle him to have dominion over them, or to pass on such dominion to his posterity. If he tries to take their properties, he is an aggressor, and thereby puts himself into a state of war against them. (Ibidem, Ch. 16 p. 109.)*

Locke is telling us that a conqueror has a limited legitimate power over the conquered. Not in the sense that the conqueror cannot dispose of the conquered' life—he has in fact legitimate despotic power over him/them—but he has no legitimate power to take anything from the people that did not participate to the war, or from the offspring of the conquered. He should not even take the estates of the people that did participate because they belong to the kids and wives that have not done anything to put themselves in a state of war. Moreover, a conqueror should not even annex the new people to his population without their true voluntary consent (not one extorted with violence). The Conqueror can *only* dispose of the life, the liberty and the *labor* of the individuals that actively participated in the war to gain restitution and reparation. Anything that goes beyond this makes the conqueror an aggressor and therefore, it makes it right to rebel against him.

The next illegitimate way of taking power analyzed by Locke is *usurpation*:

As conquest may be called a foreign usurpation, so usurpation is a kind of domestic conquest. But the equivalence is not exact: a 'domestic conqueror' might have right on his side, but an usurper can never do so, because an action counts as a usurpation only if it involves getting possession of something that someone else has a right to. A usurpation, as such, is a change only in who has the government, not in the forms and rules of the government. If the usurper ·goes further, and· extends his power beyond what rightly belonged to the lawful monarchs or governors of the commonwealth ·whom he has dislodged·, he is guilty not merely of usurpation but also of tyranny. (Ibidem, Ch. 17 p. 110.)

A usurper is someone that puts himself illegitimately in power by substituting whoever was chosen by the people to play that role. Usurpation, therefore, designs only an illegitimate change in personal, not a change of the rule of law or of the form of government. Usurpation is ultimately illegitimate because only the people can decide who can represent them and, therefore, rule. Any self-appointed member of the government is a usurper and, therefore, does not really detain any power, which means that the people have no obligation to follow him. Rather, they have a duty to remove him from power.

There is one more example, probably the most dangerous one, of illegitimate means of taking and keeping power: *Tyranny*.

Whereas usurpation is the exercise of power to which someone else has a right, tyranny is the exercise of power to which nobody can have a right. That is what happens when someone employs the power he has in his hands, not for the good of those who are under it but for his own private individual advantage. ·It is what happens· when a governor, however entitled ·he is to govern·, is guided not by the law but by his own wants, and his commands and actions are directed not to preserving his subjects' properties but to satisfying his own ambition, revenge, covetousness, or any other irregular passion. (Ibidem, Ch. 18 p. 112.)

Tyranny is, simply put, abuse of power. Whenever a governor employs power not for the good of the people, but to satisfy whatever want or need he has, he becomes a Tyrant (no matter how he has received his power). Locke here goes against the classical view of tyranny. If you remember, since Plato we have equate Tyranny with a degenerate form of monarchy; and even Hobbes, by denying that government degenerate, equates it with monarchy. Locke, instead, warns us and writes that it is a mistake to think that only monarchies can transform into tyrannies: every form of government where the power given by the people to their representatives is misused (i.e., used not to preserve the natural rights of the people) can become tyrannical. The only difference would be in the numbers of the tyrants. Even more explicitly,

Locke writes that wherever the law ends, tyranny begins. If one misuses the authority given to him, or exceeds the power give to him, he becomes a tyrant. Tyranny does not depend on the scope of the abuse of power or on the level of the magistrate: whenever there is abuse of power there is tyranny. This is very significative because it seems to attribute the possibility of tyrannical act to everyone who exercises any sort of power. If we take Locke seriously, we have to accept the possibility that wherever there are relations in which there is any sort of power involved, there is the possibility of a tyrannical use of this power. We can have tyrannical politicians, obviously, but also tyrannical police officers, or tyrannical bureaucrats; or even tyrannical teachers or wives and husbands. Power, we will see in the following chapters, is one of the nebulous concept that are fundamental when it comes to analyzing human organizations.

5.6 Power to the People!

If any form of government can degenerate into a tyranny, there is no guarantee that, if we choose wisely at the beginning and pick, for example, representative democracy (Locke's favorite form of government) we will not find ourselves in a less than ideal power struggle with a tyrant. For this reason, Locke feels the need to analyze and explain when and how people should rebel against the government and restructure the society that they have created. This entire section of Locke thought can be seen as an absolute opposition to Hobbes view that no matter what happens people should never rebel against the government, and that a day as a slave in a civil society is better than an entire life of freedom in the state of nature.

We know that Hobbes main preoccupation when establishing the principle that it is irrational to have revolts and revolutions was the inevitable bloodbath that civil war brings every time they happen. Now, Locke is well aware of the element of violence that can come with rebelling against the authority, and for this reason he specifies that the prince and the laws can be disobeyed with force *only* when force is being used unjustly and unlawfully. The people are justified to use force in response to force that has been used by the tyrant in power. More specifically, no violence should come to the person(s) of the ruler(s), unless he is clearly going against his people: in that case the state can be considered dissolved and he is not a ruler anymore, but just another man in the state of nature, where anything can happen, and there are no real positive laws in place. In a civil society, in a place where the ruler is liable for his mistakes like everyone else, it will be the law that will take care of unjust and unlawful conducts of the ruler or his associates; only in situations where people cannot be vindicated by the law, then they authorized to use force. Note how the principle of self-defense follows the same logic: I am allowed to kill someone only if my life is endangered directly (the reason being that the law cannot vindicate me if I am dead!); in all other cases I cannot even harm my offender otherwise I can be persecuted by law.

Locke is the first philosopher that we have studied that seems to be interested to some sort of a theory of rebellion. He is the first one that explicitly put in place rules and regulations to establish the rightness or the wrongness, but also the opportunity or not opportunity, to rebel against the authority.

> If an official uses his power to maintain his unlawful acts and to obstruct the appeal to law for a remedy, this is manifest tyranny and there is a right to resist it; but even in cases like this, if the harm is slight there won't be resistance that will disturb the government. For if the trouble concerns the cases of only a few private men, though they have a right to defend themselves and to recover by force what through unlawful force has been taken from them, they will be disinclined to exercise their right by engaging in a contest in which they are sure to perish. ·And they are sure to perish·, because it is as impossible for a few oppressed men to disturb the government when the body of the people don't think themselves concerned in it as it is for a raving madman or headstrong malcontent to overturn a well settled state. (Ibidem, p. 117.)

Locke is here suggesting that people have to resist and fight tyranny . . . if they are the majority that perceives the specific kind of oppression as an issue. If the minority is being oppressed, in fact, and there are no chances of change because the majority does not perceive the issue, then oppression is justified to continue, mainly because while the oppressed have the right to rebel, they will never succeed. Locke is, involuntarily, justifying institutionalized behavior like sexism, racism, and any kind of minority oppression possible. If the majority of the people does not perceives an institutionalized conduct as oppressive, then even the minority should avoid rebelling, and maybe (but Locke does not say this explicitly) use its energy trying to convince more people to join the cause. On the other hand,

> But suppose these illegal acts have affected the majority of the people, or have affected only a few but seem to set a dangerous precedent threatening everyone, so that the people are persuaded in their consciences that their laws are in danger and—along with the laws—their estates, liberties, and lives, and perhaps their religion too. When that happens, I can't see how the people can be hindered from resisting the illegal force that has been ·or threatens to be· used against them. Such resistance is a difficulty that will confront any government in which the governors have managed to become generally suspected by their people. It is the most dangerous state that governors can possibly put themselves in, but they don't deserve much pity

because the trouble is so easy to avoid. If a governor really does intend the good of his people, and the preservation of them and their laws, the people are bound to see and feel this, just as the children in a family will see that their father loves and takes care of them. (Ibidem.)

The right of the people to fight against injustice is absolute and right, and the rulers that put themselves in the position of being hated by their people bring their misfortune on themselves. We have seen that Hobbes, in the previous chapter, warns us against any sort of rebellion because it might lead to the dissolution of government and the consequent return to the state of nature and its misery. Locke thinks differently and having postulated an intermediate layer between the state of nature and the government—that he calls the Commonwealth—he is able to think about the dissolution of a government without necessarily having to fear the return of a chaos. When we talk about the dissolution of government, then, we need to distinguish it from the dissolution of society. Society, mainly, is dissolved only when a foreign force invades and conquers. Whenever a society is dissolved, the government of that society it is dissolved as well. Dissolutions of societies are traumatic because they send people back to fend for themselves. Obviously, if the society is gone, dispersed, the government instituted by that society it is also gone. The opposite, however, is not true: government can be dissolved without dissolving the society that has created it. Governments are dissolved (differently from societies) from within and it happens mainly because someone has usurped the power that belongs to the people. In any situation where the legislative is broken or altered, the government can be considered dissolved. When the people in power abuse their power, then, the trust is broken, and the government is ended at least in the sense that the people have no more obligations to abide the laws. This is very different than society being dissolved, and it is a less traumatic, but not necessarily a less violent event.

Another way in which the government can dissolve is when the supreme executive power neglects or abandons the charge: if there is nobody to enforce the laws then there is anarchy, and a government without laws cannot exist. Interestingly enough Locke equates the existence of government not just with the existence of a constitution or a set of laws—which is typical of the classical views of government—but also with the application of the laws: theoretical laws without applications are not enough to have a government, and the result is chaos.

Probably, though, the most important reason for the dissolution of government resides in those occasions when the government itself takes (or tries to) away the natural rights from its people. When the Legislative does that, it is declaring war to the people, and the people have the right to fight for their rights. The same goes for the Executive: if it acts in such a way using its powers to take away the properties of the people, then the government is dissolved. We know that there are certain natural rights that are inalienable and the safeguard of them is the only reason why people created a society and a government. If the government is taking them away, then it is declaring war to the people and the people *must* defend themselves. Locke is very aware of the usual criticism that the position that he is taking regarding rebellion against the government. The most popular objection to the possibility of rebellion against a government states that if we authorize such rebellions, then people will change government any time they do not like something about their government: the caprice of the people becomes more important than the stability of the government. Locke clearly believes that this is not true. People, he writes, tend to stay with what they know even more than what they should, as it is demonstrated by how few changes in the form of government have happened throughout history. Locke reasoning here seems correct. If we look at England, for example, we can see how they still have monarchy, even if it is not an *executive* monarchy. People have the tendency to stuck with the know rather than experimenting with the unknown.

This view, Locke specifies, is not a fomentation of rebellion. Actually, when people are subjected to the distorted usage of arbitrary power and feel powerless, that is when rebellions happen. So, giving them the theoretical and political tools to avoid such situations of powerlessness delays and in many cases prevents the rebellion itself. In addition, people do not rebel for mistakes in ruling or inconvenient laws and mistakes that a human can make; they rebel when they see a clear design of abuse. If anything, again, including a "rebellion" clause in a constitution might prevent rebellions: the fear of rebellion might be the best antidote against rebellion. If it has been established that the government is the one that is responsible, most of the times, for rebellions, if it fears it, maybe it would not engage in abuses of power. Even etymologically it should be clear that the rebels are not the ones fighting the government (they are rather the ones that act in agreement with the spirit of the social contract). *Re-bellare*, in fact, literarily means going at war again. Therefore, the rebels are the ones that lay the conditions for the rebellion, namely, the bad legislators. Whoever invades someone else's natural rights is culpable for the bloodshed, mischief and desolation that comes from the rebellion that comes after that. And the magistrates are no exception. They can be as culpable as the others.

> *To conclude, the power that every individual gave to the society when he entered into it can never revert to the individuals again as long as the society lasts, but will always remain in the community; because without this there can't be a community, a commonwealth, and that would be contrary to the original agreement. So also when the society has placed*

the legislative power in any assembly of men, to continue in them and their successors with direction and authority for providing such successors, the legislative power can never revert to the people while that government lasts; because having provided a legislature with power to continue for ever, they have given to it their political power and cannot get it back. But if they have set limits to the duration of their legislature, and given this supreme power to some person or assembly only temporarily, or if it is forfeited through the misbehaviour of those in authority, at the set time or at the time of the forfeiture the power does revert to the society, and then the people have a right to act as supreme and to continue the legislature in themselves; or to set up a new form of government, or retain the old form while placing it in new hands, as they see fit. (Ibidem, Ch. 19 p. 137.)

Toolbox

America, A Lockean Experiment

It is no mystery that the American constitution was written with Locke's theories in mind. What is interesting, though, is that American society in its entirety seems to be founded on Lockean principles. If we think about the idea, for example, that private property is a *natural right*, we should be able to understand how and why material wealth is so important in American culture. In addition, considering that according to Locke we are naturally industrious, and that our right to property comes from labor, it is easy to understand why American society, in general, dislikes any sort of program that "rewards" with money or property somebody who does not work. All social programs such as, food stamps and unemployment compensation are suspect because they don't follow the Lockean pattern of labor-property, breaking the natural bond between the two in favor of "lazy" individuals that want to reap the benefits of the social agreement but that are not willing to work for them. This is just an example of Locke's influence on American society, but really every aspects of the traditional American values can be traced back to Locke.

CHAPTER 6

The Good Savage

6 The Enlightenment and Its Origins

During the 1700s, the dominating school of thought in Europe takes the name of Enlightenment. It is important to understand that this way of thinking is not just a specific school of thought proper of *one* influential group of philosophers. Rather, the enlightenment is a cultural atmosphere that influences almost all philosophical currents. Even Philosophical schools that are traditionally rivals share, in this period, some common characteristics that we could call generally *Enlightened* that seem to reflect the innovative spirit that inhabited the great part of the European society.

The first of these characteristics is, without a doubt, the strong faith that people have in reason during the enlightenment. In fact, reason is considered to be the instrument that can solve all of men's problems: from philosophy to religion, from science to politics, reason is considered to be the cure of all evils. For this reason, it is possible to perceive in the culture of the time the general presence of a scientific spirit. We can say that this is the time when our way of intending knowledge, truth, and science takes the shape that it has now: the scientific method acquires the characteristics of *truth-giving*, infallible tool that it has now.

Secondly, enlightenment means critique of the traditional values. There is an accurate search for a new set of moral and political values during this period that expresses a *revolutionary* spirit in open contrast with the traditional view of society and religion. The philosophers of this time want to find out the inconsistency of some traditional values to open some space to new customs and ways of thinking; from this perspective, the French revolution has the merit to summarize best the new values proposed by the enlightenment in its slogan *Liberté, Égualité, Fraternité* (freedom, equality, brotherhood). These values are considered in contrast to the value of the old regime that, according to the enlightened philosophers, promoted intolerance and obscurantism, and conservatism.

Finally, the enlightenment is characterized by a generalized optimism regarding the betterment of the human condition. The advancements proper of this epoch give reason to believe that humanbeings will live in a better world (a world with less superstition and more science, with less ignorance and more knowledge) and that humans themselves will become better and, with the help of reason, they will be able to live longer and more peacefully.

The beginning of the Enlightenment movement can be traced back to the philosophy of Locke and the science of Newton. These two giants of modern philosophy have an enormous influence on the English enlightenment and on the enlightenment in general. The place where the movement had his larger development—especially regarding his socio-political side—was, however, France, where a series of historical conditions (especially the repeal of the *Nantes Edict*) helped the movement to develop greatly, and to foster a philosophical-political radicalism unknown to that era. In this chapter, we will analyze, briefly, the thought of Montesquieu (a classic thinker of the enlightenment), while we will indulge longer of the thought of a more controversial philosopher, Rousseau.

6.1 Montesquieu and the Spirit of the Laws

Charles-Louis De Secondat, baron of La Brede and *Montesquieu* (1689–1755) is interested, chiefly, about the civil problem typical of the French society (and by extension of societies in general) of his times. Regarding these issues, he expresses ideas that today we would define as moderate. He did not believe that the solution to many of the problem present in society required a radical mutation of the philosophical concepts or of the social structures of the time. He was a reformist more than a revolutionary and he believed that in order to find a *rational* explanation of the great event in humanity one must look at history.

This way of thinking is in contrast, for example, with the explanation of the relationship between State and Individual given by thinkers such as Hobbes and Locke. As we have seen, the two British philosophers thought that the State was an artificial construction (dictated by reason) based on a contract that was established to impose order on the irrational and chaotic set of behaviors proper of individuals. In other words, the social contract is an arbitrary pact is contrast with the *natural essence* of human beings (the state of nature). Montesquieu, instead, believes that the formation of a state is a long and slow process. It is the necessity of food and preservation that leads the first men to gather together and it is the environment that surrounds this primitive groups that will determine the customs that, as it is evident, differ from population to population.

These customs, which at the beginning are not yet laws, will eventually be formalized in rules that are not arbitrary or artificial. The laws of any population are in close relation with the way in which different groups obtain their means of subsistence. More laws, according to Montesquieu, are necessary for those populations in which business is the main way to procure resources, compared to those population that gain their resources from agriculture. At the same time, more laws are required for a population of farmers than it is for a population of herders, and, in turn more laws are necessary for the later than for a population of hunters. The formation of states and governments is connected to the formalization of the rules and regulations that have become norm in the customs of the different populations.

Montesquieu assigns to *climate* great importance when it comes to the vicissitudes of humanity, to the point that he believes that climate determines (more or less directly) certain factors that he calls *moral* and that are important when it comes the customs of the people.

Cold air constringes the extremities of the external fibres of the body; this increases their elasticity, and favours the return of the blood from the extreme parts to the heart. It contracts those very fibres; consequently it increases also their force. On the contrary, warm air relaxes and lengthens the extremes of the fibres; of course it diminishes their force and elasticity. People are therefore more vigorous in cold climates. Here the action of the heart and the reaction of the extremities of the fibres are better performed, the temperature of the humours is greater, the blood moves more freely towards the heart, and reciprocally the heart has more power. This superiority of strength must produce various effects; for instance, a greater boldness, that is, more courage; a greater sense of superiority, that is, less desire of revenge; a greater opinion of security, that is, more frankness, less suspicion, policy, and cunning. In short, this must be productive of very different tempers. Put a man into a close, warm place, and for the reasons above given he will feel a great faintness. If under this circumstance you propose a bold enterprise to him, I believe you will find him very little disposed towards it; his present weakness will throw him into despondency; he will be afraid of everything, being in a state of total incapacity. The inhabitants of warm countries are, like old men, timorous; the people in cold countries are, like young men, brave. If we reflect on the late wars, which are more recent in our memory, and in which we can better distinguish some particular effects that escape us at a greater distance of time, we shall find that the northern people, transplanted into southern regions, did not perform such exploits as their countrymen who, fighting in their own climate, possessed their full vigour and courage. This strength of the fibres in northern nations is the cause that the coarser juices are extracted from their aliments. Hence two things result: one, that the parts of the chyle or lymph are more proper, by reason of their large surface, to be applied to and to nourish the fibres;

the other, that they are less proper, from their coarseness, to give a certain subtilty to the nervous juice. Those people have therefore large bodies and but little vivacity. (Montesquieu, *The Spirit of the Laws*, p. 146–147.)

The influence of climate, though, decreases with the progress of civilization and its laws and customs become truly independent and partake, by themselves, to the advancement (or sometimes regress) of the nations. In other words, it is the moral and legal patrimony acquired in the past that moves and directs the future history of a population. Different things, according to Montesquieu, govern men: climate, religion, laws, etc. all these things together create a *general spirit of the population*.

This spirit is analyzed by Montesquieu in great detail, through acute observations of the Roman empire, the Chinese population, and the modern nation states. The spirit of the population gives our philosopher the common denominator to understand the history, the civilization, and the ethics of the mentioned populations. Montesquieu study has the merit of showing us the transitory and relative nature of the institutions of any society. Societies are built, in fact, not on abstract principles (natural or arbitrary), but on complex long specific histories that are realized in the specific institution that we are analyzing at that particular moment.

Given these premises, it becomes easier for Montesquieu to delineate the problem (and the solution to this problem as well) of the relationship between the individual and the state. In fact, the issue can be tackled without trying to find some metaphysical premise, and without discussing some sort of abstract way in which we can solve it. The only thing to do is to directly observe (with a scientific eye we can say) human history. For this reason, Montesquieu is concerned with the study of specific forms of government and with the principles that are the bases of such governments. He believes that there are three fundamental forms of government: Monarchy, Republic, and Despotism. The state is born from the necessity to find a solution to the state of war created by men, which from being meek and peaceful in the state of nature become aggressive and belligerent as soon as they acquire self-consciousness. On this theoretical foundation, Montesquieu builds his analysis of the three forms of government and to each one of them ascribes a specific characteristic or principle: typical of monarchy is *honor*, typical of democracy is *virtue*, and typical of despotism is *fear*. This does not mean that these principles are always present in the respective forms of government, but only that they should be. Unfortunately, in other words, it is possible to have democracy without virtue or monarchy without honor.

Montesquieu divides his sympathy between monarchy and republic: in both forms of government, he believes, men are capable to realize an authentic freedom. The way to realize and keep this freedom is the separation of the powers that exist in every government: legislative, executive, and judicial.

Separating these powers, men create a balance in their contraposition, and create the premises for a reaction to a possible usurpation of power that can come from a representative of any of these powers. This principle the separation of powers will become very influential in the XVII and XIX century and will have a practical application during the American Revolution.

6.2 Rousseau, a Different Take on Enlightenment

While the works of Montesquieu fall unequivocally under the category of "enlightenment," the thought of Jean-Jacques Rousseau (1712–1778) is difficult to place in the pure historical context of that cultural atmosphere. On one hand, in fact, he can be considered as working in the same line as Hobbes and Locke; on the other hand, he is one (if not *the*) philosopher that is the symbol of the revolutionary spirit of the enlightenment. Rousseau is interested, in fact, just like the mentioned British philosophers, in the evolution of societies, and in analyzing the moment in which human beings come out of the state of nature and unite in what has been called a social contract. His contribution, though, is quite original in that he completely reverses the positions that were very commonly accepted at the time; especially when it comes to the reasons for the contract and the characteristics of human beings in the state of nature. Two of his works are directly connected to the issues of politics and society: *The Social Contract* (SC), a classic study of the social pact that is in line with the tradition of Hobbes's *Leviathan* and Locke's *Treaties on Government*; and the *Discourse on Inequality* (DOI), an in-depth analysis of the origin of inequality amongst men that revolutionizes the idea that people had about the reason for the existence of government, and the life of humans in the state of nature. Other two of Rousseau's works are strictly connected, also, to the issues of social living even though they are concerned about slightly different topics: the self-explanatory *Discourse on the Science and Arts. Whether the Restoration of the Sciences and Arts Has Contributed to the Purification of Morals* (DOA) and the *Emile* (EM), a treatise on education. Considering that the *Discourses* are the oldest of the works and that they can be considered as some sort of theoretical antecedent to the *Social Contract* and the *Emile*, while fully acknowledging the importance of these last two works, we will concentrate more on the analysis of the discourses.

We were saying how Rousseau is difficult to collocate just under the umbrella of Enlightenment thought, and the main reason for this difficulty is his critique of the thoughts of other enlightenment era philosophers and, in general, the critique of some general principles typical of the enlightenment. One of these critiques is evident already in Rousseau first ever published work the DOA. The thesis stated in the *Discourse*, in fact, is that what we call progress in knowledge and in the arts and sciences has not contributed to the betterment of the human condition. This is a clear anti-enlightenment point of view: we have already seen how the enlightenment, as a whole, considers scientific progress *the* most important factor in human betterment. But why does Rousseau think that progress does not contribute to the improvement of the human condition? He writes that, although it is undeniable that scientific and technological progress bring human beings comfort, it is also undeniable that these forms of progress bring vices and corruption. If we look back at the ancient civilizations, Rousseau argues, if we look back at the Greek city-states and at the roman republic, we can see that people in those eras lived a simple meaningful life. When we compare their lifestyle with the one of the modern age, it is obvious how people that call themselves modern are much more corrupted and selfish.

Rousseau furthers his idea of progressive corruption of human beings in his second *discourse* (DOI) where he employs a terminology and a conceptual apparatus with which we are more familiar: the starting point in this case will not be the ancients but it will be the *state of nature*; the arrival point will not be the modern society (in a sense) but the *civilized society*. The explicit goal of the entire discourse is to understand where inequality came from: is inequality a direct consequence of the state of nature? Is it a residue of our *savage* condition?

Rousseau analysis starts with the consideration that all philosophers have made a constant mistake when describing the relationship between people in the state of nature and in a civilized society. Specifically, no philosopher has understood the state of nature: some of them have given men natural rights of any sort, others have called them brutal. They speak of *Savage Men* but describe *Civilized Men*. The polemic targets here are immediately clear, Locke has given men in the state of nature numerous natural rights, while Hobbes has indicated that men in that state are brutish beings prone to violence and destruction. What also seems to be immediately clear is the fact that Rousseau considers *natural rights* and *brutish nature* as possible characteristics not of people living in the state of nature but of people living in civilized societies. This is an evident inversion of values when it comes to Contractualism; we will see the extent of this inversion throughout the chapter.

Rousseau continues his analysis by making a first fundamental distinction when it comes to establish the origin of inequality. We need to distinguish, he writes, between physical and political inequality: the first consists in differences in age, health, strength of bodies, and quality of minds; the second one depends on a sort of convention and it is established by men's consent. This distinction has the dual purpose of refuting the argument that people are *inequal by nature* because they are physically different, and to affirm from the very beginning that political inequality is fruit of a convention and, again, not a matter of *natural development* of politics: inequality is not a residue, a typo, in our otherwise perfectly virtuous system. In order to make these points, Rousseau, takes an *historical* approach to the matter and tries to follow the development of civilization. The initial point of analysis, for this reason, should be the dawn of humanity and specifically the moment in which human beings start looking and acting like human beings: when studying the history of men, we should start with when men look physically like men, when they are bipedal, using their hands like we do, walking upright, etc. It is fascinating to see how Rousseau here, more than fifty years before the publication of Darwin's *On the Origin of Species* proposes an idea that seems in tune with evolutionism. In order to speak about men, Rousseau thinks, in a proper way that we need to consider only those animals that exhibit characteristics compatible with what men look and act today. In other words, we cannot look at an ape and think that *primitive* men must have been just like apes and, therefore, start building a theory of men in the state of nature according to the characteristics of apes. That would be a mistake, Rousseau would say. The correct way is, again, to consider men in the state of nature more like *savage* people—people that do not partake in Western civilization—that look and act like *civilized* people, but that do not partake in societies the way the West intends them. When analyzing the era of the first men, it is important to make this distinction because otherwise men and beasts are very similar. Just like other animals, in fact, human beings are *wild* and *untamed*, and live in a *pre-social* world. Here is the first crucial difference between the state of nature conceived by Hobbes and Locke (and by many other philosophers at the time) and Rousseau prospective on the state of nature. For the French philosopher, in fact, the state of nature is not the social base on which we can build civil societies, but it is a pre-social stage of humanity. When the other philosophers speak of the natural state, they already consider it some sort of society with its characteristic: Hobbes thinks of it as a society where people are in constant contrast with each other, while Locke believes that people are enjoying in it certain natural rights. But both of them think that the state of nature is some sort of society before the *legal* society of the social contract. Rousseau in the contrary believes that people at the beginning of human evolution were not social at all. For this reason, he refuses the idea that institutions like the family or private property should be considered natural. Only very specific events led to the birth of primitive societies that can be considered, at the same time, the beginning of social living and the beginning of human decadence. Human beings are better off in their wild state, and society, even the most primitive one, leads men to the road of corruption. To prove this point, Rousseau will try to show his readers that human beings are the most fitted animals that live in nature, and that, therefore, the state of nature was the perfect place to be for them. Rousseau begins by taking in consideration a series of comparisons that can be made between *men* and *other animals* and between *savage men* and *civilized men*.

First of all, human beings surely are not as strong as other animals but are obviously more organized than other animals. Secondly, men don't have any specific instincts but copy the instincts of all other animals and are omnivorous. For these reasons, men are at an advantage over other animals: men are less rigid and are better nourished because they can eat different things. And a better nutrition is the stepping stone of a better rate of survival.

Rousseau and Darwin

Rousseau seems to anticipate Darwin in linking the superiority of men to a better rate of survival: only the fitted, Rousseau explicitly writes, survives in nature. Besides appearance, though, the difference between Darwin and Rousseau is great. Darwin, as it is known, links fitness and survival to the ability of an individual to reproduce as much as possible, while for Rousseau, instead, nutrition is the key factor in survival. Also, Darwin postulates the exact opposite of what Rousseau wants to prove here: in On the Origin of Species men lose their special status amongst all other beasts becoming just one mutated being amongst the others, while Rousseau is trying to establish that men are the fittest and the best amongst all animals.

Men are superior to beasts even if both are *ingenious machines*. The other animals are completely ruled by nature whereas men contribute to their fate through their free will. So, beasts cannot deviate from their destiny even when it would be for their advantage, while men sometimes deviate from it to their detriment. Free will is the decisive factor in the distinction between men and beasts; animals are unable to exit the trajectory that nature as provided for them even when it would be crucial for them to do so, while men can always change their course of action, even when this change is not necessarily advantageous for them.

Rousseau, as we said before, is also interested in comparing savage men and civilized men. To do so, he starts by observing that in the state of nature, men are dispersed among them and live within a nature that is lush and abundant. So, men do not see other men everyday and are immerse in a nature that provides them with all they need. Obviously, in this state technology is not available and the body of the savage man is his only tool. This fact too shapes the lifestyle of the first men: they are physically stronger than modern men are because they have to exercise their muscles much more then what modern man have to. Technology has made modern men weak, in comparison with the first men, self-preservation is men' only care; their senses are hyper developed and, overall, savages are stronger than civilized people. This point is evident; in fact, all animals (men included) are stronger in their wild state than in their domesticated state. Rousseau really thinks that modern lifestyle is the cause of a lot of our issues, and he also believes that a lot of illnesses and general ailments that we have today where unknown to the first men. The modern lifestyle of men is rooted in excess and in practices that are *unnatural* to them. People eat too much, sleep too much, they exercise too little, and they are always worried about keeping these excesses going. This is evident, according to Rousseau, if we consider that all doctors do is to prescribe a return to a more *natural* lifestyle whereas savages do not need medicine except for wounds. Medicine in nothing but an art to reestablish the natural balance in our body, therefore, modern men are often unbalanced by their excesses, while the savage men get unbalanced only by *accident*, by wounds.

In conclusion, for centuries philosophers have painted a picture of the state of nature that is not conform to reality. Men in the state of nature are not miserable: they are free and healthy, they are the "kings of the jungle," they are better suited than any other animal to survive in the wild. They are at an advantage not only in comparison to the other beasts in the state of nature; they lived a better life even when compared to the people living in modern societies. In modern society, people complain more, people are unhappy whereas in the state of nature the savage lives according to his instincts. Spontaneity, living in agreement with nature, is a blessing for the savage who does not know as much as a modern person, and because of that lives a happier life. In nature, there are no moral relationships: there is no idea of good and bad. It is with society that evil starts.

6.3   Passions and Morality of the State of Nature

Hobbes mistake, according to Rousseau, was adding to the savage men passions that are proper only of civilized men. Savages do not know beauty or love or property, therefore, they do not fight for them. Ignorance of vice is better than knowledge of virtue. The only natural passion that all animals, and especially men, seem to have is pity. Vices are absent in nature because people do not put themselves in comparison with each other; pity instead seems to be omnipresent: everywhere there are signs of it, even ancient theaters reproduced it and wild animals display it—think of the fact that horses do not want to step on whatever creature is defenseless on the ground. Rousseau believes that pity is the foundation of all other virtues (generosity, clemency, humanity, friendship, benevolence etc.) and that it seems to be nature's way of countering and balancing self-love, in order to make the preservation of the species easier. Notice how human virtues are not connected, like they were in Aristotle, with reason or practice, but with passions. Therefore, Rousseau writes, pity inspires not the reasoned justice maxim *do unto others as you would have them do unto you*, but rather the natural goodness maxim *do your good with the least possible harm to others*.

Generally speaking, according to this view of the state of nature, it is almost obvious that the reasons why men would be living a miserable life in it—as considered by Hobbes—make little sense. Men in the state of nature have no need to be aggressive toward each other because they do not use reason to compare to each other and prefer to move on rather than compete for something that can be found somewhere else. They also do not enter in competition for the rights to mate. In fact, sex is not something that men would fight over in the state of nature. It is actually "moral" love that leads to violence. This is because in society people establish the idea of singularity and exclusivity of sexual access that in nature does not exists. Free sexuality is common, Rousseau writes, amongst savages whereas the civilized men will fight over a mate because of jealousy. Families are not a thing of the state of nature, they are not *natural institutions*, rather they are a product of the first forms of society. Finally, inequality is almost inexistent in the state of nature because nobody can really gain advantage because of it (what is the use of being cunning if people do not deal with each other because they live far away from each other?). *Oppression* is an invention proper of society: in nature nobody obeys anyone; everyone is free, there is enough space for a man to move away from trouble without needing a fight. Absolute freedom is the solution against oppression according to Rousseau; it is not the root of problems such as violence and anarchy. If people are free to roam wherever they want there is never an issue: you try to oppress me, I will move away in a place that is exactly like this minus you. This, evidently, can only happen in the state of nature.

A question at this point, one might say, is more than legitimate: why, if men were living such a beautiful life in this pre-social state of nature, did they end up constituting societies? What made them decide to group together? Rousseau answer is unequivocal: men grouped together because of necessity. Some natural disaster, some years of scarcity of natural resources, and the invention of agriculture to avoid such famines were at the origin of social living. And such group-living leads to the birth of those activities that we call properly human: arts, technology, language, work. Only at this point, inequality can become a thing: when some enter in possession, through different means, of the existing means of subsistence, and force the others to work to survive. Inequality has a twin, private property, and on these twins is built the state in order to sanction these relations of inequality.

The first man who, having enclosed a piece of ground, bethought himself of saying This is mine, and found people simple enough to believe him, was the real founder of civil society. From how many crimes, wars and murders, from how many horrors and misfortunes might not any one have saved mankind, by pulling up the stakes, or filling up the ditch, and crying to his fellows, "Beware of listening to this impostor; you are undone if you once forget that the fruits of the earth, belong to us all, and the earth itself to nobody." But there is great probability that things had then already come to such a pitch, that they could no longer continue as they were; for the idea of property depends on many prior ideas, which could only be acquired successively, and cannot have been formed all at once in the human mind. Mankind must have made very considerable progress, and acquired considerable knowledge and industry which they must also have transmitted and increased from age to age, before they arrived at this last point of the state of nature. (Rousseau, *Discourse on Inequality*, part 2.)

6.4 The Birth of Civil Society

We have seen how Civil Society begins with a fence around a piece of ground and someone saying, "this is mine!" and other people believing it. But what was the need for that? Why did men, at a certain point, needed to claim something has theirs in the state of nature? We have already said that people group together out of necessity. We now have to see what kind of necessity that was and how living in groups is conducive to the emergence of private property and all the evils that follow it.

If we look back in time, Rousseau thinks, it is easy to characterize men as *problem-solving machines*. Men, in fact, were a bundle of instincts, of passions, tuned just to achieve survival. Consequently, they start solving the problems presented to them by their environment and start building tools apt to reach this goal. But, if this is true, it becomes evident that the environment where they live poses a specific set of problems to them, and that people that live in different places find solutions to different problems. For example, people living close to a big body of water have to learn fast how to contain that water when it rains, and how to use the resources that the water brings them; they build hooks to fish and boats to sail. People that live on mountainous environments, instead, learn to deal with the specific issues that their environment presents them—the cold at night, the landslides, the mountain lions—and to use the resources offered by it. They build spears to hunt and defend themselves, and more insulated huts. When, because of the needs mentioned in the previous section (Natural disasters, famine, etc.), people come in contact with others, they end up arousing the mind of these others. By looking at the solution founded by their neighbor, they start comparing and reflecting: they start to reason. Thanks to this process, men become superior to the other species and a sense of pride comes as a result; first as a species then as individuals. Reason is a product of comparison of practical solutions that eventually leads people to become superior to other animals: a constant race to a better solution characterizes the life of humans while it is absent from the life of the brute beasts.

Considering that our intellectual life is born, and it is based, on *comparison* it is easy to understand how pride can arise: comparing the achievements of the humans with those of other species, men become proud of themselves. And comparing the different achievement among men, they become individually proud.

Living together, though, does not simply starts the process that we call reasoning and the instinctive pride that comes with it. It also produces the understanding that "there are others like us!" Men, at this point in their path toward civilization, recognize the others of theirs pecies and immediately become aware that they could and *must* find a way to use the others (as tool) to their advantage;they realize that they can form temporary alliances with the goal of fulfilling a certain need. At the same time, they understand that they might be, from time to time, in competition with their fellow humans and that they might need to fight each other sometimes. The possibility of war and peace is born with the newly acquired faculty of reason.

The initial progress just described leads to more use of reason, which in turn leads to more progress and more tool-making. Property is born here with the ability to yield more from the same piece of land occupied. The first fights for property are born, probably, but still there is enough free land that people just move "over" and occupy a different portion of land. This new sedentary life brings into existence what we would call proper families: living together for extended periods of time sparks the feeling of love for the mate and the offspring. Families, only at this point, become the first rudimentary societies where the first gender roles are established: male and female start doing different things. In sum, property and families are the first elements of a civil society. Notice the radical difference between this approach and the Hobbesian (or Lockean): families and private property are the nuclei of civil society, but they are not part of the original state in which men live; families and property are already a step into civil society and a step outside the state of nature. Again, men in their natural condition live isolated and disperse in a lush and plentiful nature. Men are not social animals—like Aristotle wanted—they are solitary beings that are forced into society by sheer necessity.

This new "family" lifestyle weakens the species and makes habits into needs. Men, for example, at first get in the habit of sleeping securely in a cave, and then with time they tend to need a cave to sleep; they feel that there is the need for a cave, otherwise they cannot sleep. Rousseau thinks, basically, that with more tools men, obviously, need to use their bodies less, which makes them physically weaker (we all know how exercising is the key to keep in shape and develop muscle strength). He also believes that new habits become, eventually, needs, pushing people to do more than what they really need. Let's make an example. In a pre-cellphones or pre-pcs era, there was no need to be always connected and always accessible. Today we feel lost the moment there is not signal for few minutes, and we claim that we *need* Internet, a cell phone, a computer, to function properly in our society. We are so used to these tools that we need them. And the need is, at this point, real.

Living next to each other, also, makes families grow, and people falling in love. Inevitably, jealousy onsets and eventually someone kills or dies for love. Living together, obviously produces group activities as well: dances and performances are organized, and people wish to excel in what they do, or to be recognized as excellent at the activity that they perform. Competitions start, vanity and envy take root, and happiness and innocence are gone forever. In Rousseau's view, Love and competition are the main causes of people loss of happiness and innocence. With envy and vanity rooted in their mind, men start fighting for *Glory* (to use Hobbes' term) and people begin to think that some behaviors must be punishable, and that vengeance should be a normal part of life.

To summarize we could say that property, work, and inequality are all born together:

> *so long as they undertook only what a single person could accomplish, and confined themselves to such arts as did not require the joint labour of several hands, they lived free, healthy, honest and happy lives, so long as their nature allowed, and as they continued to enjoy the pleasures of mutual and independent intercourse. But from the moment one man began to stand in need of the help of another; from the moment it appeared advantageous to any one man to have enough provisions for two, equality disappeared, property was introduced, work became indispensable, and vast forests became smiling fields, which man had to water with the sweat of his brow, and where slavery and misery were soon seen to germinate and grow up with the crops. (Ibidem.)*

Iron and wheat ruined mankind. At this point of the evolution of civilization, the downfall of humanity starts picking up speed. Consider, for example, that specialized labor, as a form of sustenance and loss of freedom is born at this point. Agriculture, in fact, is the cause of specialized labor: cultivating the fields is time-consuming, therefore, people need someone else to perform other tasks for them. At the same time, because after so much work people need to be able to enjoy the fruits of their labor, land is divided, and it is now owned by someone: the rights of property come from the labor. Just like Locke, Rousseau believes that what gives the right to property is labor; the difference, though, is that while in Locke this right is natural, for Rousseau is acquire at the expenses of human freedom, innocence, and ultimately happiness. Thanks to reason, as we have seen, people start the comparison and the ranking of other people and abilities and, in order to be better ranked, they want to portray themselves differently from what they really are. To be and to appear become different. At the same time, men realize that they are not free anymore: they depend on others (even the masters depend on their serfs). The ambition to be "more" leads to the inclination to harm others: all these evils come from property.

Land is private at this point in our path towards civilization, and some form of inheritance is probably in place. Land is not as readily available as it used to be and some fights for "space" (which meant wealth) are now common. *The poor* are now being born: they are the ones that did not change their lifestyle, the ones that lived still from natural means and that now do not have anything because everything belongs to someone else; they become bandits, outlaws. A fight for power and resources begins. The state of war comes just as the state of nature ends.

6.5 Government and the Interest of the Wealthy

Rousseau, evidently, contradicts Hobbes: the state of war comes not from the state of nature, but from the first societies. It is when people are organized in groups that thanks to familial love, agriculture, and property in general war and chaos start. Reason, communities, ingenuity, and even love are far from being the evidence of a better living; they are the root of the unhappiness typical of civil societies, and the base for the foundation of government that will institutionalize inequality. Why is Rousseau thinking that governments make inequality legal and permitted? The answer is easy to guess: who is more damaged by the new state of chaos and war, the people that do not have anything to lose—the poor—or the people that have properties and wealth? Rousseau thinks that the rich at this point are the most worried about the state of war, especially because they realize that there is really no good reason to justify their claim for property. To avoid the inevitable bad outcome for them and their property, they propose a social contract and institute the regulations that they call Justice.

> With this view, after having represented to his neighbours the horror of a situation which armed every man against the rest, and made their possessions as burdensome to them as their wants, and in which no safety could be expected either in riches or in poverty, he readily devised plausible arguments to make them close with his design. "Let us join," said he, "to guard the weak from oppression, to restrain the ambitious, and secure to every man the possession of what belongs to him: let us institute rules of justice and peace, to which all without exception may be obliged to conform; rules that may in some measure make amends for the caprices of fortune, by subjecting equally the powerful and the weak to the observance of reciprocal obligations. Let us, in a word, instead of turning our forces against ourselves, collect them in a supreme power which may govern us by wise laws, protect and defend all the members

of the association, repulse their common enemies, and maintain eternal harmony among us." (Ibidem.)

People sensed an advantage in this political unity but did not foresaw its danger: freedom was gone, and the rich gained a perennial advantage. The social contract normalized the status quo, property, and inequality are now the norm, and spread to societies all over the world. Now the political bodies do the fighting in what is called the state of nature: wars and murders begin as a result of the birth of political societies. Just like Hobbes and Locke, Rousseau thinks that the newly instituted political bodies are now fighting instead of the individuals, but differently from them he believes that wars and murders are not the direct consequence of the state of nature; they are rather the result of the institutionalization of privilege (namely property).The social contract, in few words, is always rigged in favor of the rich. It was an idea of the rich to normalize an otherwise unjustifiable appropriation. We will see how Rousseau believes that, considering this ancestry made of inequality and privilege, government as an institution cannot be repaired and needs to be completely reset in order to function as a true democratic organization. Modern societies cannot be cured with internal reforms (through the progress of arts and sciences), but do need a radical transformation, a revolution to reestablish the innocence of the state of nature.

What did government look like at very beginning? Probably, Rousseau thinks, government at his inception did not have constant regular form, and the issues that came from it were dealt on an "as needed" basis. Laws were few and could be evaded easily because all the people were judges and witnesses, and everyone thought of their own interest. This state of affairs convinces people that there is a need for representatives to be put in place to administer the law: they are called *magistrates*. Government is insecure, inefficient, and messy at the beginning, producing problem to which people do not have an immediate response. Because solving the issues produce by the institution of government is difficult and time-consuming, people establish magistrates that have to administer and enforce the law.

In addition, Rousseau seems to be sure that if there is a form of government that could have not existed at the beginning of civilization, that form of government is monarchy. In fact, the whole idea that monarchy is an almost natural form of government derived by the servile nature of men or modeled on the authority of a father in a family, it is for Rousseau absurd. Politicians, in fact, say that men are inclined to servitude that they need to be herded, because they look at the way people have become in the civilized society. In the state of nature, men fight and don't bend to keep their freedom.

An unbroken horse erects his mane, paws the ground and starts back impetuously at the sight of the bridle; while one which is properly trained suffers patiently even whip and spur: so savage man will not bend his

*neck to the yoke to which civilised man submits without a murmur, but
prefers the most turbulent state of liberty to the most peaceful slavery.
We cannot therefore, from the servility of nations already enslaved,
judge of the natural disposition of mankind for or against slavery; we
should go by the prodigious efforts of every free people to save itself from
oppression. I know that the former are for ever holding forth in praise
of the tranquillity they enjoy in their chains, and that they call a state
of wretched servitude a state of peace: miserrimamservitutempacem
appellant.[6] But when I observe the latter sacrificing pleasure, peace,
wealth, power and life itself to the preservation of that one treasure, which
is so disdained by those who have lost it; when I see free-born animals
dash their brains out against the bars of their cage, from an innate
impatience of captivity; when I behold numbers of naked savages, that
despise European pleasures, braving hunger, fire, the sword and death, to
preserve nothing but their independence, I feel that it is not for slaves to
argue about liberty. (Ibidem.)*

As for paternal authority, it cannot be the model for government: the dominion of the father ends, in fact, when the child is able to survive on his
own, and the relationship is based on respect and not obedience. In reality, it
is civil society that with the laws of familiar living, gives power to the father;
not vice versa. Paternal authority, in other words, cannot be considered the
model for government and to justify absolute power of a monarch because it
works in a very different way, in comparison with monarchy; also, because it
is not a real natural institution: the power that the father enjoys is given to
him from the social institutions in which he lives. The only legitimate form of
government is the one that, according to Rousseau, establishes the political
body as

*a real contract between the people and the chiefs chosen by them: a
contract by which both parties bind themselves to observe the laws
therein expressed, which form the ties of their union. The people having
in respect of their social relations concentrated all their wills in one, the
several articles, concerning which this will is explained, become so many
fundamental laws, obligatory on all the members of the State without
exception, and one of these articles regulates the choice and power of
the magistrates appointed to watch over the execution of the rest. This
power extends to everything which may maintain the constitution, without
going so far as to alter it. It is accompanied by honours, in order to bring
the laws and their administrators into respect. The ministers are also
distinguished by personal prerogatives, in order to recompense them for
the cares and labour which good administration involves. The magistrate,
on his side, binds himself to use the power he is entrusted with only in
conformity with the intention of his constituents, to maintain them all in*

the peaceable possession of what belongs to them, and to prefer on every occasion the public interest to his own. (Ibidem.)

This is a rudimentary definition of social contract as intended by Rousseau. Few points can be taken from it: (1) everyone is under the law, nobody is above it. Therefore, the idea proposed by Hobbes that the Sovereign should enjoy special privileges is not even taken in consideration; (2) the laws are the representation of the general will of the people; and (3) the magistrate can use their power only to enact the will of the people. We will see in the next section what are the specifics of such understanding of the social contract. For now, we need to go back to the analysis of the different forms of government.

If the only legitimate form of government can come from such pact among the people, it might seem strange that we can see, in history, so many different forms of government. We should not be surprised, though, the different forms of government come from the different level of inequality present at the moment of the inception of these governments. If one person is superior to all others in wealth, power, or prestige then people will see the rise of monarchy; if few are equal and superior to all others, people will have an aristocracy; if there is no sufficient inequality people will have democracies. What is important to understand here is that, except for when people live in a direct democracy, *people* are transformed into *subjects*. This transformation is the final stage of a progression of inequality that has its roots in the first communities and in the institution of private property.

When we look at humanity diachronically, in fact, we can appreciate this progression of inequality: first comes property, second the institution of Magistracy, finally the conversion of legitimate power to arbitrary power. These stages are defined by the evident subdivisions that can be observed amongst people: first we see the subdivision of humanity in rich and poor, then in powerful and weak, and finally in master and slave. People don't realize until is too late that the same vices that made politics necessary, make its abuse inevitable. If, as the rich propose at the beginning of government, we need to institute rules to avoid that the powerful take advantage of the weak, it is only normal that the new powerful—the people made powerful by the institution of government—will take advantage of the new system to enhance their power and dominate the others. Politics, because is born on such premises, is dangerous and produces oppression and domination of people over people.

Political distinctions necessarily produce civil distinctions. The growing equality between the chiefs and the people is soon felt by individuals, and modified in a thousand ways according to passions, talents and circumstances. The magistrate could not usurp any illegitimate power, without giving distinction to the creatures with whom he must share it. Besides, individuals only allow themselves to be oppressed so far as they are hurried on by blind ambition, and, looking rather below than above them, come to love authority more than independence, and submit to slavery, that they may in turn enslave others. It is no easy matter to reduce to obedience a man who has no ambition to command; nor would the most adroit politician find it possible to enslave a people whose only desire was to be independent. But inequality easily makes its way among cowardly and ambitious minds, which are ever ready to run the risks of fortune, and almost indifferent whether they command or obey, as it is favourable or adverse. Thus, there must have been; a time, when the eyes of the people were so fascinated, that their rulers had only to say to the least of men, "Be great, you and all your posterity," to make him immediately appear great in the eyes of every one as well as in his own. His descendants took still more upon them, in proportion to their distance from him; the more obscure; and uncertain the cause, the greater the effect: the greater—the number of idlers one could count in a family, the more illustrious it was held to be. (Ibidem.)

From this new extreme condition of inequality, the chiefs will gain an advantage: they will try to put the citizens against one another to keep their power: all governments at the end become tyrannical, and only blind obedience is left to the slaves (citizens). But at last, in tyranny, equality rises again: all people are nothing, all people find themselves in a new "state of nature" where obedience to a despot is the norm. But because force alone maintains the despot in power, force alone can dethrone him. Only a violent revolution can end tyranny, according to Rousseau. There is no fixing the system, only uprooting the entire institution and starting all over again might serve the purpose of finding some new freedom. Only a return to men' primitive state can grant back lost innocence and freedom to the people. As it stands, the difference between the Savages and civilized men are so vast that they could very well be two different species, one devoted to happiness, the other affected by the disease that we call "misery."

The former [the savage] *breathes only peace and liberty; he desires only to live and be free from labour; even the ataraxia of the Stoic falls far short of his profound indifference to every other object. Civilised man, on the other hand, is always moving, sweating, toiling and racking his brains to find still more laborious occupations: he goes on in drudgery to his last moment, and even seeks death to put himself in a position to live, or renounces life to acquire immortality. He pays his court to men in power, whom he hates, and to the wealthy, whom he despises; he stops at nothing to have the honour of serving them; he is not ashamed to value himself on his own meanness and their protection; and, proud of his slavery, he speaks with disdain of those, who have not the honour of sharing it. (Ibidem.)*

Rousseau has established that the corruption of men is tied to the very same activities that we connect to the development of civilization: arts, sciences, and social institutions are nothing but the historical evidences of men progressive depravity. Men seem to be doomed to a life of progressive misery and inequality that will eventual explode into a violent revolution, only to restart the cycle all over again. The question is, at this point, can men be saved? Can men be freed from the endemic and congenital that afflicts the society where they live?

6.6 The General Will

The questions left open by the *discourses* are fundamental to establish any sort of legitimacy of a sovereign power and a consequent government. The dichotomy observed between individual and society seems, in fact, too vast to find some sort of reconciliation. The challenge is to find, according to Rousseau, a way in which society could defend and protect the well being of each associate and in which each individual can still only obey to himself and stay as free as he was before. In other words, the challenge is to transform society so that it does reinforces the freedom of each associate rather than dissolve it.

Rousseau thinks of men, as we have seen, as animals that are characterized essentially by their freedom. Everyone is born free, and freedom is what makes men what they are. So, if men give up liberty they would give up their humanity: renouncing freedom is incompatible with human nature. This seems to be an unsurmountable difficulty when it comes to establish some kind of civil society: traditionally, in fact, living in a community has always been linked to some sort renunciation of freedom. Living in communities, most thinkers of Rousseau's time thought, means to give up freedom in exchange for order and security. This is the essence of any social contract theory written before Rousseau. Surprisingly enough the French philosopher, in order to reconciliate the needs of the society and the freedom of the individuals, maintains that the social contract is the best theoretical tool that can be used. His interpretation of the social contract, though, is profoundly different than the vision presented by the previous philosophers.

Firstly, Rousseau considers the social contract not as an historical fact, but as an intellectual tool, as reference to use in order to establish the fundamental principles of social living. Second, and more importantly, he understands the social contract essentially as a *moral* agreement, and only secondarily as a legal/political agreement; political facts, he thinks, have no meaning if they are separated from the moral necessities of human beings. This is in stark contrast with the preoccupations typical of Hobbes and Locke. We know that a good chunk of their work and energy was devoted, in fact, to establish the reciprocal limits between the power of the state and the rights of the citizens. This way of thinking, according to Rousseau, has brought forward the distinction between *man and citizen, subject and sovereign* that is expressed in technical terms in the distinction between *pactumunionis*—the agreement expressed in the commonwealth, where people pledge to unite and govern as peers—and *pactumsubiectionis*—the agreement between the Sovereign power and its subject that was delineated differently by different philosophers. Rousseau thinks, instead, that the journey that goes from the state of nature to the civil society, in order to be legitimate, has to be the meaning of a change in human behaviors: human beings move from a stage in their evolution where they were chiefly concerned with themselves to a situation in which they need to act based on different principles, a situation in which they need to listen to reason and not their passions.

In other words, the *social contract* marks the passage from a human behavior that is essentially instinctive and selfish to a *moral* behavior. Obviously, intended this way, the social contract assumes characteristics that are unsuited for the explanation of the relationship between state and individual given by the previous philosophers and especially by Hobbes. In fact, if the social contract has to be based on this change of heart described by Rousseau, any contract that unites people based on purely *external factors* (like coercion in the case of Hobbes) can be considered absurd and null. It is impossible to produce an effective change in the individual will that will keep its primitive independence and selfishness underneath the appearance of obedience solely through force. A true pact, a true union, can be founded only on free consent and on reciprocal respect for freedom. A social pact is valid only if the individual is not obligated to obey it, and only if he submits to it spontaneously.

Joining the social contract, the people, renouncing their prerogatives do not alienate their freedom. They just decide to substitute the needs and wants of the individual wills with the needs and wants of the *General Will*. It is important to distinguish, Rousseau writes, between the General Will and everyone's will: the latter might be contingent to a momentary convergence of individual egoistic interests; the former, instead, is the expression of the universal will—of the collective good—and it cannot be selfish or evil. The freedom that the individuals maintain in the social contract does not corresponds to a futile agreement with the will of the sovereign, but it is, instead,true submission to the sacred and severe law of the General Will. Every individual imposes on himself such law, and through this submission people can affirm their authentic human personality. With this submission rises, in fact, a *positive* concept of freedom that does not consists in a pure expression of individual impulses, but as a domination of these impulses in the name of reason. Only moral freedom, according to Rousseau gives men true control over their being: instincts and impulses are a form of slavery, while obedience to the law prescribed by the General Will is true freedom. It should be clear that Rousseau is crafting a new idea of liberty: not anymore some sort of anarchic emancipation of the individual but an autonomy of the individual under the discipline of reason. On this concept, Rousseau further develops his political theory.

From the social contract originate the various forms of government, which are legitimate only if they respect the General Will that is at the origin of the contract. Rousseau believes that democracy is the most perfect form of government, but he admits that taking in consideration times and places it is possible to justify other forms of government; what it matters is that the different regimes do respect the General Will and that they don't try to suffocate it. In any form of government, the Sovereign is based on the General Will, which always belongs to the people. The real Sovereign, the people, can give the govern of the state to the entirety of the citizens, which will produce a democracy; to a small group of citizens, which will produce an aristocracy; or to a single magistrate, which will result in a monarchy. In any case, Rousseau affirms, the people invested with the authority assume their role only temporarily. Sovereignty is nothing but the exercise of the General Will and cannot be alienated. This means, obviously, that Sovereignty is always under the control of the people and that no government can suppress the sovereignty of the people. Less intuitively, though, this means, also, that the power cannot be divided: Executive and Judiciaryare emanations of the Sovereign power, and therefore of the Legislative power. No separation of powers (in the sense intended by Montesquieu) is legitimate.

The consequences of this point of view evidently express the fervor that few years after Rousseau's death would lead to the French revolution (1789): Rousseau abandons classic Liberalism to embrace a form of political democracy that is not formal, we can say, but substantial (direct democracy) that will inspire the leaders of the French revolution. Infamously, at least some of these leaders, considering themselves interpreters of the General Will did risked transforming democracy in dictatorship.

Toolbox

Language: a Mean of Inequality

During the progression that leads to the rise of inequality, Rousseau pays special attention to the origin of language. People learn how *speak*, our Swiss philosopher seems to suggest, by necessity: language is a byproduct of social leaving, and it is a step out of the natural realm. It is interesting to note that this means that human beings are not, in this system, linguistic animals, but that language is a pure tool, an artificial mean that solves a specific need. The need for language arises from environmental causes: the new condition of *sociality* is what produces and stimulates men to find a tool to govern this new situation. Just like men figure out a better way to respond to the natural event of "water in proximity" by building, for example, huts that are elevated from the ground to avoid flooding; they also respond to the natural event "living in proximity to other humans" by creating a tool that we call language. The implications of this view are multiple, we will mention just a couple. (1) The existence of the others is a problem to solve. This means that sociality is not a natural trait of humanity. It is interesting to see that language and social living seem to be closely tied: in systems of thought where one is natural, the other one follow as natural as well; in systems, like Rousseau's one, where one is unnatural the one also is. (2) This view of language is not in agreement with our "scientific" understanding of language today. What seems to be missing in Rousseau's view is the distinction between a *natural* language (e.g., English, Italian, Chinese, etc.) and a Language in general. Today we think, in fact, that while it is true that there is no natural *Natural* language, all human being posses naturally the ability for a Language. What does this mean? It means that today we believe that while nobody is born with the ability to speak a specific language, let's say English, everyone is born with the ability to speak *a* language. We believe that the kind of language that individuals end up speaking depends of the kind of environment that surrounds us (if a baby grows up surrounded by people that speak Chinese she will speak Chinese, but if she is socialized among Italian speaking people she will speak Italian), but we also believe that the ability to learn a language (any language) is universal and the same for everyone; it is natural.

Finally, it is worth noting that for the second time in our journey through the various political theories of the past, we encounter language as a meaningful vehicle of inequality: Aristotle and Rousseau both believe that language is an agent of inequality, but while the former uses it to justify the naturality of it, the latter explains that by nature language is a stepping stone for the construction of the institutions that will formalize inequality.

CHAPTER 7

Political Economy and Its Detractors

7 Adam Smith and the Physiocratic Economists

During the enlightenment, as we saw in the previous chapter, we witness a rebirth of the arts and sciences, and a renew faith in the ability of human beings to solve the issues regarding the mysteries of nature. Consequently, the natural sciences are usually considered the center piece of this new spirit that is pervasive of the modern era; classic sciences such as Physics, Chemistry, and Mathematics come out of this period rejuvenated and acquirethe shape that they have now and that is familiar to us.

Another aspect of the extraordinary vigor of the *enlighten* thought is the birth of a brand-new science: *Political Economy*. This discipline, in fact, becomes autonomous during the enlightenment thanks to the so-called *French Physiocratic School* and thanks to the efforts of the Scottish philosopher Adam Smith (1723–1790). This new science is concerned with a specific field of observation, *production*, and it aims to explain the elements that make up the economic system, and the relation between those elements.

François Quesnay (1694–1774) is considered the most important of the Physiocratic economists. His doctrine considers the *soil* the primary source of wealth. In his book *Economic Table*, Quesnay organizes the Physiocratic theory in a systematic way; He describes the economic mechanism as a dynamic circular structure that has the agricultural activity as its engine. Agriculture, thanks to the natural fertility of the soil, produces a *wealth surplus* (Quesnay calls it *net product*) that is necessary to sustain the economic system and to make it larger. According to Quesnay, the farmers are the only *productive workers* whereas the merchants and the artisans a *sterile class*. Merchants and artisans do not produce wealth, but merely distribute and transform it.

From this theoretical approach, the Physiocratic school derives a series of political and technical consequences. Considering, in fact, that production is a natural activity (derived from a natural material—soil), it is necessary to recognize and second its spontaneous tendencies, and to avoid any changes in its natural development. With this in mind, it is evident that to the Physiocratics there is a need for reforms of the economic organization in order to favor a capitalistic agriculture. Free trade, abolition of any sort of tariffs on the import–export of goods, and suppression of any kind of monopoly are some of the many reforms proposed by the physiocratic school.

In simple terms, the approach of this school to political economy is that the production, distribution, and circulation of wealth follows natural laws and that, therefore, the government should only play the role of the *protector* of these laws and should not interfere with them. In addition, with this new economic science is born the idea that the analysis of the mechanisms of production was a privileged lens that can be used to understand the entire social organization.

Heavily influenced by physiocracy, Adam Smith is considered the funder of what will be called *classic economy* and the first to theorize a laissez-faire approach to economy. Smith career starts as moral philosopher, and specifically as follower of David Hume. The latter believed that morality cannot be justified rationally, but that it can be explained only if linked to the natural instincts that we call emotions. Sympathy (but also other feelings) can be considered a starting point to ethics. When people see themselves in the others, they are likely to treat them like they would like to be treated if they were in the other's position. Smith also believes that human beings are motivated by emotions, but he considers *gain* as the central instinct that drives humans.

To be more precise, Smith believes that human beings are motivated to live in a society (and to do anything) simply by what he calls "self-interest and social-interest". In his work *An Inquiry into The Nature and Causes of the Wealth of Nation*, he postulates the existence of a natural order in which, if every individual would be left to act according to his or her own interest, he or she would contribute to the social well-being and to the happiness of the whole group. In other words, Smith believes that human beings would be naturally guided by some sort of *invisible hand* to behave in a way that benefits them, but that also benefits the society as a whole. The good of the individual, according to this view, can only be attained within the good of the whole group (or at least of the majority of the group).

The core of Smith's economic theory is, like for the Physiocratic school, the concept of productive labor. Productive work, in fact, is what gives any commodity *exchange value*. This means that, according to Smith, the price of goods is determined mainly by the value that we give to the work that goes into that object exchanged. This value is the only origin of social (and individual) wealth. Differently from the Physiocratic economy, though, he believes that productivity (and its expansion) is not linked to the soil and agriculture. On the contrary, productivity (and therefore, social well-being) is guaranteed by the growing division of labor, by the constant reinvestment of profit, and by technological innovation.

Finally, Smith believes that free trade and a free market will guarantee maximum economic growth; he also believes that if we leave the market to auto-regulate organically, without artificially steering it one way or another with any sort of governmental regulations, the whole nation will prosper. Free market means, for Smith, a market where the single individuals are left free to search profits without any limits: no tariffs, little or no taxes, no State regulations, etc. Only if we organize our society in these terms, the individual will find the best way to satisfy his or her impulse to profit, and thanks to this freedom the general wealth of a nation (of the group) will grow.

We can clearly see how the economy, beginning with Adam Smith's work, is now fully integrated in politics and society. Political economy, in fact, proposes itself as the science that more than any other is interested to understand how we can build a socio-political system that could guarantee the happiness of the individual within a group. It is worth noting that, since the birth of this new science, we have progressively identified happiness and wealth, which was (at the time) a brand-new way of understanding happiness. Economic success and happiness, in fact, have not always been synonymous, and they start to be linked in our minds and cultures only from this point on in history. We will see shortly how this optimistic view that links the satisfaction of individual impulses and general happiness, though, was not exactly quietly accepted by other economists, and that the system that was generated by this view (*Capitalism*) was not a-critically received.

7.1 David Ricardo: A Less Rosy View of Political Economy

David Ricardo (1772–1823) is usually considered, together with Smith, the main founder of classic political economy. His views, though, are quite different than Smith's, and we will see how these views will greatly influence thinkers such as Marx and Engels.

To fully understand Ricardo's work, we need to keep in mind that during the enlightenment, thanks to the industrial revolution, we have a rise of the *middle class*. The entire mode of production is changing in that period of time, and economist and intellectuals are confronted with a completely new world: new forms of energy are used (coal is used in factories and to fuel boats and ships), factories start to be mechanized (especially when it comes to the cotton industry), new industries arise (metallurgy), etc.

Ricardo was a "progressive" thinker, which means (in England at the time), that he believes that political economy—as a science—should be separated from any State influence, and that it should be fully organized around the concept of free market. This economic view was, obviously, completely antagonistic compared to the one of the *ancient régime*, where the economy was by definition regulated by the sovereign power.

Ricardo's progressive view consisted in the idea of refusing any priority or privilege given to agriculture (which was traditionally associated with the ruling class). This meant that Ricardo refused the idea that governments should *protect* any sort of agricultural product. In fact, he thinks, the income that comes from owning land is not earned. The land owners just benefit from the fact that some pieces of land are more productive or that are better situated. There is a divergence in interest when it comes to what the land owners want and what the capitalists want, and Ricardo sides with the latter. He noticed, in fact, that *protectionism* (especially of grains) made bread more expensive, and, in turn, made uneasy that segment of the population that was fundamental for the development of the new middle class, and of the new capitalistic society that was just born. The *laboring poors*, as Ricardo calls the class of people that live on a salary, were often unable to buy bread and forced to live outside the cities where the only possible occupation was, for them, working the land for some land owner. This condition, Ricardo thought, was slowing down (and risked to completely arrest) the development of the new society that capitalism, competition in general, the new market, the new technology, and a general movement from the country to the city were trying to foster.

Protectionism, in general, was for Ricardo an economic measure to reject. It favors collusions among lobbies and governments impeding on the separation between State and economy. Protectionism, therefore, incentivizes dependence from the government (and the collusion between the government officials and the lobbyists) and depresses the initiative and the will to take risks of the investor (of the capitalist) that is the core of the new system of competition that we call capitalism. In economic terms, protectionism artificially manipulates the prices compromising the *rational* way in which the market would adjust if it would be left alone.

The natural difference in prices between goods, and between goods and services are dictated, according to Ricardo, by the quantity of labor necessary to produce such goods and services. For example, if to produce a yard of cotton we need 3 *quantities of labor* (this is the way Ricardo calls the amount of work needed to produce something), and to produce a pound of steel we need 6 quantities of labor, the free market will auto-regulate in a way that if someone wants to exchange cotton for steel, she will need two yards of cotton to get a pound of steel. Therefore, there is a natural exchange/price proportion that would establish itself if there wasn't any disturbance created by State legislated measures.

It is interesting to note how this view, that puts the quantity of labor at the core of the economy, could be interpreted as favorable to the workers' interest. At the end of the day, in fact, the workers, the ones that work for a salary, are the ones decreeing the cost of all goods. The worker could be considered the protagonist of capitalism, and it could be theorized that he or she should be the one to reap the larger benefits from it. While Ricardo himself did not go in this direction, a group of economists usually called *Ricardian Socialists* did. They tend to remark the central role that the worker plays in the capitalistic economy, and the inequality of condition and wealth between the capitalist (the rich middle class) and the worker (the laboring poors).

After Ricardo's analysis, the optimist image of the new society described by Adam Smith is, to say the least, seriously compromised. It is clear how within the new system—capitalism—are at work forces that will naturally produce a series of harsh conflict between the social classes that exist inside it: the relationship between the old aristocracy, the middle class, and the working class will be the center of attention of many economist and social and political philosophers.

7.2   A Radical Critique of Political Economy

The *Ricardian Socialist*, we just saw, are the first ones posing the problem of the relationship between the capitalist and the worker. Their analysis, though, was limited to the signaling of the unjust condition in which the worker found himself or herself. Their idea was that, as we explained before, the workers should reap the benefits of the wealth that comes with capitalism, but they are, instead, forced to live in miserable conditions. What is puzzling, when reading these analyses, is the fact that technically none of the Ricardians are able to explain the origin of the worker's condition. They decried the injustice of the capitalistic production and the exploitation of the working class, but they were unable to explain what the exploitation consisted of. In other words, while political economy used a scientific method to outline forms of social/political conducts to enforce to make society better, the Ricardian Socialists—and in general all *utopian socialists*—seemed to *feel* the injustice and exploitation but could not scientifically explain what it was or why it happened.

We could say that the critique of capitalism made by these socialists was superficial and non-scientific, and therefore, destined to be of scarce importance for the development of a real revision of political economy. The philosophers and economists that considered inadequate the socialist critique of the new economic system were not only the purists of political economy (the ones that followed the letter of Adam Smith), but also—and especially—some philosophers that were also critical of political economy. Notoriously, Karl Marx (1818–1883) and Friedrich Engels (1820–1895) are considered to be the most influential of the philosophers that critique very harshly the basic assumptions of Political Economy *and* Utopian Socialism. Their name is usually associate with the birth and the development of the socio-economic theory called *Communism*. This system is intended as a scientific response to political economy, a response that tries to explain why and how the working class is exploited in the capitalistic society. Amongst the other critiques (lack of scientific methodology, misunderstanding of the relationships between economy and politics, etc.) that Marx and Engels pose to the social utopists there is the idea that they are unable to understand that the capitalistic economy could not change without a radical political transformation. In other words, Marx and Engels accuse the *Utopists* to want to keep the capitalistic society and to want to just eliminate the *working poors* by giving them better life conditions. What they are missing—the Utopist that is—is the impossibility of a better society without a complete revolution of the socio-political system. Marx and Engels see as their philosophical goal to move socialism outside of *Utopia* and bring it into science. To properly explain how they are able to do so, we will need to analyze the evolution of their political and philosophical thought.

7.3 Of Human Alienation or *the Feuerbach Connection*

The Beginning of Marx and Engels' Philosophy can be traced back to the search for the essence of human beings. What they are looking for, though, is quite different from what philosophers such as Hobbes, Locke, or Rousseau were looking for. In fact, our German philosophers are not interested in discovering if human beings are good or evil by nature, if they are selfish or altruistic in the state of nature. Marx and Engels are concern with understanding which characteristics constitute the essence of a human being. In other words, they are looking for some traits or activities that define human beings on a fundamental level; traits or activities without which a human being would feel dehumanized and essentially unhappy.

They are not the first ones to try to find such essence. Before them, German philosopher Ludwig Feuerbach analyzed, amongst other things, the origin of human unhappiness, which he believed it had to be found in religion; and the fundamental trait that he considers the essence of human beings, which he believes to be solidarity. Because Marx and Engels will use and criticize Feuerbach's philosophy, it is important for us to briefly take a look at it.

Feuerbach is convinced that Philosophy should not be concerned with abstract ideas and lofty realities. Rather, philosophers should make the object of their research the concrete human being. The reason for this *Humanism* is simple: any sort of lofty metaphysics puts the essence of the human being outside the human being itself, with the result of taking meaning away from her life. Especially pernicious, among metaphysical systems, is religion and, especially, Christianity.

Feuerbach says that Religion is an anthropomorphic construction where human beings project their thoughts and needs. When they invent religion, humans create a fracture within themselves, separate themselves in two pieces by posing in front of their earthly selves a *divine self* that they call God and that plays the role of some sort of antithetic being. This means, for example, that when we consider certain attributes proper of God, we are in fact looking at projections of human needs or wants presented in a form that is unattainable to human beings. Let's think about the idea that God is all-loving. According to Feuerbach, this divine attribute is nothing but the projection of the human idea that there is nothing better than a loving disposition. Human beings want love, well, God is love. Another example could be the belief that God is infinite. Again, this is a projection of a human desire: the desire of infinite power. Human beings want to achieve infinity, God is infinite. If we consider now all the characteristics and attributes that God has, we can easily see how this process of projection is repeated for all these attributes. The result of this process is, Feuerbach says, *Alienation*. Alienation is the fictitious elaboration of another world (Heaven and its personification: God) where human beings imagine their dreams to be realized. Now, this fantastic world is the most comfortable way to evade the real problems of earthly life. This is also the reason why human beings are always miserable; they have "forgotten" that they invented *religion*, and while they are obviously aware of their desires and needs, they are deeply disturbed by the fact that only a being that *is not* them can fully satisfy these wants and needs. The goal of philosophy has to be then, according to Feuerbach, to help human beings to rid themselves of religion and to develop a true understanding of the *real* essence of human beings. Feuerbach's idea is pretty simple: human beings need to understand that their nature is not that of a creature that depends for meaning and essence on a God, and, consequently, they need to understand that they can fulfill their essence within their earthly life. But what is the essence of humans? According to Feuerbach, this essence is the communion, the unity, of a human with another human. Human beings can be lonely, finite, and limited; or they can be together, free, and infinite. Social solidarity, as Feuerbach calls it, is the instinct that makes every individual *feels* that all humans share an impulse toward happiness. And from this solidarity is born the *political instinct*, which is realized in the constitution of all sorts of super-individual institutions. To summarize, Feuerbach believes that there is a fundamental union between human beings that leads them to happiness through common organization. In order to achieve such happiness and true social organization, humans need to get rid of religion, so they can realize that they have all the means to be happy on Earth, and that there is no need to *alienate* themselves by creating false realities or entities (God).

Now, Marx and Engels do agree with Feuerbach that the source of human misery is alienation, and that in order for human beings to be happy they need to realize that they have to live in agreement with their essence. What they disagree on is the origin of human alienation, and the nature of human essence. Specifically, Marx and Engels are convinced that there are different forms of alienations, but that there is one on which all others rest. This means that there is a form of alienation that produces all the others and that if we want to bring back human beings to their original *humanity,*we need to get rid of this fundamental kind of alienation. This form of alienation is, according to them, economic alienation: if we suppress it, all other forms of alienation will disappear.

Religion Is the Opiate of the Masses

One of the most famous quotes from Marx is probably his take on religion. He famously said that Religion is the opiate of the masses. *The problem with this quote (and with most famous quotes, to be honest) is that it is usually taken out of contest. If you have heard this quote before, you most likely connect it with the idea that religion was created to keep the masses, the people, calm and sedated while the powerful do what they want. Nothing further from the idea that Marx is trying to convey. What Marx is really saying here is that, considering the miserable condition in which the majority of the people in the world live, religion serves a very important role, the one of painkiller. Like an opioid medication relives the pain caused by a wound, religion alleviate the spirit of the people living in misery. Christianity, especially, with its promise of an afterlife of eternal joy for the last of the people and the oppressed plays the role perfectly. Religion is not the real enemy for Marx and Engels, in fact, they think that the moment people will be allowed to live a more comfortable life religion will disappear on its own.*

Just like it was for Feuerbach, for Marx and Engels the object of philosophy has to be the real human being and not any sort of metaphysical reality. Consequently, the first thing that a philosopher should do is to understand what the essence of human beings is, what is the main characteristic that makes them different form any other species. According to Marx and Engels, such characteristic is labor. Specifically, Marx and Engels believe that through labor humans get in contact with nature, and from it acquire their means of subsistence; also, through labor humans enter in relation with other humans establishing social grouping; finally, still through labor, humans express themselves and develop their thoughts, and acquire self-awareness. This idea leads our philosophers to believe that the main form of alienation needs to be, consequently, the alienation of labor, economic alienation. In fact, alienated labor disrupts the relationship that human beings have with their work. Labor, we said, is the way humans make sense of nature, of the others, and ultimately of themselves. Capitalism transforms this activity in just a mean to survive, it alienates human beings from their labor intended as what gives meaning to their existence and shape to their surroundings. This theory of alienated labor is called in Marxist terms *Historical Materialism.*

Marx and Engels are convinced that the first historical activity of human beings, the very activity that distinguishes them from any other animal, we could say, is the production of the means to satisfy their needs, the production of their *material* life. This way human beings can be considered essentially *practical productive activities*. That is to say that they can be considered essentially *Homo Faber*, beings that have as their main essence the ability to create, to do. If we agree with this description, it is easy to understand that the main form of proximity between human beings cannot be, like Feuerbach wanted, a general social solidarity. Rather, the main bond between humans is labor, production: it is the bond that binds men and women in *classes*.

Classes are, for Marx and Engels, real entities, factors that determine society. They can be described as the subdivision of people in groups according to their activities and economic condition. Historical Materialism is nothing but the recognition of the fact that the history of humanity is just a history of the struggle between classes regarding the production and the distribution of wealth. This consideration is made clear in the early parts of Marx and Engels's *Communist Manifesto* where this struggle is revisited historically: the struggle between dominant and dominated classes is pin pointed with extraordinary clarity, for example, when Marx and Engels describe the primitive communist society, the Feudal society, and finally the bourgeois and capitalistic society.

If history is considered this way, and labor is the essence of humanity, it is obvious that the dominant class will always be the one that ends up controlling the means of production and distribution of wealth. Politics, Ideologies (but also philosophies and arts) are mere *superstructures* that rest on the *structure* that is, the economy. This means that who controls the economy controls everything else, and that to really change the miserable condition of the dominated classes, we need to revolutionize the way we organize and distribute economic power. Let's make an example. Many people believe that if there is a specific party in power, if there is let's say, a government that has power to make laws and regulations, a society could rectify its course and produce better conditions for the less fortunate. The truth is, according to Marxism, that while we might see some laws being implemented in such sense, we can clearly see that no matter what the problem that led the less fortunate to be so was, it has not been solved. Nothing, in fact, can be solved politically, or philosophically. A real solution could come only through a modification of our economic rules, specifically, Marx and Engels would say, the only possible solution would be a revolution that eliminates capitalism. Why? Because until then the people that make the laws and regulations are either capitalists or are manipulated by capitalists (think of lobbying).

That is not all, though. Things like arts, sciences, or any sorts of recreational activity are superstructure as well: they represent constantly the value of capitalism. Why? Because only the capitalist has the means to finance arts and sciences, and therefore, she will always finance products and projects aligned to her views.

Understanding all of this is crucial to realize that the world cannot be changed by reforming the system in which we live through laws and regulations. Only through real social action things can change. This has been, Marx and Engels say, the main mistake of all philosophers: *they have analyzed the world in different ways, while we should try to change it.* Changes can only come through a revolution which can be ignited solely by the development of class consciousness. Only when the workers will organize and act united, they will be able to seize control of the economic power and eventually build a classless and stateless society. This is why the *Communist Manifesto* ends with the exhortation *Workers of all Countries Unite! You have nothing to lose but your chains!*

This unity will bring a revolution that will defeat the capitalists and that after a period called the dictatorship of the *proletariat*, will produce a classless and stateless society. This means that when the working class (proletariat) will finally defeat the class of the owners (*bourgeoise*) there will be the need for the vanguard of the revolution (for the people that have clear the ultimate goal of the revolution) to seize power and reshape politically, economically and culturally the relationships that can be created among people. This is necessary in order to avoid that the proletarians might fall prey to the temptation of wanting to simply put themselves in the position of power and to reproduce the capitalistic logic, with just them at the top. The dictatorship of the proletariat is instituted for this reason, to simply avoid the risk of a new class structure. After this dictatorship period, a new era will begin for human beings. A classless and stateless society will be born. A society where there is no need for a government and where everyone is free to produce what they want according to their desires, and not according to someone else's profit agenda. We will talk more about this point later.

7.4 Political Economy vs Marxism

A series of legitimate questions, considering the Marxist political program could be the following: "why should we care about the workers? Why should we be concerned with the faith of a specific group of people especially when a science (political economy) tells us that capitalism is beneficial to the wealth of a nation as a whole? After all, shouldn't we look for the benefit of society rather than the betterment of a specific class? Finally, isn't part of the capitalist system the possibility of betterment for all individuals?"

As we said these are legitimate questions. Marx response here is especially instructive. He says, in so many words, that he too agrees the fact that we should use science to understand what is beneficial to a society; but he is also convinced that the science called political economy is contradictory in various points, and that if we truly *scientifically* examine capitalism according to the main axioms of political economy, we will find that the capitalistic system is not efficient in producing real wealth for the nation. Ultimately, Marx believes, political economists have forgotten to factor in the main piece of data: real people that live within the system. Let's see what proofs Marx has to believe that political economy is mistaken.

The analysis of these mistakes is exposed by Marx in his *Manuscripts of 1844* where he uses the methods and the principles of political economy to examine political economy itself. Marx starts with one of the assumptions that we make about the capitalist system that was embodied by the last question that we asked at the beginning of this section (*Isn't part of the capitalist system the possibility of betterment for all individuals?*) which implies that the system is in itself fair. Everyone, we think, can succeed. The problem with this assumption is that, Marx notes, political economy itself tells us otherwise. Firstly, there is an obvious essential distinction between the class of the landowners, the class of the capitalists, and the workers. The landowners and the capitalists can make use of the profit that they obtain to augment their revenues; the workers, on the other end, have neither rent nor the capital gain to supplement their income. The situation of the worker, therefore, is very peculiar: he or she cannot increase his or her pay in any way. The only mean of subsistence that he or she has is his or her body, his or her material work. This evident separation of capital, rent, and labor puts the worker at a disadvantage at the very heart of the capitalistic system. In addition, the rules of capitalism recommend that a worker gets paid the lowest and only the necessary wage rate.

> *The ordinary wage, according to Smith, is the lowest compatible with common humanity, that is, with cattle-like existence.* (Marx, *Economic and Philosophical Manuscripts* of 1844.)

According to the rules of political economy—and Smith in particular—workers need to be paid just enough to be able to have sufficient food and energy to go to work, reproduce, and keep the class of workers alive. This, evidently, takes away from them the possibility of moving up the social ladder.

The one just described, though, is hardly the only impediment on the fairness of the system. Marx, in fact, points out how the capitalist is essentially in a different position, in comparison with the worker, when it comes to shifts, radical changes, and/or turmoil within the marketplace. The capitalist can always direct his capital—his investment—toward another enterprise. This financial move, though, either renders the worker, who is specialized to a specific kind of labor, destitute, or forces him to submit to every demand of the capitalist. In other words, if a company starts failing who suffers the most is the worker, not the capitalist. The capitalist can pull his investment and make money somewhere else. The worker, instead, is ruined because he is specialized in that restricted line of work. Specialized labor, that was considered the stepping stone of the wealth of a nation, is also the cornerstone of the workers' ruin. We can think, for example, of all those workers that were employed by the *Bell Telephone Company* in 1879. Many of them where specialized in making parts useful to the construction of telephone's landlines; others were just operators (the people that would *physically* connect your calls). As technology advances, obviously, many of the skills necessary for these jobs became obsolete, and many workers found themselves unemployed. One might think that this change in technology might have hurt also the capitalists that had invested in the company. One, though, would be mistaken: the capitalists simply invested in new technology and redirected their capital toward more lucrative fields; this is why, still today, the company is alive and well (it is now called AT&T).

We might be tempted to believe, Marx says, that at least when a company is doing well the worker will also reap the benefits of such increased wealth. The truth is, however, very different. The worker does not necessarily gain when the capitalist does, but *he necessarily loses when the latter loses.* Consequently, when the capitalist makes more money, the salary of the worker, generally, stays the same, but when the capitalist loses money, then the worker will see his pay reduced or his position eliminated. In addition, generally speaking, the cost of life raises much faster than any salary, making the workers every year poorer.

Furthermore, another evident disparity when it comes to capitalist and worker comes from the difference in value that we put on labor and capital. Marx states that:

> *The labor prices of the various kinds of workers show much wider differences than the profits in the various branches in which capital is applied. In labor all the natural, spiritual, and social variety of individual activity is manifested and is variously rewarded, whilst dead capital always keeps the same pace and is indifferent to real individual activity.* (*Ibidem.*)

This means that different jobs promise different salaries (different professions are paid differently) and different social classes (depending on the job/career that someone has, it will depend also the consideration that we have of the individual), while the capitalists all gain the same way, independently from the kind of investments that they make. In other words, the worker is defined by what he or she does (one is a carpenter, or a chef, or a hairdresser, etc.) and his or her character is defined by it. The capitalist, instead, is just an *investor* and he or she is not identified with any specific characteristic proper of a job. An example of the difference between the two concepts can be this: the single soldier that kills enemies for a living is identified with his or her job, killings, duty as a protector of the nation, and so on. We think of him or her in a certain way, as fundamentally different from a baker. But when we think of someone who owns a big chain of bakeries and someone who owns, let's say, a company that makes guns and bullets, we do not make the difference in character between them, we consider both entrepreneurs. What they do is the same, they both invest money, they are both, essentially, capitalists.

From what Marx has shown us up to this moment, it should be clear that there are numerous *essential* differences between the condition of the capitalists and the one of the workers. It should also be evident that the capitalist system is not fair in terms of equality of opportunity. Although this critique of capitalism is associated, rightly so, with Marx and the Marxist philosophy, we don't have to forget that our philosopher is using the arguments proper of political economy and that very often he quotes word for word Adam Smith's work. But going back to the questions asked at the beginning of this section, even if there is a class that suffers the most, *shouldn't we look for the benefit of society rather than the betterment of a specific class?* Marx will address this issue as well, still using political economy against itself. In order to get to do so, he will need to make one more point regarding the miserable condition of the workers in *any* economic stage of society.

7.5   The Condition of the Worker and the Betterment of Society

The political economist, the fervent Smith's adept, would respond to the accusations that Marx has moved against capitalism that the Marxist analysis is too abstract, at least at this point. If we really take in consideration all factors, Smith's follower would say, there are phases within the market oscillations where all parties involved suffer—the worker like the capitalist—and phases where all parties involved benefit from the system. This view is pretty naïve, but still widespread. Marx counter argument to this idea is not to respond using abstract theories and good-hearted sentiments; rather, Marx uses once more the same scientific method used in political economy to make his point.

Marx proposes, in fact, to take in consideration what he calls the *three chief conditions in which society can find itself* and to analyze the situation of the worker in them. These three conditions are (1) the wealth of a society is in decline; (2) the wealth of a society is increasing; and (3) the wealth of a society is at its peak. Let's see what happens to the workers in these cases.

1. If the wealth of society declines, Marx says, the worker suffers most of all. In fact,

   although the working class cannot gain so much as can the class of property owners in a prosperous state of society, no one suffers so cruelly from its decline as the working class. (Ibidem.)

   It is Smith himself to say so, and with reason, according to Marx. When the economy crashes, the worker is the one that has no parachute that can ease the fall. No savings (or very little) no plan b as to where to allocate resources. The worker just loses his or her job, and sometimes his or her life. This certainly does not come as a surprise. It seems an obvious market law that if things are not good economically everyone will suffer some consequences, and it is also obvious that the people that are the lowest on the economic ladder will lose the most.

2. Let's analyze now a society in which wealth is increasing. This condition should be favorable to the worker and, at least in part, it is. Competition between capitalists is in place in this stage, consequently the demand for workers is greater than the supply. But what does this translate into?

   Firstly, the wages rise giving the workers the opportunity to make more money. And many workers will take advantage of this situation by working more (the capitalists would offer the opportunity for overtime, after all he needs people!). The more they wish to earn, the more they have to sacrifice their time and carry out *slave-labor*, losing all their freedom, *in the service of greed*. Workers work more and have little time outside of work. They are in a craze that stresses them. They take the least amount of time off (no matter if sick or if there are other important things to do outside of work). They try to make the most out of the situation. Inevitably, they shorten their lives. The fact that individual workers live less is a *favorable* circumstance for the working class as a whole, because this way an ever-fresh supply of labor becomes necessary: more deaths equals less workers. Less workers equals better wages.

   The class of the workers then has always to sacrifice a part of itself in order not to be wholly destroyed. (Ibidem.)

   In summary, even in times of overall prosperity the working class gets the short end of the stick. While the capitalist just sits back and enjoys the fruit of his or her capital (note: not of his or her work, but of his or her capital!), the worker, if he or she wants to take advantage of such period of prosperity, needs to work more and more. This will cause stress and premature deaths. This increase death rate amongst the workers is good for the working class in general, because it means that there will be less worker and less competition, but more competition amongst capitalists to get workers.

This is not all. If we analyze further the situation where society is prospering, and the wealth is increasing, we will notice even more disparity between the condition of the capitalist and the worker. Consider this, Marx writes, *when does a society find itself in a condition of advancing wealth? When the capitals and the revenues of a country are growing.* But this is possible only if: (a) the worker produces objects that are owned by someone else and that are out of his or her economic reach. The more the worker produces and gains, the more the capitalist has control over his or her means of existence. This is evident if we look at the fact that, even today, when the economy is good, prices rarely go down, they actually tend to go up. Think of the price of crude oil: a depressed oil market is usually a bad economic indicator whereas a high price of oil is usually an indication of a healthy economy. Consider now someone who lives on a fixed salary. Evidently, the good economy would make it more difficult for the worker (living on a fixed salary by definition) to *buy* oil, and therefore, it would make him increasingly poorer. This is true for all sorts of products that the workers produce with their labor. In addition, a country is able to grow its capital only when (b) this growth of capital produces a diversification of labor (the workers get more and more specialized), and the diversification of labor, naturally, increases the number of workers. Conversely, the diversification of labor increases the accumulation of capital (the more the worker is specialized the more he will produce for the capitalist). With this diversification of labor on the one hand and the growth of capital on the other,

> *the worker becomes exclusively dependent on labor, and on a particular, very one-sided, machine-like labor at that. Just as he is thus depressed spiritually and physically to the condition of a machine and from being a man becomes an abstract activity and a belly, so he also becomes ever more dependent on every fluctuation in market price, on the application of capital, and on the whim of the rich. (Ibidem.)*

So, in a society that is advancing in wealth, the labor becomes more and more specialized and the worker becomes a machine-like being left at the mercy of the will of the capitalist and of the specific task that he can perform. Moreover, he becomes dependent on the products that he can buy and therefore vulnerable to the fluctuations of the market prices.

Finally, (c) *In an increasingly prosperous society, only the richest of the rich can continue to live on money interest.* Everyone else has to carry on a business with his capital and risk to lose it. Therefore, the competition between the capitalists becomes very intense. The concentration of capital increases to the point that

> *the big capitalists ruin the small, and a section of the erstwhile capitalists sinks into the working class, which as a result of this supply again suffers*

*to some extent a depression of wages and passes into a still greater
dependence on the few big capitalists. The number of capitalists having
been diminished, their competition with respect to the workers scarcely
exists any longer; and the number of workers having been increased,
their competition among themselves has become all the more intense,
unnatural, and violent. Consequently, a section of the working class falls
into beggary or starvation just as necessarily as a section of the middle
capitalists falls into the working class. Hence even in the condition of
society most favorable to the worker, the inevitable result for the worker
is overwork and premature death, decline to a mere machine, a bond
servant of capital, which piles up dangerously over and against him, more
competition, and starvation or beggary for a section of the workers.
(Ibidem.)*

Even in a prosperous society, then, only the richest can live as capitalists:
the ferocious competition between capitalists brings more accumulation of
the capital on fewer hands. Consequently, some ruined capitalists will slip
down into the working class bumping some workers into misery. In addition,
the increased number of workers cheapens the skill and lowers the salary,
bringing back the worker to their usual miserable condition.

At this point, Marx introduces the third possible condition form a society.
It analyzes what would happen to the workers in a society that is at its economic peak. To do so, he uses Adam Smith's words:

3.   *In a country which had acquired that full complement of riches both the
wages of labor and the profits of stock would probably be very low, the
competition for employment would necessarily be so great as to reduce
the wages of labor to what was barely sufficient to keep up the number of
laborers, and, the country being already fully peopled, that number could
never be augmented.* (Smith, *The Wealth of Nations*, Vol. I p. 84.)

This means, according to Marx, that even in a fully developed society, the
workers would be in a not so great position: their wages would be low and
the competition for employment would be very harsh. This is not news for
Marx, nevertheless, what it is more important is rather another consequence
of what Smith says. According to Smith, (and political economy in general)
the pinnacle of capitalism, the moment when the economic system of a society reaches its apex, coincides with poor profits and a plateau in sustain-
ability when it comes to the number of people that can be housed in such
society. This stage will cause, according to Marx widespread unhappiness.
In addition, we have to remember that to arrive at the apex the society must
have gotten through that phase of growth that leads to the accumulation of
the capital in the hands of very few people, leaving the *majority* of the inhabitants of the society living in miserable (workers-like) conditions.

This conclusion is, Marx writes, undisputable, and it leads to an enormous contradiction within political economy. Smith, in fact, says that a society where the majority suffers cannot be not happy. This means that capitalism goal, since it aims to achieve the greater amount of wealth in the way we have seen, is the unhappiness of society. The capitalist system, the way it is presented to us by Smith, to say it plainly, seems to have as its objective the unhappiness of the majority of the people, and therefore, the unhappiness of society; if, like Marx wants, capitalism inevitably leads to the accumulation of wealth in the hands of the few.

Finally, we can see why answering the question *shouldn't we look for the benefit of society rather than the betterment of a specific class?* is pointless within capitalism. In this socio-economic system, the majority of the people ends up belonging to a specific class, the class of the workers. This class will be by definition exploited to benefit the minority within the society; and according to political economy itself, this is not conducive to a happy society. As big of a contradiction this might seem, it is not the only one in capitalism (and political economy). We will see some of the other ones in the next section.

7.6 Rent, Profit, and Wages. The Contradictions of Political Economy

Marx, uncovered the main contradiction in political economy, decides to dig deeper by analyzing the foundational concepts and theories of it. He starts with what he thinks it is a basic short-circuit at the origin of the science itself. Political economists theorize clearly that *naturally* the whole product of labor should belong to the worker. This means that who works at something, the worker, should enjoy the fruits of his or her work. This concept as we know is hardly new; already Locke established that private property is a byproduct of labor. Private property, in fact, was considerate legitimate by the British philosopher only because human beings mixed their labor with it. What is new (and specific of political economy) is that, while telling us that the fruits of labor should belong to the worker, political economy tells us, at the same time, that in actuality what the worker gets is the smallest and barely indispensable to survive part of the product. The worker gets only what is necessary for his existence, *not as a human being but as a worker*, and for the survival, not of humanity, but of the class of workers.

We can clearly see the logical inconsistency here. It is political economy that establishes that the worker is supposed to be the *owner* of the product that he makes, but that in reality he gets just enough to keep alive not as a human being but as a worker. This distinction between human beings and workers is a crucial one. Marx is implying that the workers are treated not as human beings that have a life and a meaning beyond their job. They are treated, rather, as means toward an end, as tools.

The concept of labor and its relationship with ownership, Marx notices, is really problematic for the economists. The very definition of *Capital* is tainted by issues concerning the concept of labor. Indeed, the political economists tell us that the only natural and real currency is labor, and that *capital is nothing but accumulated labor*; but at the same time,they tell us that the workers, far from being able to buy everything they want, must sell themselves and their humanity to survive. The laws of political economy do establish that all capital is accumulated labor. This means that capitalism is justified and not considered a form of parasitism just because *Capital*—the money invested by the Capitalist that is—represents labor that has been accumulated. We can think of capital as a container full of labor that has happened before, and of the capitalist as the one that eventually decides to apply all this previously accumulated labor in a specific field (this is what we could call an investment). The money used by the capitalist is, in few words, nothing but the representation of a specific amount of labor accumulated. The illogical aspect of this way of thinking, Marx reflects, is the fact that who is doing the work is not the capitalist but the worker; and yet the accumulated labor (the capital) goes for the major part to the capitalist.

Labor is also the center of another issue within political economy. According to this science, in fact, it is exclusively through labor that human beings enhance the value of the natural products. Labor is, therefore, human beings' active possession. And yet, according to this same political economy the landowner and/or the capitalist, which don't really produce any labor and can be considered privileged and idle beings, are *everywhere superior to the worker and lay down the law to him*. Here is another logical inconsistency with the way political economy uses the concept of labor: labor is what brings value to things, but the *laborer* is somehow "inferior" to the capitalist and the latter is the one who can decide the destiny of the *laborer*. If we look at labor coherently, we should also agree that it should be the only unchanging price of things. But, Marx writes, there is nothing more accidental than the price of labor, nothing is exposed to greater fluctuations.

We need to understand that Marx here is not advocating for the price of labor to always being the same, in a monetary sense. He is saying, simply, that the only thing that remains constant when *evaluating* any goods (when establishing the price of them) is the fact that labor is needed to make those goods, and that this labor is what gives value to the product (remember the exchange value between cotton and steel presented in Section 7.1?). At the same time, he says, the amount of money paid to a worker, the working wage, fluctuates greatly. This is another contradiction of political economy one that makes us confuse.

Because of it, for example, we start believing that wages are some sort of expenditure, some costs, that we need to deduct from the profit that the capitalist or the landowner make. The truth is that *rent of land and profit on capital are deductions suffered by wages*. If we take seriously the idea that labor is the only thing that gives value to all goods, and if we take seriously the definition of capital as accumulated labor, then we should easily understand how logically whenever the worker is producing something, he or she has in his or her hands the whole capital. When the capitalist reaps the monetary benefits of such capital and pays the worker a wage, he or she is taking away from the wage, he or she is deducting from it the majority of the monetary value present in it. In simpler terms, the capitalist will always need to underpay his or her workers to make a profit, otherwise he or she would not see a penny. The value of the product, in fact, resides only in the labor *produced* by the worker. This means that the profit is something that comes out of the wage, which should represent the value added by the worker to the product.

Another, related, confusions that comes out from this strange concept of labor that political economy holds, has to do with another way we think of profit in relation to wages. We have the tendency to believe that the profit is some sort of *bigger* wage, proportional to the investment, that the capitalist pays to himself. The profit or capital gain is, completely different from the wages, in reality. This difference can be seen in two ways: firstly, the profits of capital are regulated entirely by the value of the capital employed, even if the managerial "labor" of the owner associated with different capitals may be the same. Moreover, in large works the whole of this labor is committed to some main manager, whose wage has no regular proportion to the capital of which he oversees the management. And although the labor of the owner is here reduced almost to nothing, he still demands profits in proportion to his capital. Profit, therefore, is not comparable to wage. Although we think that earning money in a way or another does not make a difference and it sums up as making money, there is a difference. We usually think that the profit is some sort of a salary that the *investor* pays himself for his investment (we think of it as the work of the capitalist). The truth is that the profit is related to the quantity of the capital invested and not to the amount of work that the capitalist puts in.

Here, we can see another misunderstanding when it comes to capitalism: we think that because the capital is accumulated labor, the capitalist investing is putting forward *his* labor. The truth is that the capitalist is putting forward the labor of someone else. In addition, the number of *hours* that the capitalist spends actively involved in the project does not influences the profit at all, only the quantity of capital will. Obviously, this is the opposite to the worker and his wages: the wage depends exclusively on the number of hours of work. The Capitalists profits the most, then, when human activities, that he *does not* performs, add value to the products that he is selling. The workers' wages stay the same or do not rise in proportion with the profit. We can say that the wage of the workers is part of the equation of the profit of the capitalist and it is used to increase the profit. We hear sometimes that a product costs more because the capitalist *must* give higher wages to his workers: think of the fact that goods manufactured in Western country are more expensive than the ones made, let's say in Bangladesh, because we are told, the wages paid in the West are higher. Technically, this is not true: the product costs more because the capitalist wants to make money on the wages. If he or she pays a worker ten dollars per hour and the product takes three hours to make, the capitalist will calculate in the price of the product not just thirty dollars, but thirty dollars plus whatever he considers enough to make a profit on it (let's say three times the amount spent on the wages: so the product will cost, just for the labor, not thirty but ninety dollars). The same happens with the materials (if the materials cost one hundred dollars, the capitalist will charge for the product three hundred dollars).

This last idea, once more, is taken by Marx from political economy (precisely from Smith).

> *Why does the capitalist demand this proportion between profit and capital? He would have no interest in employing the workers, unless he expected from the sale of their work something more than is necessary to replace the stock advanced by him as wages and he would have no interest to employ a great stock rather than a small one, unless his profits were to bear some proportion to the extent of his stock. (Ibidem, p. 42.)*

The capitalist employs workers *only* because he or she can profit from their work, Smith writes, he or she would not employ anyone if the worker was just a cost to be reimbursed. In other words, the capitalist wants to make a profit from the labor of the workers by selling the workers' labor for more than what he or she pays the worker. The capitalist does the same thing with the materials used. Men and things (materials) are used the same way, as simple tools to make a profit. An important point here is the pure selfishness on which the capitalist acts; Smith says—and Marx highlights—that the only engine of capitalism is the will to have more typical of the capitalist. No profit, no capitalism.

The fact that the workers are comparable to materials, in the sense that they are both tools to increase the profit, leads to the consideration that, according to Marx, the political economy has of the workers in general.

> *It goes without saying that the proletarian, i.e., the man who, being without capital and rent, lives purely by labor, and by a one-sided, abstract labor, is considered by political economy only as a worker. Political economy can therefore advance the proposition that the proletarian, the same as any horse, must get as much as will enable him to work. It does not consider him when he is not working, as a human being; but leaves such consideration to criminal law, to doctors, to religion, to the statistical tables, to politics and to the poor-house overseer. (Marx, Economic and Philosophical Manuscripts of 1844 pp. 19–20.)*

Political economy, Marx notices, considers the workers only as proletarians, not as real human beings. This view can be explained by the analysis of the way of saying "it is business, nothing personal." When we say that we intend that even though some consequences of an action might seem unfair or evil, we need to understand that there is no malice intended in the action, but that it is solely a matter of profit. In the same manner, the treatment of the proletarian from the capitalist is nothing personal, it is just business. All consideration about the *real* life of the proletarian need not be part of the calculation of the capitalist.

At this, Marx believes to have shown that political economy is contradictory, at best, if not illogical. Considering this, he asks two questions that try to address the issues that derive from this separation between proletarian as workers and proletarians as people, and the solution that are usually proposed (by the socialists of his time) to solve these issues.

(1) What in the evolution of mankind is the meaning of this reduction of the greater part of mankind to abstract labor? (2) What are the mistakes committed by the piecemeal reformers, who either want to raise wages and in this way to improve the situation of the working class, or regard equality of wages (as Proudhon does) as the goal of social revolution? (Ibidem, p. 20.)

These two questions, and especially the first one, are very important to understand Marx's proposed philosophy. The first one asks, basically, what is the purpose of a socio-economic system where the majority of people have to live like animals to satisfy the greed of a very small group of people. The second one addresses an issue still present today when it comes to alternatives to the capitalist system: there is a group of economists/politicians that believes that it is possible to solve the issue of the workers just by raising their wages (just like today people want to raise minimum wage) and another group that believes that we can solve it by equalizing the wages (just like today people consider scandalous CEO's bonuses or athletes salaries and want to make the wages of the workers proportional); Marx believes that both of these approaches are wrong, and that we need a different way if we want to achieve a social revolution to build a society where the proletarians don't live in misery.

Before we take a look at the alternative proposed by Marx, though, we need to take a look at one more bias regarding the status of the capitalist vs the status of the worker. This bias was present during Marx times and, we could say, it is still present today. The idea is pretty simple. We are led to believe that the capitalist is in the position in which he is because he *deserves* it. In other words, we think that there might be a quality that the capitalist has, which makes him or her successful, that the workers are lacking. We might think, for example, that the capitalist is smarter or more courageous, when it comes to investing money. Or maybe we could think that simply the capitalist has worked harder. We already know that the last belief is not well founded, considering that the capitalist, by definition, reaps the profits of someone else's work and not of his or her own. But what about the other biases? To answer this question we need to consider, Marx writes, what happens when someone acquires capital (one way or another). Once again, Marx leaves Adam Smith talk for him:

> The person who [either acquires, or] succeeds to a great fortune, does not necessarily [acquire or] succeed to any political power [. . .]. The power which that possession immediately and directly conveys to him, is the power of purchasing; a certain command over all the labor, or over all the produce of labor, which is then in the market. (Smith, *The Wealth of Nations*, Vol. I p. 26–27.)

Capital is just governing power over labor and its products. The capitalist possesses this power, not because of his or her personal or human qualities, but because he or she is an owner of capital. His or her power is the purchasing power of his or her capital, which nothing can stop. Given Smith definition of capital, we can clearly see how the capitalist has the power of purchasing political and economic influence, lawmakers, entertainment programs, and opinion makers, etc. And this is not because he or she has some special qualities or because he or she is a particularly good human being. In other words, the people that we can call capitalists do not have any special traits, they are not necessarily smarter, or more versed in business, or better in any sense when it comes to human qualities. They are able to do what they do—buying more power for themselves—only because they can spend their capital to gain influence and more capital.

It is now time to look at Marx proposed alternative to the capitalist system and political economy.

7.7 A Different Version of Socialism

The general rules put forward by political economy to justify capitalism lead people, according to Marx, to behave in wicked ways without even realizing it. Moreover, what is probably worse, it makes people believe that the only way in which people can live a decent life is by obey the rules of capitalism. The issue is that in capitalist societies the number of people that will live in decent conditions, Marx says already in 1844, is very small and it will get smaller and smaller. This happens not as an unwanted consequence or because of some sort of glitch within the system. This happens because, we can say, it written in capitalism DNA. Let's consider once more the attitude of the capitalist. Paraphrasing Adam Smith: What motivates him or her to invest (and how to invest) the capital accumulated? Obviously, the consideration of his or her own private profit is the sole reason which determines the capitalist to employ it either in agriculture, in manufactures, or in some particular branch of the market. The quantities of families that will be involved in the enterprise (read: the number of employed people), and the contribution of the investment to the GDP of his or her country, never enter into his or her thoughts (Adam Smith, WON, Vol. I, p. 335). The decision about how to employ capital for the capitalist will be made on the basis of, risks being equal, what yields him the greatest profit. Evidently, this investment might not be, and it is not always the most useful for society. To summarize, then the only motive for capitalistic investment is profit. Public utility, the condition of the workers, fair wages, and the advancement of society in general never cross the mind of the capitalist when it comes to deciding how to invest his or her money. The most useful employment of capital, for the capitalist, is the one that can more surely give him or her the biggest profit. This doesn't always coincide with the most useful employment of capital for a society.

Moreover, the plans and speculations of the capitalist regulate and direct the entirety of the organization of labor involved with the enterprise, and profit is always the only end for all those plans and projects. The problem is that the amount of profit does not rise with the prosperity and fall with the decline of the society like wages, for example, do. On the contrary, profit is low in rich countries and high in poor countries for the capitalist, and it is always highest in the countries which are going fastest to collapse economically. The interest of the owning class, therefore, has not the same connection with the general interest of the society as that of the class of the workers. *The particular interest of the capitalists in any particular branch of trade or manufactures is always in some respects different from, and frequently even in sharp opposition to, that of the public.* The capitalist, therefore, directs all the operations regarding his or her investment to simply gain profit: profit is the end game of an investment of capital. The rate of profit, though, opposite to wages, does not rise when a country is doing better and falls when a society is doing badly. On the contrary, a capitalist does better in societies where the living conditions are miserable, and profits are even better when a society is rapidly crumbling. This is why companies and capitalists want to invest, always, in places where the living conditions are poor. Not only because they can pay less in wages, but also because the profit that they can make on these wages is higher (a capitalist will always charge, for example, five hundred dollars in labor for a specific product, independently for the fact that he or she pays for labor thirty dollars or five dollars). It is clear, for Marx, that people that choose to be capitalists have interests that are often in contrast with the good of the society, and that, in general, these people have an interest to deceive and oppress all others.

Considering that this is the norm when it comes to the way we organize our society; can we even think of a real non-utopian alternative to capitalism? Marx believes that it is possible only if we revolutionize the way we think of the economic system. Only this way, we can create a new society and a new political system. But what does this revolution entail?

First of all, we need to understand what revolution really means. Marx is convinced that all socialist before him can be considered utopists. This is because they believed, wrongly, that it was possible to make some changes within the capitalist system (higher wages, better working conditions, proportions between profit and wages) in order to better the condition of the dispossessed majority that the proletariat represents. Marx believes that it is not possible to salvage capitalism because it will always revert to its true nature: the few are always going to exploit the many, and the life condition of the workers, in comparison with the one of the capitalists, will always be miserable. So, when we think of a revolution, we need to think of a completely new system that would guarantee the well-being, if not of all, at least of the majority of the people.

Having clarified what revolution means for Marx, we can now concentrate on more substantial issues. Again, capitalism is the norm, how do we proceed out of it? How do we start the revolution? Marx writes that the revolution cannot be imposed top-down. He believes that capitalism will crumble, and the revolution will begin by necessity. There will be a moment (not too far in the future according to Marx) where the ever-growing mass of dispossessed people, that is inevitably produced by capitalism, will develop a class consciousness and rebel against the capitalistic order. This coupled with the implosion of the contradictions (of which we have seen some) inherit in capitalism will lead to the toppling of the ruling class (the bourgeoisie) and the beginning of the revolution.

Marx has no illusions about the peacefulness of this moment. He is very much conscious of the fact that violence will probably play a role in the revolution. The bourgeoisie will not leave its position of power without a fight, and the proletarians will be so feed up that they will put as much energy as possible in this class war. But Marx is certain of it, in the end the proletarians will win. The issue is, at this point, what then? Are the proletarians to become the new powerful subject and substitute the bourgeoisie, while the latter becomes the new oppressed class? is it just a matter of exchanging one oppressor for another? Marx believes that there might well be the will, at the beginning at least, to do so. After all, we have been all brainwashed for a long time to believe that being successful and happy means to be a capitalist. We all have been trained to believe that the lifestyle and the wants of a capitalist are the ones to have. It would be only normal, Marx believes, if the proletarians would want to be the new ruling class.

This, though, cannot be the faith of the revolution. What do we do then, to avoid that the oppressed becomes the oppressor? Marx thinks that in order to avoid a new capitalist system with just different people in charge there will be the need for a period of time where only the people that have fully developed a true understanding of the purpose of the revolution will be in charge. These people will put in place rules and regulations that will favor a completely new way of conducting business. Meanwhile, the means of production (think of big factories and industrial equipment) and the natural resources (think of oil, natural gas, gold mines, etc.) of the country will be collectivized. This means that the entire society will profit of them. This period of time is called by Marx *Dictatorship of the Proletariat* and it is described as a necessary period to reboot our societal values and to purge away from the people all the false aspirations that capitalism has built in our minds.

After this period, Marx writes, when the people finally rid themselves of the values of which we talked about, the dictatorship will dismantle itself and the people in charge will resume living like everyone else in the world. What kind of life will these people live once they are voided of their capitalistic desires? Marx answer is simple. They will leave in a *Communist* society.

The characteristics of such a society are interesting and pretty clear. Firstly, as we have seen, the means of production and the natural resources will still be communal. This means that everyone will have a share in them. Secondly, this society will not have different classes of people, it will be *classless*. Everyone will be part of one class, the class of *human beings*. This people will not be defined by what they do, and they will not be ranked depending on their occupation. A communist society is a society where everyone creatively produces what he or she wants to produce, because he or she wants to produce it. Marx is not worried about the fact that people will all want to do the same thing (some of us might think that if we all could do what we want all of us, for example, will be musicians), he believes that people have such different interests and so different ways to express their creativity that there is no risk of an excess of conformity. Finally, a communist society will be *stateless*. No one will need to oversee anyone else. The government and the State in general will be a thing of the past. People will self-regulate and live fully satisfying existences.

Marx believes, and this is probably his main issue, that all these changes will happen by necessity because history moves inevitably in that direction. He believes that all that he has said can be proven scientifically, and he think he has done so in his book called *Das Kapital* (The Capital). He is certain that eventually the right side of history will prevail, and that the entire world will be organized in a giant communist society.

Toolbox

Communism, an Abused Word

Considering what we have learned during this chapter, the mental image that we had of communism might have been slightly different from what Marx was really proposing. It important, though, to realize that throughout history the word communist or communism has been associated to various entities that have shaped our prejudices toward this term. Chiefly, communism has been associated with the Soviet Union. It is important to understand that while the Russian revolution (which led to the Soviet Union) was inspired by Marxist principles, Lenin (the leader of the revolution), and later Stalin clearly set themselves apart from Marx (Lenin conceives a different system of society that is not the mirror image of the Marxist one). China is another communist country. And yet again the kind of communism implemented was not modeled on Marx's principles, but on a Chinese reformer teaching, Mao-Zedong. Then we have Cuba and numerous other Communist dictatorships. Marx would say of some of them that they are not really communist societies (because they have simply removed an oppressor to create another one); while of others he would probably say that they are still on the *dictatorship of the proletariat* stage. There is one thing, though, that all society that have called themselves communist have in common. They all have developed huge governmental bureaucracies where all the power has been allocated. In one form or another most self-proclaimed communist countries have been a social-political-economic failure. While these countries, we have said, have no real ties with the Marxist ideology, the fact that who uses Marx ideas could pervert them to the point of creating a society that reflect quite the opposite of what he intended, should give us pause when considering the functionality of the Marxist ideology. And, more importantly, it should make us understand how powerful philosophical idea could be when they find practical application.

CHAPTER 8

Philosophical Anthropology

8 Indetermination and Human Nature

At the beginning of the twentieth century in Europe, we assist to the birth of a new way of doing political philosophy. A new *science*, in fact, is born: philosophical anthropology. This science tries to explain what many philosophers have used as the cornerstone of their philosophy, Human Nature, in scientific terms. Many of the philosophers that adhere to philosophical anthropology draw their conclusion by putting together results taken from sciences like Biology and Linguistics using a methodology that is a combination of sociology, anthropology and philosophy.

One of the main representants of this new branch of philosophy is Helmut Plessner (1892–1985) whose works are especially important for political philosophy. Amongst other things, his philosophical system tries to understand what the real nature of human beings is. According to Plessner, figuring out what possessing such nature entails is fundamental not necessarily because we need to build a political system that is in line with it, but because the concept of human being is at the base of every culture's foundation. This means that Plessner is convinced that to understand human societies we need to understand what concept the inhabitants of these societies have of themselves as individuals. He believes that we need to understand what these people believe their nature is. This implies, according to Plessner, that the essence of human beings is their history: humans qualify themselves in terms of appropriation of their history. History in this context has to be intended as individual/collective evolution, individual or collective becoming throughout life. As a population, people consider their nature whatever their past has shaped them to be, and as individual they think of their *personal* nature as what their evolution throughout their life has been. This simple idea is very powerful and explains, somewhat, any sort of politics that reinforces national identity. The Americans *feel* that being American means to co-participate in a certain history, to self-identify as, for example, Christian, country-loving, hard-working,

173

humble, and honest people. Other people will identify with different values, but all people will identify with some values that are considered the backbone of being part of that group. This happens also at the individual level. How many times have we heard somebody saying, for example, "I am good at cooking, it is in my blood". Whenever somebody says something like this, she is expressing, naively, exactly Plessner's point. These individuals, in fact, identify with their historical evolution of becoming great cooks.

This means, obviously, that specific national identities and specific individual identities are relative to the specific history of a population and to the specific history of an individual. Plessner, though, is not content with identifying the relative nature of the specific histories of people, he aims to find a *common* trait present in all human beings. To do so he draws exactly from the relativity of the specific histories. He thinks that if all humans can build their nature starting from historical facts about their life (communal or personal) it is obvious that all of them have a characteristic in common. They all *can* do so, they have the ability to build their nature the way they see fit. In addition, the evident diversity visible among people is proof of the fact that the content of life is variable, and that we can have different experiences and identify with them independently from what they really are. Human beings, Plessner says, are *immanence open to acquisition; life is undetermined*. This means that man is *power*, *know-how*. Human beings are simple possibilities, they do not have specific characteristics that rigidly develop, for example, from their biology. And yet, the number of possibilities that they have is delimited from the infinite possibilities that exist. A good way of understanding this is thinking of our language. A human can speak whatever language he or she is socialized to speak or no language at all, but he or she cannot communicate through ultra-violet signals. This means that there are infinite ways in which we can combine sounds to speak to each other, but this infinite is still delimited by everything that is *not* a perceivable signal and that still might exist. If we accept the idea that *humans are possibilities* and not a determined kind of being, then it is possible to accept diversity and consider human essence as "power to . . .," "Know-how," etc.

Plessner's idea is interesting for multiple reasons. Firstly, he proposes that the only trait that we can consider human nature is the indetermination and the openness to possibilities that humans have. This means that Plessner believes that what makes human beings different from all other animals is their freedom to become whatever they want. A cow is driven by a certain number of instincts that will make it become, more or less, like any other cow. Humans, instead, evolve, individually and as a group, in significantly different ways. In Plessner's words:

Man is different from all other creatures because he can influence history, and not just being influenced by it. (Plessner, *The limits of community*, p. 97.)

Secondly, Plessner is convinced that if we really understand the fact that we are different because we are indeterminate, it is possible to embrace the other, the different, on the basis of our ability to understand that the other is nothing but one version of what we could have been if put in other material conditions. If Plessner is right, humans are an open question, an historical product, and even the most widespread form of identity, "Western culture," is not the way of the world, but a simple expression of what he calls "European spirit."

8.1 Familiar Faces: Building Identity through Differences

As we discussed in the previous section, the natural indetermination of human beings can lead to the understanding of the diversity that comes in the form of what philosophers call the *other*, the *stranger*. While this is true, Plessner remarks, we also need to analyze more closely how this recognition happens, and what are the consequences of such understanding.

Human beings are so undetermined that they are in a constant fight to build pockets of familiarity. Surrounded by infinite possibilities, by the chaos of a universe (which includes them) that can always develop in some unexpected way, they need to find something familiar to stabilize their life and to build their determinate history. This stabilization implies that humans need to differentiate themselves and keep away from what is different. This is a necessity for human beings, as for them to determine themselves they need to differentiate from others. Like a picture needs to stand from the background to exist, a human being needs to determine himself by contrast to others.

Living, in human terms, means to struggle to find some stability, it consists in a constant contrast of familiarity and foreignness, of friend and enemy. These dichotomies are essential to the constitution of a human being. In their being undetermined to themselves, humans configure a peculiar horizon inside which everything appears to be known, familiar, natural, conform to their essence and necessary. They build homes, families, and activities that make their world predictable e determined. While outside of such horizon everything is unknown, foreign and unnatural, against their essence and incomprehensible. People, outside of their "comfort zone" feel like everything is unnatural and strange. Outside of the world that they build to be their own everything is incomprehensible; trying to live there is like trying to live in a place where everyone speaks a foreign language that nobody can understand or translate.

What it needs to be clear, according to Plessner, is the fact that these boundaries, the position of these demarcation limits between familiar and unfamiliar are not established by nature and are not fixed once and for all. Humans, in fact, cannot predetermine where this horizon will lay, and they will set it either by accepting a line already marked or by rebelling to a line already marked. The nature of this horizon is always historical.

> *Every association and every commonality, whatever shape it takes, for purposes of cohabitation, for economic purposes, love, reproduction, or religious worship, are determined by the friend-enemy relation. A familiar circle opposes an unfamiliar elsewhere.* (*Ibidem,* p. 101.)

All relationships are determined by the will to create a familiar place. Human beings strive to stability because their nature is unstable, and finding these pockets of stability is essential for their survival.

It is crucial to understand that Plessner conceives this idea of *enemy* in a radical different way when compared with Hobbes. The latter, in fact, believes that people fear the enemies because of the damage (mostly physical damage) that they can do to them. Plessner, instead, thinks that enemies are not such because of the fear of the damages that they can do, like Hobbes seems to think, but because of the fear of the other as a *perturbation* of their familiarity. In order to understand better what Plessner means, it is better to use the term *stranger* and not the term *other*. In fact, a rock is the other in comparison to humans, but they don't fear it.

Human beings only fear the stranger, a being where they see difference and, at the same time, can recognize some familiarity. Simply put: the stranger is what can perturbate our familiarity, and that is why we fear it. When immigrants come, for example, they can bring these *strange* practices that will impede on our familiar way of doing things; they are disturbing the quite of my *familiar* life. The fear is that they will bring chaos *not* to society, but to our personal being, they might make us regress to a state of pure possibilities where we have to rethink the ways in which we can become. If an individual or a population is capable of understanding, though, that the stranger is just another possibility of existence (technically a way in which they could have become as well) then we have the simple recognition of different people, culture, and customs. Thanks to this recognition, Plessner writes, we build the different concepts of races, populations, nations, cultures and individuals. But this discovery can easily lead (if we don't keep considering human beings as simple *possibilities*) to a unilateral manipulation of a historically determined humanity to contrast all that a group considers different. If we just take at face value the differences, without connecting them with the concept of human nature as pure possibility we might find that it becomes easy to justify the belief that there is one *true* way of existing—the one familiar to the individual in question—and many *wrong or false* ways of living. Regardless of the recognition of possibilities, though, it is vital for human beings to keep differentiating between familiar and unfamiliar, friend and enemy in order to live a meaningful life.

The friend—enemy dichotomy can be also considered from a political prospective. The premise of the political definition of the dichotomy is, obviously, the fact that the perturbating effect of the *stranger*, of the enemy, is historically variable: the enemy takes different forms in different times. Thus, political fields and alliances are variable and historically determined. Understanding the friend—enemy opposition, though, means to see *the political* as a human behavior tending to insure and increase power by limiting or annulling the scope of power of the *stranger*. In this sense, politics is everywhere. Friend—enemy is not political in a technical term, rather friend—enemy is a category of existence for all humans in the sense that it has to do with the possibility to exercise power and to limit someone else's power. Politics is defined by the existential characteristic of humans; and one of these characteristics is to enlarge as much as possible the pocket of familiarity of the group to which one belongs, while trying to eliminate as much as possible the space of unfamiliarity.

8.2   Carl Schmitt and the Political Connotation of Friend and Enemy

Building on the concepts of philosophical anthropology and working especially on the political considerations derived from it, is German philosopher and political theorists Carl Schmitt (1888–1985). The main aim of Schmitt philosophy is to fully understand what makes politics different from everything else. We will see how his view of politics rests on a peculiar anthropological version of human beings and how his concept of what he calls the "political" will influence multiple political philosophers after him. According to Schmitt, the concept of the Political is fundamental if we want to justify and truly understand concept like state, sovereignty, liberalism, conservativism, etc.

In order to understand what a State is, and how other political concepts that seem sometimes obvious to us really work, we need to understand, firstly, what is the *essence* of politics. Schmitt, in fact, declares that the concept of State, which might seem the primordial concept when we talk about politics and society, presupposes, in reality, the more basic concept of the *Political*. But what constitutes such concept? The Political is intuitively identified, according to Schmitt, as the negative part of a dichotomy: politics and morality, politics and economy, and so on; the Political is also, usually mentioned in relation with the State. We need to be careful, though, when trying to pinpoint exactly what the Political is, especially in today's political system. When State and Society penetrate each other, like it happens in a democracy, the equation state/politics becomes deceptive. When social matters (the so-called social issues, in today's political lingo) become affairs of State and vice-versa, then everything seems to pertain State and Politics. Sometimes even fields that should be by definition antithetic to the political in a democracy (like religion, culture, or science) are englobed by democratic states in their politics; this once again, Schmitt writes, produces some confusion when it comes to trying to understand what the essence of politics is, what is the political.

How should we proceed to understand what the political is, then? Schmitt proposes that we, as our first move, try to identify the most general political categories that we can find. What our philosopher is trying to identify here is what we can consider the final concepts to which we can refer when trying find the scope of politics. Let's make some examples: in ethics this final distinction—the one to which all ethical dilemmas can be reduced to—is definitively good and evil. In Aesthetics this distinction is beautiful and ugly: Aesthetics aim is the distinction between these two general categories. What about the political? What is the final distinction within the political realm? Schmitt writes that the specific political distinction to which we can reduce political actions and motives is the one between *Friend* and *Enemy*.

While, evidently, this distinction recalls the one made by Plessner, Schmitt's version of it is more specific, and definitively less grounded in the biological aspect of human life. The distinction of friend and enemy, according to Schmitt, *denotes the utmost degree of intensity of union or separation, of association and dissociation.* Specifically, the *political enemy* doesn't need to be evil or ugly or an economic competitor. These other categories are not political ones therefore they are not implied by the definition of enemy. The political enemy is, rather, the *Stranger* whose nature is existentially different. This existential difference justifies the possibility, in extreme cases, of conflicts. In a similar way, the friend is not necessarily the good or the beautiful; it is simply whomever we share our existential nature.

It is important not to fall for the idea that friend and enemy, for Schmitt, are abstract categories that should be understood only theoretically. It is quite the opposite. Friend and enemy need to be understood in a proper and existential way, not as metaphors of any sort. When we speak of this dichotomy here, we are speaking of the greatest degree of friction or fluidity that can be among people and not about some lofty ideal *feeling* that exists only in the hearts or the minds of philosophers. In addition, when we speak on enemy, we need to understand that we are not referring to an economic competitor or to a debating adversary. These other "entities" are often conflated into the political by liberalism, but putting these parties together is simply wrong and confusing. The only enemy is the *existential enemy*.

Another important distinction that Schmitt makes, when defining the friend–enemy couple, is the one between private and public enemy. In the sense of the Political the only enemy is the *public* enemy. A political enemy exists only if a fighting collectivity of people can confront (at least potentially) a similar collectivity. The distinction between this sort of public enemy and a private kind, is made evident, for example, within Christianity. The exhortation "love your enemy!" in fact, is intended—even by the purest of the Christians—as "love your individual enemy," your private one. On the other end, in over a thousand years of fighting against Islam, never Christianity thought of surrendering to the Saracens or the Turks. Christians fought their public enemy hard, while loving their private ones. This does not constitute a contradiction, rather it exemplifies for us the distinction between public and private enemy. The former being the political one, the one to which Schmitt refers to.

Antagonism is, then, key to understand all politics. All political words, in fact, presuppose the understanding of the friend—enemy dichotomy. Words such as republic, state, society, and party only acquire meaning in light of this original dichotomy. Characterizing an adversary as political or non-political has an antagonistic meaning; even characterize oneself as political or not has such meaning. Once again, Schmitt writes, we need a clarification. The friend and enemy antagonism is not exclusive of relationships between people that are part of different States, rather, this dichotomy can be observed also inside one single State. Parties, for example, as usually identified in political partisan politics, can be considered the product of this internal antagonism. When inside the State, amongst parties, the internal antagonism is intensified, and it achieves its peak we have the friend—enemy dichotomy on an internal level. At that point civil war is possible. The true possibility of combat starts being present among the groups inside the same state. This possibility is essential for the birth of public enemies, and combat must be always present in politics. They are essential to it.

8.3 The Possibility of War as Essential to Politics

More than once Schmitt clarifies in his book *The concept of the Political* that when he uses terms like combat or war, he means it literally, not metaphorically. The combat to which he refers is the kind in which someone can always die, a combat where there is real killing involved that is why war is the most extreme consequence of enmity, it doesn't have to be common or desirable in politics, but it needs to be possible. The possibility of conflict is what fuels politics.

This, of course, does not mean that war is the aim of politics, nor its content. It is rather a way in which humans act and think *politically*. To be precise, the possibility of war is what keeps politics in existence. *Politics exists as long as there is the possibility of war.* The interesting point about this way of thinking is, obviously, that it seems to be countering the general idea that politics exists to avoid war or to, at least, limit it. Commonly we think that wars are political failures (meaning that the parties in questions were unable to politically come to an agreement), or that wars have "hidden" motivations that justify them (motivations that are not strictly political like economy, religion, etc.). What Schmitt is telling us here is, instead, that war (its possibility) is *essential* to the existence of politics itself. All wars are political wars. There are no such things as purely moral, religious or economically motivated wars. These other interests can only reinforce the political motive. The only justified war, he writes, is the *political* war: the war that is motivated by an existential threat to a people way of life.

These ideas lead Schmitt to the consideration that every religious, moral or economic antithesis can become a political one under certain conditions. This means that he believes that there are certain situations in which some antagonistic views about, again, religion, ethics or economy can become a matter of real conflict. According to Schmitt, these conditions exist only if the antagonism between the factions involved is strong enough to group them effectively according to the friend and enemy dichotomy the way it was previously described. The political does not resides, therefore, in the battle itself, but in the *mode of behavior* which is determined by this possibility. This means that the essence of politics is not the *art of war* but the ability to correctly evaluating a concrete situation and distinguish promptly real friend from real enemy. Therefore, communities that are able to make such distinctions are to be considered political communities regardless of their actual participation in actual combat. For example, a religious community that wages war against other communities (religious or not), it is obviously more than a religious community, it is also a political one. It is evident, in fact, that this community has the power to group people in friend and enemy. In the same way, if the same religious community is able to successfully forbid to its members to participate in a war against some other community, it is also to be considered a political community. This community is capable to promote the decisive step of denying the *enemy* quality to a certain adversary. In other words, the community is able to declare someone *not* an enemy. This is true not exclusively of religious communities, but also of organized communities like labor unions or social classes intended in a Marxian way. If the antagonistic feeling becomes so powerful that the groups enter in a real war (civil war would be in this cases) with the declared enemy (Respectively, the bosses and the antagonist social class), these groupings become effectively political groupings.

It should be evident from the previous paragraph that the political might derive energy from different and various fields of antagonism. Religion, economy, class, etc. are all fuel that it is utilized by the political, but they cannot be identified with it: wood or oil both fuel fire but are not fire. In brief, if a political entity is in existence it supersedes any other grouping. This does not mean that the political entity must define (or de fact defines) every aspect of an individual's life or that a central political system should encompass all other organizations or corporations. It means, instead, that the real friend—enemy grouping is so *existentially* strong that the moment another grouping becomes political all other antithesis become subsidiaries of the friend—enemy one. The existential threat posed by an enemy, for example, is much stronger than my cultural affinity with someone who is part of the enemy grouping. Therefore, Schmitt concludes, the political entity is *sovereign* as long as there is a concrete grouping of friend–enemy.

8.4 The State as the Only Legitimate Political Entity

Schmitt writes that the typical incarnation of the sovereign, as the legitimate entity able to successfully group friend and enemy, can only be the State. To the State, in fact, belongs the *Jus Belli*, the right to declare war. For this reason, the State is the only entity that we can call *fully* political. Schmitt believes that, having the Jus Belli, the State obviously possesses an enormous power, it has the power of disposing of the life of many individuals. Only a State can legitimately send individuals to kill others or to be killed by others. The State has the ability to legitimately decide of the life and death of individuals and groups. This is true for external menaces and for internal ones as well. The State is in charge as much of declaring war as it is of keeping peace and tranquility within its borders.

If the State has, as Schmitt thinks, the legitimate power to declare war, it also has the ability to successfully declare the enemy. This means that the State has the power to declare someone or a group an existential threat to the existence of the people grouped inside of it. Every state has a specific formula to declare external or internal enemies, but whatever the formula is the goal is to declare someone as incompatible with the existential traits proper of the citizens of that particular State. The goal is to declare an enemy. While it is clear that when we talk about the external enemy such declaration consists, normally, of a declaration of war, there are different dynamics at work when The State declares an internal enemy. The internal enemy declaration can come in the form of *ostracism, expulsion, or simple outlawry*. In any of these cases, though, the result is the same: the subject is now considered a *mortal* enemy, an existential threat, a Stranger. It is important to pay attention to the internal enemies, according to Schmitt, because when it comes to them the reaction of the subjects of this declaration of enmity can be crucial for the destiny of the State itself. If the ones declared enemies, in fact, pose themselves in direct contraposition to the State and fight back the declaration of enmity in organized manner— declaring the State as the enemy of the people for example—we have the possibility of civil war. This possibility becomes an actuality if the enemy of the State is successful in grouping enough subjects as friend in contraposition to the State. If a civil war starts, Schmitt writes, we have the dissolution of the State as an organized political entity that provides peace inside its border.

This definition of the State as the only legitimate power that is in control of the enmity among people can leave some of us perplexed; especially when we think that there are other non-political entities that seems to be obviously in charge of the life and death of people. Let's take, for example the case for religious communities. A religious group, we can observe, has often requested its members to die for their faith. Specifically, numerous religions have exhorted—rarely they have obligated—a member of their faith to die for her belief and become a martyr. This request, though, is not a political request. The reason for martyrdom is always the salvation of the individual soul, and never the glory or the integrity of the religious community intended as an earthly power. If and when a religious community requests the sacrifice of someone's life for earthly purposes, that community is no longer a religious community, but it has assumed a political dimension.

Another example could be an economic system; we can see how within it there are a whole series of means to neutralize and eliminate—usually non-violently—the unsuccessful or the inferior competitors. If there would be an industry that would ask of a human being to kill or to be killed so trade and profit may flourish for the survivors, we would conclude that the request (and the *requestor*) is crazy and sinister. The right to declare enemy is an exclusive prerogative of the State as a political entity, and if the State gives that prerogative away, that entity ceases to be political.

8.5 The Pluriverse of Politics

It should be clear at this point that, according to Schmitt, a political entity can exist only if a real enemy exists. The implications of this reasoning are not to be underestimated. If a political entity can exist only in a real contraposition to an enemy, then the political world always presupposes at least two of such entities to be in existence. Therefore, a universal state (such as the idea of a global empire or a global democracy) that would encompass the entire globe and that would have the whole humanity as citizens is impossible by definition. *The political world is a pluriverse not a universe.* Without enemies and therefore without the coexistence of multiple sovereign entities there is no politics.

This concept is critical to understand the fact that, while it is important for the existence of the political to create a strong unity amongst the individuals that are part of the friend grouping, it is equally important to keep in existence a certain group that we can call Enemy, otherwise the first grouping (Friend) disappears. The idea here is pretty simple, and it borrows from Plessner's definition of the friend—enemy dichotomy. The Political needs the Stranger to come into existence, otherwise the friend grouping will stay indeterminate and unable to produce any real-life consequence in the existence of the individuals. It is worth noticing that, if Schmitt is correct here, whenever we ask ourselves why in the past (or in the present) some political identity have not obliterated completely their mortal enemy the answer could be: "because they need *that* enemy in order to justify their existence." Even more interesting is, we should notice, that the practice known as *scapegoating* exemplifies Schmitt's idea: in order to reinforce its power, a political entity creates or better declares someone as a mortal political enemy in order to justify its existence in the eyes of its citizens. It is important to remark here that such scapegoat, in order to become really an enemy, needs to have at least the potential of becoming the antagonist to the political entity in question; it needs to be the Stranger, otherwise the people would not recognize it as an Enemy. A powerful State will always be able to make its citizens (or at least the majority of it) recognize the proposed enemy.

To be even clearer, Schmitt writes, the very concept of *humanity*, intended as the totality of human individuals living on our planet, is antithetic to the existence of the political because it excludes in principle the concept of enemy. An enemy, in fact, is still a human being and cannot cease to be one no matter what a State says. This is why, evidently, whenever a State fights a war in the name of humanity, whenever it fights against the *inhumane* atrocities of another group, it is not fighting for the sake of *all* humanity. Rather, Schmitt states, it is usurping a universal concept (humanity) to use it against its military opponent. This sort of usurpation, obviously, is not exclusive of the concept of humanity. In the same way a State can misuse the concepts of *Peace, Justice, Progress,* and *Civilization* by claiming them as proper characteristics of its own existence while denying the same to the Enemy. Excluding the Enemy from the realm of justice or progress is obviously problematic and dangerous. Riskier is, though, to exclude the enemy from humanity: to monopolize such a concept, Schmitt claims, to deny the enemy the quality of being human and declaring it *unhuman,* a criminal against humanity, leads to the most inhumane and extreme variety of war that can be fought. In such cases, the enemy will not deserve the treatment that people would reserve to other fellow humans. Using an analogy, we can say that the difference in treatment during a war with an enemy that is deprived of its human quality and one who still has its human quality is similar to the difference between a criminal that can be considered redeemable and one that is not. A criminal that can be reformed is usually considered as someone just like the rest of the people living in society. The only difference is that this specific individual has made a mistake: the punishment for these individuals is usually a fine or some time spent in prison. People give to these individuals many names: criminals, outlaws, offender, etc. Whenever people deal, instead, with someone that they consider irredeemable, immediately the *quality* of the individuals in question appears different. These individuals are not people just like the rest of the people living in society, they are, rather, beasts impossible to tame. The punishment for these individuals is usually death or life in prison (social death), penalties that in society people would rarely apply even to non-human animals. But these incorrigible individuals are not humans in the eyes of society: they are, as we said, savage beasts, pests, dangerous animals that, by nature, cannot be controlled, and that therefore cannot be treated just like any other person; they are not human. Now, Let's elevate this way of thinking to the level of a war between States. The obvious result is that if a group considers their Enemy not to be in possession of the quality of humanity anything goes during a war against such foe. There is no more obligation to use the "humane" rules of engagements, and definitely no obligation to use weapons and tactics deemed acceptable amongst human beings. Unconventional attacks that involve the death of civilians rather than military personnel, attacks on non-military targets like hospitals or schools, the use of chemical weapons, and so on, are all permissible actions in a war against a non-human enemy.

According to Schmitt's view of the concept of humanity, every time a State lunches in an activity in the name of such concept, it uses the name of it to justify other means or causes. In fact, Schmitt declares, Humanity, in itself, is not a political concept. More, Humanity is antithetic to politics. If someone would be able to materialize the ideal of humanity, indeed, the world would be organized in a universal society where there are no nations and/or political entities and, therefore, no friend–enemy grouping. Such a universal grouping would mean necessarily a total depoliticization of the world and the disappearance of the entity called State. *Pluriversity* is the specific characteristic of politics.

8.6 The Anthropology of Liberalism and Other Theories

During his analysis of the concept of the Political, Schmitt reflects on the political theories and theorists of the past in order to show us of the necessity of the friend–enemy couple when considering what is the political. He begins his analysis by stating that all theories of State and Political could be grouped together according to their anthropology. Political theories can be divided, according to Schmitt, in two general categories: the ones that consciously or unconsciously presuppose humans to be evil by nature and the ones that consciously or unconsciously presuppose them to be good by nature. The only exception that Schmitt can find to this general rule is the case of Plessner who considered human beings, as seen at the beginning of this chapter, an *open question*—not good nor bad.

Truth be told, most political theorists believe that human beings are dangerous and evil (among the names cited by Schmitt there are Machiavelli and Hobbes—whose philosophies are presented in Chapters 3 and 4 of this volume), while very few believe that humans are good natured. This is, Schmitt thinks, because the political can only exist where there is enmity and therefore, the perception of evil is necessary.

Among the few political theories that consider humans good, Schmitt recognizes Anarchism and Liberalism. Of the first one very little is said by our philosopher. Anarchism presupposes men to be good in their natural state and considers Government and State to be oppressive and damaging to individual and collective freedom. The rebuke of Anarchism proposed by Schmitt is simple, Machiavellian, and powerful: people, he writes, are optimist until everything is calm. They refuse, at that moment, all sorts of political truths in the name of some individual discipline and consider political theories amoral, uneconomical or unscientific. They fight the existence of the political, that is, until an existential threat presents itself. At that moment the political grouping friend–enemy will present itself as well, and the rosy conception of human beings as individually good will dissipate.

Liberal and Liberalism

We need to be careful when reading about Liberalism in Schmitt's works. The way he uses the word, in fact, is radically different from the use that we commonly give to the word, especially in the United States. Today, when we talk about Liberalism, when we call someone liberal, we most likely refer to something or someone that we consider progressive, that believes that the government should play a central role in the lives of the people, and that it is concerned with the equality and the welfare of the people. A liberal person appears to be concerned with ethics over economics; simply put, at least in principle, for the current day liberal, her economic growth comes after values like equality, solidarity, freedom of expression etc. Now, while some of these values were already present in the original definition of Liberal to which Schmitt refers to, the order in which these values have to be respected and the reasons for this respect are radically different. The Liberalism to which Schmitt (and generally speaking all philosophers of his time) refers to is a peculiar political-economic-philosophical tradition that has at its core the values of freedom and private property. The father of such Liberalism is considered to be John Locke (see Chapter 5 of this volume) who famously considers Liberty and Private property natural rights. This classical way of intending Liberalism, specifically, proposes that liberty is fundamental to acquire as much wealth and private property as possible. Therefore, any sort of infringement on absolute free trade and economic prosperity—even if it comes from genuine political preoccupations—must be avoided. To simplify, in what we call liberalism today ethical and social issues supersede the economic prosperity; in classical liberalism (the one analyzed by Schmitt) economic power and prosperity supersede ethical and social issues. In both cases, though, the State and the Government are slaves of Society intended as the result of ethical and economic forces that might, sometimes, be at odds.

Liberalism, on the other end, will be analyzed in depth by Schmitt who introduces it by declaring that Liberalism also presupposes humans to be good, but it tries to make the State work for society, meaning that the State and the Government must be controlled by society in a pure liberal system. After this concise introduction, Schmitt goes on to give Liberalism its dues: Liberalism, he writes, has changed the political way of thinking in a systematic fashion. Liberalism, in fact, has neutralized and depoliticized successfully the strata of the political (education, economy, etc.) in a significative manner. Liberals have done this in a very "political" mode by allying themselves to illiberal political movements helping to build all sorts of totalitarian states. But, aside from this political method, *no specific political idea* can be deducted from an untainted form of individualistic liberalism.

The absence of political ideas is, Schmitt writes, due to the negation of the political as a category that is typical of all forms of individualism. This refusal of the political leads, almost paradoxically, to a political practice of distrust toward all conceivable political forms, but never produces its own politics. Liberalism, seen this way, is simply a *pars destruens*, a negative force that denies the existence of something (in this case the political) without proposing an alternative. We need to be careful when looking at the works of Liberalism though. It might be easy to mistake, in analyzing Liberal systems and proposals, what we can call *policy* for the political. There are, evidently, Liberal policies of antithesis against the State, the Church, or other institutions that by definition limit the individual freedom; there are also liberal policies that regulate religion, education, trade, etc. but there is no *Liberal politics, only liberal critique of politics*. The only political practice that can be attributed to liberalism is a sort of methodology conceived to hinder and control the State's and the Government's power for the sole purpose of protecting the freedom and the private property of the individual.

It is interesting to briefly take a look at how Liberalism is able to conduct political business without actually producing any real political theory. The game played by the liberal ideology is fairly simple: the goal is to evade State and politics by moving back and forth between two heterogeneous "non-political" spheres, namely *ethics and economics, intellect and trade, education and property*. The only part of the State and Government that the liberal individual accepts is confined to protecting liberty and eliminating all sorts of obstacles to the enjoyment of individual freedom. For the liberal, private property is the center of the universe, and ethics and economics are the contrasting forces that emanates from this central pole. In liberal terms a battle becomes competition in economics and debate in the ethical realm. This is, probably, the greatest difference between liberalism and politics: in case of need the political entity, as seen before, must demand the sacrifice of the life of the individual. Such demand is obviously not justifiable under the flag of Liberalism, it would be the greatest infringement of individual freedom.

This way of looking at communal living, as a simple warranty under which people can affirm their individual liberty without risking their life, it has been the appeal of liberalism, according to Schmitt, to the point that the liberal thought has created a distrust toward political institutions that it is still visible today.

Under Liberalism the State ceases to be a State and turns into a *Society*. This means that the way people look at successful forms of aggregations becomes different. On one end there is the ethical discourse that transforms the political into an *ideological humanitarian conception of humanity*; on the other end there is an economic-technical system that is concerned just with production and traffic. Consequentially a politically determined people turns into a culturally interested public and/or into a mass of consumers. Politics, power and government turn into propaganda, mass manipulation, and control. Any sort of political institution that tries to limit individual freedom becomes repressive and necessary instruments of the political, namely war, become obsolete and negative.

Schmitt critique of Liberalism ends with a warning. While it might seem desirable, a world where war and conquest are deemed negative elements does not equate to a world where these two things are considered wrong. The reason why Liberalism tries to avoid war and conquest, in fact, is not grounded, for example, in the abhorrence of violence. Rather, war is considered bad business. War does not produce amenities or comfort, it is not useful, and even the victorious ones are bad business. The *trade people*, in Liberal societies, *have subjugated the warring nations*. But under the ashes of a world burning with Liberal economic competitions rests a political fire: economic antagonisms can turn into politics again. Politics and State, according to Schmitt, are like the Phoenix they are cyclically born again from their own ashes, they cannot be exterminated.

Toolbox

The State and Society. The Risk of Global Warfare

Schmitt's idea of war as a necessary instrument of politics might seem either naïve or antiquated in an era where the most powerful nations of the globe rarely engage in face-to-face wars, and where we have in place many political entities that where created to avoid wars (think of the UN or even NATO). Schmitt is aware of how his idea might sound to the reader, and, in fact, he addresses the issue. Schmitt states, in fact, that there has been a shift in our vocabulary (partially to accommodate liberal instances) to justify violence that is not considered "war." We often talk about *sanctions, punitive expeditions, pacifications, international police,* and all sort of measures to ensure that peace remains intact. The foe is not called an enemy anymore, but rather someone that wants to disturb the global peace and economic prosperity. The Enemy is now an outlaw of humanity. What we used to call wars are now crusades for the salvation of humanity; war obviously waged to expand and protect economic power are, thanks to propaganda, sold as ultimate cultural clashes. This is the product of the polarity between ethics and economics expressed by liberalism, a product that presents itself as anti-political but that will produce, according to Schmitt new friend—enemy grouping, and that therefore, cannot escape the logic of the political.

PART 3

POLITICS AND SOCIETY

Premise to Part 3

The last part of this volume is structured differently compared to the previous two. The first two parts, as the reader has seen, follow a chronological order and explore the thought of a specific author at a time. This last part, instead, privileges a more *thematic* approach: the reader will find that the chapters are subdivided according to themes and not authors. In addition, the chronological order is not fully respected, and the chapters are noticeably smaller.

The reason for these changes is simple. The closer we get to our contemporary history, the more difficult it is to identify specific thinkers that can emblemize a certain topic. Many authors nowadays contribute to the same topic, and the topics themselves are more liquid and less definite. In addition, many of the authors mentioned in this last part (with few exceptions perhaps) are less "famous" than, let's say, Plato, Machiavelli, or John Locke.

The topic analyzed in this part of the text are: *Human nature* and its implications for the formation of a just society; *Neo-marxism* and the relevance that it might have today; A critique *Democracy* conjugated in all of its forms; *Power* as a socio-political tool; and finally *Revolution* as seen through the lenses of Hanna Arendt.

The chapters, while connected with each other and with the previous parts of the book, can also be read by the more experienced reader as standalone explanatory pieces.

CHAPTER 9

One More Stab at Human Nature

9 Human Nature

Throughout the previous chapters, we have often mentioned the concept of *human nature*. The way in which we have talked about it, though, might have reinforced a stereotypical and unidimensional understanding of it. Commonly, in fact, when people discuss about human nature, they habitually try to understand if human beings are "good" or "evil" by nature. This was the debate, to a certain extent, among Hobbes, Locke, and Rousseau when they are trying to describe the "state of nature." Reducing the debate regarding human nature to behavioral or ethical terms would be, though, partial and arbitrary. A larger debate, of which we saw a glimpse when we were describing Plessner's Philosophy, has been at work for a long time. This discussion tries to pinpoint what makes human beings what they are, what is essential to their being, rather than discussing what sort of behavior they kept before civilization existed. Just like the discussion over the "ethical" nature of humans, though, this other version of human nature's debate has obvious political ramifications. If we could find out what are the main characteristics of human beings, what makes them radically different from all other beings, then we could probably figure out what a social organization should look like in order not to be oppressive and repressive for humans. If there is something that makes us what we are, in fact, then repressing or having a government that prevents us to fully realize the ability that makes us humans, would make it intrinsically oppressed.

In 1971, two of the most influential intellectuals and philosophers of the twentieth century meet for the first (and last) time in Eindhoven, Netherlands, to discuss about human nature and its repercussions of politics. The debate was televised as a part of a series of debates titled "The International Philosophers' Project." The two philosophers in question were **Noam Chomsky** (1928–) and **Michel Foucault** (1926–1984).

The debate is an interesting tool to dig deeper through the concept of human nature and it is representative of a philosophical divide that has not been breached yet. It is the divide between philosophers that think, like Chomsky, that the biological aspect of human beings has to take precedence over the social, historical aspects of human life, and the philosophers that believe, with Foucault, that while the biological aspects of human beings are important, they are not central when it comes to understand the way we function as individuals and/or as a group. Let's try to understand better what these two "camps" are about by analyzing Eindhoven's debate.

Chomsky, asked to start the debate, in order to explain what he believes human nature is, introduces the audience to the main point of his linguistics. Chomsky's linguistics, simplifying, theorizes that every single human being is equipped with what we can call a *faculty of language*. This means that human beings share an innate ability not only to learn a language (any language), but also that this ability is unique when compared to other species. We can talk because, in summary, we possess this faculty of language is part of our mental structure. In a sense, for Chomsky, the faculty of language corresponds to human nature, it is that *biological invariable* that gives human beings their specificity. There is more. Chomsky is also convinced that the faculty of language is characterized by an element of creativity. Every speaker is able to make an infinite use of finite means. We don't learn all the sentences that we can utter from someone else, we are able to create new—never-uttered-before—sentences because we have an innate ability to do so. Creativity is, then, innate and derived from a series of mental structures that help us make a creative use of rules and elements that cannot change and that we all share.

Foucault's response to this idea is at first circumspect. He replies that he doesn't like to use the notion of human nature because it seems to him that this notion is not a real scientific concept. Foucault, in fact, does not see the concept of human nature as an object of scientific research, and he thinks that when we mistake it for one, we are misunderstanding the entire concept. Human nature is nothing but an *epistemological indicator*, it has the simple function to mark the "borders" a field of research, distinguishing it from others. The notion of human nature serves as a methodology, but it is not itself an object of knowledge. As for the claim that creativity is confined to innate mental structures, Foucault is categorical: the schemes and the structures on which creativity works are not individualistic, they are intersubjective, and therefore historical. All rules from which the individual deviates or to which she conforms are products of the economic, social, and political structures that are historically contingent. In summary, there is no such thing as human nature, there is only the specter of it, used erroneously by some theorists to declare something as immutable and unchangeable, when it is obvious, according to Foucault, that there are no such things as immutable unchangeable human structures.

9.1 Justice vs Power

This theoretical disagreement becomes practical when the two philosophers, during the second part of their debate, try to connect their specific philosophies to political practices and views. It might be instructive to know that the two philosophers were in full agreement when it came to some political objectives (both of them were against the Vietnam' war, both of them were on the side of the most radical workers' fights for better work conditions, etc.), but they vehemently disagreed when it came to try to establish a model of society based on certain characteristics that we can call human nature. This is an important disagreement, because it will lead our philosophers to completely different views on society, state, and politics in general.

Chomsky, when asked to describe the goals of his political activity and theory (libertarian socialism), makes an explicit connection between the creativity implicit in human biology and political ideals. It is a fundamental element of human nature, he claims, the need for creative work, for free creation. This can only happen without the arbitrary limitations posed by coercive institutions. It follows from this that a decent society should maximize the opportunity for the individual to express her creativity and realize this main characteristic of human nature. Chomsky goes on to describe the main elements of libertarian socialism: the existence of a federate, decentralized system of free associations which would encompass also economic and other social institutions; the re-evaluation of agency in human affairs, that is the idea that people do not need to be cogs in the machine of production anymore (thanks to technological advancement). We can achieve all this by promoting a society of free associations where freedom is paramount, and where the creative need that is intrinsic to human nature can be fully realized in whatever forms it will take.

Foucault, at this point of the debate, starts to show us that he is not in agreement with these political ideals. He states that the most important political task that he can think of is, at the moment when he is speaking, to indicate and uncover all the relationships of political power which control the social body and oppress or repress it. Foucault exemplifies this by pointing out how, in western societies, people consider power as localized in the hands of the government, and exercised through institutions, such as the army, the police, and in general, the entire state apparatus. It is obvious that such institutions exist to create and transmit a certain number of decisions in the name of the nation. Now, Foucault says, this is not all. Political power also exercises itself also through institutions that at first sight might have nothing to do with the State. These institutions seem to have nothing in common with political power, but they are hidden places for it to propagate. Institutions like the family, higher education—but really all teaching systems—, and all institutions of care (like medicine) are good examples of it. Let's look more closely at the education system. When we look at it, we are often fooled in thinking that the only function present in it is the dissemination of knowledge. In reality, it is pretty evident that this institution also tries to achieve the goal of maintaining a certain social class in power (for more on this see Chapter 10 of this volume).

Foucault is convinced that the role of a philosopher, politically, should be to criticize the mechanisms of the institutions which appear to be neutral and independent; this attention to these institutions needs to be maintained in order to unmask the political violence which they usually exercised obscurely. This way we can fight the violence of the system where it is really happening. Only this way, we can truly fight oppression and repression. Political power, in fact, is everywhere and it is at work in places where we won't expect to find it.

Chomsky, during the debate, readily agrees with Foucault that one should unmask political power whenever it is exercising itself obscurely. However, he adds, we would be falling short in our political actions, if we would not try to draw a connection between human nature and political institutions. The goal of politics should be to create a social structure that is founded on freedom, dignity, creativity and other fundamental human characteristic. The goal of political action, in summary, should be to allow humans to realize their natural potential.

Foucault sees a danger here:

> *Then isn't there a danger here? If you say that a certain human nature exists, that this human nature has not been given in actual society the rights and the possibilities which allow it to realize itself [. . .] if one admits to that, doesn't one risk defining this human nature [. . .] in terms borrowed from our society, from our civilization, from our culture?*

Foucault worry here is an important one. He is concerned that whenever we identify something as human nature we are simply using our cultural categories in order to highlight a specific trait that is not necessarily natural, but that our society presents to us as natural. An example should clarify. People have a horrible history of considering natural traits that are obviously not natural and elevate them to "what makes us human" or to pinpoint an "unnatural" characteristic that one might find in another individual or culture and declare this individual or culture not human enough, or in need to forced "humanization". Chomsky thinks that we need a society that allows creativity because it is in our nature to be creative. But what if, in twenty years, a group of intellectuals declared that it is in our nature to be subjected to someone else's will? What if someone declared that it is human nature to be "sheeply" following few leaders, and that freedom is not within our nature? should we then build a society on these "natural" principles?

Chomsky insists that when such uncertainty about human nature strikes us, we need to plow through because whenever we are trying to build a free and just society we will always be confronted with doubts and indecisions, but in the end it is more or less easy to find the route to the just action. When we are fighting the "oppressor" we might commit illegal acts (Chomsky was heavily involved in civil disobedience during the Vietnam war), but we do that to move toward a Just society.

Foucault is quick to point out that this idea is quite strange. He says that what the MIT professor is saying here is that we are justified to defy justice (intended as the catalogue of the law of a nation) in order to achieve a *purer* higher justice. It is true, Foucault continues, that in all social struggles there is a question regarding justice, but it is also true that justice in such contexts is an instrument of power, not an ideal notion. Whenever we are "involved" in a war, we are not merely fighting it because we think we are fighting a just war. The truth is that people fight wars not because they think they are just, but because they want to take power. And when they finally acquire this power, they will consider the war just. *One makes war to win, not because it is just*, Foucault concludes.

Summarizing the debate on human nature in few words, we can see that, when it comes to political issues different concepts of human nature lead to different ways of thinking of society, political struggle, and justification of the political struggle. If we believe that there is such a thing as a fixed, biological, human nature, then we are justified in believing that we should create a society based on this nature. Conversely, if we believe that human nature is a social construct, a concept that is proper not of biology, but of history; if we believe, that is, that notions like human nature are proper only of our civilization, of our type of knowledge, then we cannot think to build a society in ideal terms, in terms of a specific "nature". We can only uncover, unmask, the mechanisms of power currently present and currently at work in a particular society and, lastly, regard any social change as a simple movement of power from one group to another.

9.2 Dissatisfaction

The reader can decide for herself if one of the two philosophers was more convincing than the other. Aside from the critiques that each of them has on the other, few *neutral* considerations on a certain dissatisfaction with both positions are, though, in order.

Although Foucault is right to point out that what we consider human nature is always influenced by our culture and the specific socio-political moment in which we live, he is probably wrong when he uses this argument to completely deny the existence of human nature. He seems to think that the fact that the notion of human nature, of some sort of biological invariable, presents itself in different forms in different cultural ages proves that it is not invariable, and therefore that it doesn't exist. The problem is that it is possible to say, using a metaphor, that Judy comes to work everyday with a different outfit without denying that it is still Judy that comes to work every day. The different outfits are not a sign of the fact that underneath the clothes there is nothing, that all there are is clothes. It is possible to conceive that the variability that we observe when analyzing human nature is not all there is: underneath the variable forms of human nature there might be a stable, minimal maybe, essence.

Even Foucault seems, unconsciously, to indicate that somehow. When he says that human nature is an *epistemological indicator*, a grid used to organize a field of research, he must admit that whenever we apply a grid the grid is applied on something. There must be an empirical reality behind the grid. Human nature might be considered as the empirical reality behind the epistemological indicator.

When it comes to the issues that one might criticize in Chomsky's position during the debate, we can immediately point out to the problematic reduction that he proposes. In fact, it is evident that what Chomsky is suggesting is that all historical variable should be reduced to biological invariables. According to him, in fact, to build a "decent" society we need to correct the disfunctions that history has thrown in the way of nature. The creativity of language is the permanent reminder that creativity is what makes human beings what they are, and that we need to correct all the systems of power created in order to re-affirm this biological characteristic. In Chomsky's view *unjust equals unnatural,* and all societies and governments tend to be unjust because they are based on principles that are unnatural instead of being founded on human nature, and therefore, on natural principles.

Just, for Chomsky, could only be a society that would be absolutely faithful to human nature. He is deducing his socio-political ideal from the biological invariant because the social and political variability are, according to him, the elements that derail every try to build a just and decent society. And this is obviously problematic because, while he claims that freedom and creativity are at the foundation of human nature, he is also implying that there are certain rigid parameters that need to be followed in order to build a just society. Any variation would inevitably lead to injustice.

Lastly, both of our philosophers seem to be blind to connection that exists between the two concepts that they contrapose to each other. Justice and power, in fact, are correlated and they imply one another while for them they seem to be completely separated. Chomsky considers justice as a direct corollary of the immutable aspect of human nature, while for Foucault power is completely independent from what human beings "should be" and it depends only on specific struggles. Justice, according to Chomsky, is rooted in the natural order; power, according to Foucault, doesn't have any legitimacy that transcends its historical incarnations. The difference between the two notions—justice and power—anyhow, regards just the preeminence that we can give to one or the other term within the necessary relationship that there is between the two. Foucault intends justice as a collateral effect of power relations; Chomsky believes that any request of more power coming from asocial class is founded on a "justice criterion" that is deduced from human nature. Depending on what version of these two relationships we believe in, our idea of power, knowledge, justice, and society can be radically different.

10

Neo-Marxism

10 Revising Marxism: On the Reproduction of the Conditions of Production

During the twentieth century, Marxist thinkers, in light of the historical events happening then, start to review Marx's writings and try to show aspects of his theory that were neglected by Marxist orthodoxy. In particular, we will see how thinkers such as **Louis Althusser** (1918–1990) or **Antonio Gramsci** (1891–1937) will concentrate especially on the cultural and ideological aspect of Marxism. Specifically, they are interested in reversing, or at least in partially modifying, the orthodox Marxist idea that all that matters when it comes to understand, and ultimately defeat, Capitalism is the economic process as a structural process that can be separated from everything else.

What philosophers like Althusser try to do is to show that the conditions of production, central to Marxism, do not exist in a vacuum and that the very existence of such conditions depends on the possibility for such conditions to be reproduced. This means that, according to Althusser, it is of fundamental importance to highlight in Marx's works the aspects that are relative to fact that social formations, whatever kind of social formation, in order to continue to exist need to reproduce the very conditions that made their existence possible in the first place. It follows that every social formation must produce, at the same time, its reproductive forces *and* the existing relations of production. Marx says clearly that no production is possible which does not allow for the reproduction of the material conditions of production. An example should clarify what Althusser (via Marx) is indicating here.

Let's think of a factory that produces electronic parts for computers. In order for this factory to keep on existing, it needs to "reproduce" its raw material, its machines etc. (i.e., it needs to buy it or repair it constantly). But it does not produce these materials and machines in its own production, other companies do: A company that refines metals, another one that produces plastic, one producing machine-tools and so on. In turn these other companies need other companies to reproduce their conditions of production, and this cycle is infinite, Althusser writes. In other words, the idea here is pretty simple: a capitalistic enterprise in order to survive needs to "reproduce" its material conditions of production. This means that in order to produce something "more than once" the enterprise needs to keep on getting the material and the machines needed for the production. These things are what Althusser (and the Marxist tradition in general) calls the material condition of production, and they need to be "reproduced", replaced, we can say, in order for the capitalistic enterprise to keep existing.

What it should not escape us is the fact that the material conditions are not the only ones that need to be reproduced in order for the enterprise to keep on existing. It is obvious, in fact, that materials and machines are not the only elements needed. There is the need for people working the machines and to perform tasks. There is a need for the reproduction of *Labour-power*, of workers. This aspect of the reproduction of the condition of production, Althusser writes, is difficult to detect because it happens completely outside of the firm. How is the reproduction of labour-power ensured? It is ensured by giving the workers the material means to reproduce themselves: it ensured by wages. The parallel with the material condition for the reproduction of production is pretty evident. The same way in which the capitalist needs to spend money to buy more material and machines (to ensure the material reproduction) she needs to spend money to pay her workers in the form of wages in order for them to be able to continue to produce. The wages are necessary for the wage-earners to pay for housing, food and clothing. In short, the wages are necessary for the worker to present herself again at the factory gate the next day, and any other day of her life. Moreover, finally, to raise and educate the children that will eventually be the new labor-power.

Another important aspect of the reproduction of the labor-power is the necessity for this labor power to be competent. It is, in fact, fundamental for the firm that the labor-power is able to perform the whole complex of productive processes. The productive forces, therefore, need to be, at any historical moment, diversely skilled according to what Althusser calls the *socio-technical* division of labor: the different jobs and posts necessary for the firm to keep on producing.

How is this reproduction of diversified skills provided by the capitalist system? This reproduction, differently for society where serfdom or slavery are in place, is ensured less and less by apprenticeship "on the spot", and more and more outside the production place. The education system and other institutions in capitalist societies provide this "service" to the capitalistic enterprises. Althusser notices how children in school, while going varying distances in their studies, all learn to read, to write, and to add. A number of techniques, he calls them, including elements of scientific or literary culture which are directly useful in the different jobs in the production belt. What they learn is a *know-how*.

Aside from these techniques, though, the children learn also something else. They learn the rules of "good behavior," or better, they learn the way in which each and every one of the agents in the division of labor should behave depending on the job that the agent is "destined" to such as morality, civic and professional conscience. In other words, they learn to respect the rules established by class domination. They learn to speak and to act toward others, for example, accordingly to their rank and role in society.

The reproduction of labor-power requires, then, not only a reproduction of its skills, but also the reproduction of its submission to certain rules of the establishment. There is the need to guarantee the reproduction of the submission to the ruling ideology for the workers and the reproduction of the ability to manipulate the ruling ideology for the agents of exploitation and repression, so that the domination of the ruling class can be reproduced. Simply put: the school (on other state institution) teaches its students the know-how only in forms that will ensure the *subjection to the ruling ideology or the mastery of its practice.*

Althusser makes it clear that this reproduction of subjection is not "supplemental" to the production of skills. In fact:

> It is in the forms and under the forms of ideological subjection that provision is made for the reproduction of the skill of labour-power. (Althusser, *On the Reproduction of Capitalism*, p. 236.)

What is new in this analysis is the existence of what Althusser calls *Ideology*. We should now see what this term denotes, considering that the word is used in our ordinary language in a much looser sense.

10.1 Repressive State Apparatus and Ideological State Apparatuses

In order for us to understand what Althusser has in mind when he talks about Ideology it is necessary to clarify one main point about Marxism that it is usually neglected. Because of what we have associated historically with communism, and because a series of governments have called themselves communist, we tend to associate Marxism with States and forms of government that control every aspect of the citizens' life. Marxism is considered a state-friendly system. The truth is, though, that in all of Marx's writing, and Marxist tradition, *the State is conceived as a repressive apparatus.* The State is a "machine" of repression that empowers the ruling class to guarantee their domination over the working class. This way, Marx says, the state enables the ruling class to exploit the working class.

The State is first and foremost what the Marxist orthodoxy has called *the state apparatus*. With this term, theorists denote those apparatuses that are specialized and necessary to keep the state alive when it comes to infringing on the laws of the land (Police, courts, prisons, but also the head of state, the government and the administration, etc.). Althusser says this quite clearly: the state, at the end of the day, is the most repressive force that exists, and its role is simply the one of an apparatus, a machine, that perpetuates domination. If we fail to recognize this and keep associating Marxism with state-centric societies, we will completely miss the point of Marx's theory.

To understand this even better, Althusser makes another distinction, the one between *state power* and *state apparatus*. The first one is the center of the entire political struggle. This means that political struggle equates to the fight around the possession and conservation of state power by a certain class or by an alliance between classes. Obviously, during revolutionary events or after any sort of discontinuity within the political real (i.e., every time that a new class of individuals seizes and maintains power) state power changes hands and can be structurally modified. State Apparatuses, instead, can resist any sort of change. In certain situations, everything might change within the state power without effecting at all the state apparatuses (i.e., the police, the army, the structure of the government stays the same).

Up to this point, Althusser has just clarified and reiterated Marxist ideas. His original contribution to the theory consists, though, in a distinction that he makes within the state apparatus. He writes that while there are some State apparatuses that are clearly repressive (and we will see which one they are in a moment), there are others that, while still being on the repressive side, must not be confused with the former. He calls these other slightly different apparatuses *Ideological State Apparatuses* (ISA from now on).

The kind of apparatuses that Althusser calls repressive (RSA from now on) are the "classic" apparatuses that we have mentioned before: the government, the administration, the police, the army, etc., the word *Repressive* here suggests that the state apparatuses in question function by "violence" (physical and nonphysical). On the other hand, the ISA are a certain number of what might seem independent and specialized institutions. Some examples of them are: the educational ISA (the system of the different public and private "schools"), the religious ISA (system of the different churches), the family ISA, the political ISA (the political system and the different parties), the cultural ISA, etc.

The ISA and the RSA are different, according to Althusser, and the differences are multiple. Firstly, the RSA constitutes an organized whole of which the different parts are centralized under one unity: the politics of the representatives of the ruling class. The ISA, instead, are multiple, separate, and autonomous. They are also able to express the contradictions that arise within the class struggle in all its forms.

Secondly, the RSA belong to the public domain while the ISA belong to the private one (churches, parties, families, unions, some schools, media outlets, cultural ventures, etc. are private). One might ask, anticipates Althusser, why do we consider (ideological) State apparatuses things that are by definition not part of the public domain? To answer this question, he introduces the thought of another philosopher, Antonio Gramsci, who shared with Althusser similar theories. Quoting Gramsci, Althusser states that the distinction between public and private is already internal to bourgeois (dominant class) law, and valid only within it. The State, that is the state of the ruling class, escapes the distinction: it is neither public nor private; rather, it is the condition for any distinction between public and private. The same can be said, the French philosopher writes, when it comes to ISA: it is not important if the institution that incarnates them are public or private, what matters is how they function. And private institutions can function very well as ISA. More on this later.

A final difference between RSA and ISA (the essential one, possibly) is represented by the fact that RSA functions *mainly* by violence while the ISA functions *mainly* by ideology. While no "purely" violent nor purely ideological apparatuses exist, Althusser warns, the proportion of the these two criteria in each institution seems to determine if they are part of the RSA or one of the ISA. Let's make a couple of examples. The army and the police obviously function mainly as repressive forces that through violence (physical and not) perform the task assigned to them; in them, though, we can clearly see some ideological elements to ensure cohesion and reproduction. There certain "values" that are shared by all police personal or by military personal that have nothing to do with violence. Let's think of loyalty, courage etc., for example. At the same time, let's consider the school as an example ISA. Obviously, schools operate, mainly, without the use of violence. But this does not mean, for example, that schools don't have means of punishment, selection, expulsion etc.; these elements are disciplinary methods that use, by definition, violence (again, not necessarily physical).

Considered this broad distinction, Althusser, finally identifies what all different ISA have in common. The fact that all of them *serve* the ruling ideology is what "unifies" them. Ruling classes usually hold state power and RSA and, at the same time, it is reasonable to believe that they are also active within the ISA. This is fundamental for the ruling class because

> No class can hold state power over a long period without at the same time exercising its hegemony over and in the Ideological State Apparatuses. (*Ibidem.*)

This means that while the state power is the objective of any class that wants to rule, ISA are the stake and the site of class struggle. In fact, even for a change to occur, within the system, it needs to be at least conceivable within the ISA. If we want now to answer to the question, "what ultimately allows for the reproduction of the relations of production (and all sorts or relations, to be sure) within a given society?", one must answer that such continuity is secured by the Ideological structure (superstructure if one wants to use a more orthodox Marxist terminology) in the form of the appropriation of state power, and the exercise of it through RSA and ISA. The role of the two entities are clear within the class struggle: the RSA secures by force the political conditions of the reproduction of the relation of exploitation. In other words, the RSA is responsible to make sure that the status quo (which can include some "controlled" progress or change) is maintained. The RSA is also responsible for the political conditions for the success of the ISA. In a sense The RSA is the shield of the ISA, which in turn secure the normal production and relation of production within the system.

Because of the historical nature of the ISA and their dependence on the Ideology of the ruling class of the time, it is obvious that in different times we might have had different ISA and that the ISA may vary in number and "kind" in different times in history. It is evident, Althusser claims, that during the pre-capitalistic era there was one dominant ISA that basically swallowed all of the others. This ISA was the Church. This is demonstrated, Althusser writes, by the fact that all ideological struggle from the sixteenth century to the eighteenth century is anti-clerical struggle. Think of the French Revolution: amongst its objectives there clearly was to attack the most powerful of the ISA, the church, which is seen as a real enemy and it is dismantled by the revolutionary government. In the 1970s, when Althusser writes, the church as lost its "grip" on the people, the philosopher argues, and the biggest ideological fight is over a new omnipotent ISA: education. Why is education the main ISA in the 1970s for Althusser? The answer is simple. School is the place where all children form every class, starting with infant-school age and for a long time, are "inoculated" with the ruling ideology. In different forms, know-how (math, sciences, literature) or pure ideology (ethics, civics, and philosophy) the children are molded into *citizens*. Depending on the level of education achieved, the "students" will be ejected into the work force to perform the role that is fit for them: the worker proper, the manager, the agent of exploitation (capitalist), the agent of repression (policemen, politician etc.), the professional ideologist (priest of any sort), each one of them with a precise set of skills and a common ideological substrate.

School is powerful because it is mandatory (at least to a certain age) and it is "free". The audience that it can reach is massive: all the children in society are subject to it for the most part of their formative years.

Another element that makes school the most powerful ISA is, according to Althusser, the hidden nature of the reproduction of certain relationships that is present in the educational system. The entire operation seems voluntary and neutral: free teachers (academic freedom) are in charge of children that are entrusted to them by free parents (they decide where to send them) and open the path to freedom for the students. This system seems today so natural and necessary that just associating it with ISA seems blasphemous. The truth is, though, that no knowledge is neutral, and that the social relationships taught and enforced in school tend to shape the relationships that one has throughout her entire life. Althusser also notes that because the school is the central ISA of his time there seems to be a perennial crisis of the educational system. The class struggle, in fact, creates crisis the closest to the center of the ideological system. Who controls the main ISA, controls the means of reproductions of the relations of production which in turns leads to the control of State power.

One thing is left for us to analyze within the revision of Marxism: the concept of Ideology.

10.2 Ideology

The word Ideology, as intended in Marxist tradition, has the meaning of *system of the ideas and representations which dominate the mind of an individual or a social group*. This means that ideology, to Marx, is the complex of ideas that are the base for a social group or an individual life. Althusser will be the first philosopher who produces a general theory of Ideology. He believes in fact that Ideology is *trans-historical* which means that, while it is connected in its incarnation to the particular social formations, it is omnipresent throughout history. In other words, Ideology could not exist if humans went extinct tomorrow, but until there are historical social formations there will be ideologies.

Althusser also proposes a slightly different definition of ideology:

Ideology is a 'representation' of the imaginary relationship of individuals to their real condition of existence. (Ibidem.)

We use the word ideology for different "objects" we talk about religious ideology, political ideology, ethical ideology, etc., what we mean by that is that people have certain *world's outlooks*. For the external observer, Althusser notes, if we don't believe in such ideologies, it will be clear that they are not real. They are imaginary. They are simple ways in which people try to explain the world, knowing though that the explanation is not completely bulletproof. The imaginary nature of the ideology, however, should not make us think that ideologies are pure *illusions*. They do have a connection to reality, the *allude* to it. A good way of thinking of them is to see them as *stories* about reality that need to be interpreted in order to discover the world underneath them or as *maps* that describe a territory. Ideologies are everywhere, men seem to represent the real condition of existence to themselves in an imaginary form routinely. Why? Why do men need to do that? Althusser identifies two ways in which historically we have answered to this question: (1) some despot invented these lies to dominate the many; (2) the material conditions of existence (which is alienation) makes human beings imagine "better" condition of existence.

Both of these answers are incorrect though. In fact, they both assume that what is represented in the ideology is actually reality unfiltered. They assume that what is represented is the actual condition of existence of men. In reality, instead, what people represent in Ideologies are the relations that they have with their condition of existence. To be more specific, what is represented is *the imaginary relation of these individuals with the real relation they live in.* What does this mean? It means that in an ideology human being create a story about their relation to the conditions in which they live and see everything through that story. The ideologies are the glasses that people wear to look at their condition of existence. An example should clarify the concept. Some people interpret what happens to them in terms of good luck, bad luck, Karma, etc. This means that anything that happens to them will be interpreted in these terms. Something unpleasant happens to them? They have bad luck. They do something "good"? They do it because it brings good Karma etc. If we don't believe in luck or Karma, it will be pretty clear that such interpretations of real events are imaginary. We will also realize that the "imaginary" aspect of it does not pertain the event themselves (something unpleasant *really* happened to them) nor the sensation felt by the subject is imaginary (something *really* feels unpleasant). The imagination has to do with the way the individual relates to the event: it is the *relation* of good luck or bad luck to be imaginary, nothing else.

Now, while we talk about luck and Karma the consequences for the life of the individual imagining such relations are marginal and personal. When we talk about the kind of ideologies that Althusser has in mind, though, the consequences of such work of imagination are much more important and mainly collective. We have seen before that Ideologies do not exist detached from their particular incarnation. They exist, to be more precise, in what we have previously called apparatuses. This means that such ideologies have real consequences for the everyday life of the individuals living in the social formations that sport the apparatuses. This will happen in different ways. First of all, the individual will act in agreement with the ideology and will participate in regular practices that the apparatus associates with such ideology. It is necessary for an individual subscribing to an ideology to participate in such activities otherwise she will be deemed "bad," "inconsistent," or "deviant." Think of religious ideologies: if you subscribe to a religion you will need to participate in certain ritual (pray, give to charity, etc.) if you don't want to be a "bad" religious person. Or think of political ideology. There are certain practices that you need to perform if you want to call yourself a member of a specific party. Ideologies, therefore, exist materially in actions and rituals that are dictated by the apparatus in which they are embedded.

Second, subjects are *acted* by the ideological system in which they are immersed. This obviously means that our agency is seriously compromised by the fact that we live within a social formation that produces ideologies. Everything that we do is dictated, at least partially, by ideologies. We are *permitted* to think in certain ways only because our ideology allows us to do so. All that is obvious to us it is so because our ideology makes it so. All that is strange to us it is so because our ideology makes it so.

Finally, Ideologies can be recognized as such only from the outside. While we live in an ideology we perceive it as such a natural way of thinking and living that we cannot recognize the imaginary element of it. Only from the outside we are able to indicate to someone else that they are living in an imaginary relation with reality. This is particularly worrisome for two reasons: we can always be living in an ideology without knowing it, and we can never consider ourselves free from any sort of ideology no matter what we do. Ideologies seem to be totalizing.

In closing, Ideology makes the individuals work for the social group, it makes him or her reproduce the very condition of existence of the domination implicit in the capitalist system. If the subjects are good, they will just follow the ideology, if they are "bad" the apparatus will employ the RSA. This is possible because, even when subjects recognize the ideological nature of the reality they are living in, they accept it to avoid repression or because they think of it as the best of the possible world. But most people live in total ignorance of the ideological process, Althusser believes, making possible the constant reproduction of the entire system.

11

Democracy

11 Is Democracy Really Democratic?

During the twentieth century, and especially after the end of the Cold War, most societies in the world seem to have accepted the idea that *Democracy* is without a doubt the best way, the fairest way, in which a people can organize themselves. As we have seen in previous chapters, this idea is relatively new and it is born with modernity and perfected throughout the centuries.

Philosophers, though, have continued to scrutinize the democratic form of government and some of them have proposed that it needs revision. We will see, in this section, how most philosophers distinguish between different kind of democracies and how most of them agree with the fact that *Western democracies are not really democratic*. Or, better, they believe that democracy, traditionally intended, is not the best way in which we can organize ourselves. We will also examine their proposal for the birth of a *real* democracy.

We can begin our analysis of Democracy by looking at the etymology of the word: *Demos* and *Kratos* mean, in ancient Greek, respectively people and power. A democracy, then, is a form of government where the population has the power. Democracy literarily means *power of the people*. While etymology does not explain everything, it is legitimate to ask if contemporary society that call themselves democratic are set up to *truly* give power to the people. In order to answer this basic question, however, we need to explore societies of the twentieth and twenty-first centuries to see if there are any differences in the conception of democracy, or if, in general, we can isolate specific "kinds" of democracies.

There is at least on kind of Democracy that all philosophers believe to be dangerous. **Iris Marion Young** (1949–2006) calls it *interest-based democracy* and describes it, together with other theorists, as a model of democracy where everyone expresses one's preferences and demands, and registers them in a vote. In this model, democratic decision-making corresponds to deciding what leaders, rules, or policies will better serve the majority of the people, and individuals define their own interest as they see fit. This model allows for individuals (or interest groups) to determine and vote for policies that will best serve their perceived interest in the knowledge that everyone else will do the same. Democratic decisions are the result of a coalition of ideas that translate in the sum of a series of self-interested votes.

While at first sight this model of democracy might seem desirable, a more in-depth analysis will immediately reveal some issues. In interest-based models of democracy citizens never have to leave their own private and limited pursuits, or recognize their fellow human beings in a public setting to address what might be a series of collective, as distinct from individual, needs and goals. Each individual citizen might reason about the best means to achieve their privately defined goals, but no real rationality is needed to put a long-term strategy about real goals and ends. In other words, everyone is always stuck in his or her private world that is made of temporary perceived desires and wants. People, in this model, never need to leave their subjective point of view and embrace a more objective or general point of view on political issues of any sort. Finally, in this model individuals cannot make claims on others about justice or the public good with reason: their private interest supersedes all of these general issues and their "rationality" is impeded by the short-sightedness of their individual desires.

By contrast, another model of Democracy called *deliberative democracy* considers the democratic process as a way to create a public "space" where the citizens can come together to discuss problems, ideas, and actions. This is obviously different when compared with the interest-based democracy: the latter promotes the private good of each individual while deliberative democracy promotes what is called the common good. Deliberative democracy establishes, in a sense that a functioning democratic state has to find a common ground to make decision about common issues. The way these decisions are made is also important for the deliberative model. Citizens (through their representatives) make decisions after a rational discussion about the issue at stake has led to the victory of the better argument.

It is evident that, when compared to the interest-based model, the deliberative one has a specific virtue. It seems to promote reason over power. Policies and rules have to be put in place not because of the most powerful private interest of a group of citizens, but because the citizens together determine the rightness of the policy after hearing and criticizing the reasons for it. This means that, in an ideal version of deliberative democracy, participants analyze a political problem with an open mind, they are not influenced or tied to the authority of previous decisions or norms or to party ideologies. In addition, the process of political discussion is guided by reason and proposes reasoned argument. Lastly, the participants to the discussion make decisions based on the better argument and not, again, on some preconception or some prejudice held prior to the discussion.

It is also evident that in this model all the participants in the democratic process have to be free and equal. If not, in fact, it is plausible that the votes of the "un-equals" can be bought or coerced. Simply put: everyone must have the same opportunity to make proposals and to criticize them. Everyone needs to be free from domination. This means that, at least during the discussion process of democracy, political and economic power need to be restrained and/or very limited.

It seems that the deliberative model tries to establish equality amongst the citizens (when it comes to the public sphere) by means of rational discussion. Once again here, we are confronted with a model that seems intuitively a good one. After all, it seems to be the political version of one of the most respected institutions of the modern West: science. We imagine, indeed, that the scientific community works exactly like the deliberative model. Scientists debate hypothesis among themselves, and as peers they decide what the most convincing one is. These discussions and decisions, we think, are made in the name of the truth and are exempt from power struggles or ideologies. Again, the deliberative model of democracy thinks that the same should happen within politics. Aside from the questions that one might have about the real status of scientific discussion (are sciences really ideology free? Do scientific discussions really promote equality amongst scientists, etc.), there are certain flaws that seem to be inherited within this model when it comes to its application to politics.

Marion Young identifies these issues very clearly. The first one, she writes, is that the deliberative model does not account for cultural and social differences. The assumption within the deliberative model is simple: democratic deliberations are culturally *neutral*, meaning that they are rational and rationality functions in the same way everywhere. We know, though, that different cultures exercise and express rationality in different ways, and that styles of speech and thought that might be considered appropriate in Western culture are not considered so in other cultures and vice versa. Moreover, since the Enlightenment (which is when the scientific discourse becomes *the* model for rationality) all "rational" institutions have been historically male dominated, white dominated, and upper-class dominated. These historical incarnations have led to a series of norms of deliberations that are specific to these dominating groups. In a formula, Marion Young writes

The norms of deliberation are culturally specific and often operate as forms of power that silence or devalue the speech of some people. (Young, *Intersecting Voices.*)

Another problem with the deliberative model is that political (and often scientific) debates are never free and open forums where all people have the right to express their claims and give reasons that are reflective of their beliefs. Only certain people can *speak*, and, the discussion is more than anything else, an agonistic form of deliberation where what people seek is not the truth but a winning argument. The goal of deliberative discussions is transformed, in actuality, from trying to find the better argument to concede defeat when the argument that one proposed is trumped by the better rhetorical skills of another.

Connected to the previous issues we have what we can call the problem of *style*. Considering the way in which the discussion is built in democratic institutions, we can say that speech needs to follow specific rules to be accepted and successful: a certain confrontational style is preferable to speech that is cautious, conciliatory or exploratory. In most cases this gives the advantage to male speaking styles. In addition, this gives the advantage to better educated white middle class people, while groups that are intimidated by the formality of these speech acts end up being frustrated in their tries to make their voice heard.

Finally, a major problem with the deliberative model of democracy is given by the assumption, implicit in this theory, that we need to construct (or re-discover) unity. Deliberative theorists describe the movement that it needs to happen among people in order to get to a true democratic approach. According to them, people need to move from a subjective self-regarding mind set to a more objective prospective to try to find a solution to the collective problems of society. They need to construct unity. This means that they need to keep a united front and "think like one" in order to deliberate correctly on the issues at stake. This way of thinking presupposes that what people have to do is rediscover this sort of lost unity that got disrupted by the emergence of private interest. This is the idea, for example, of philosophers like **Jürgen Habermas** (1929–) who believes that even though some values might appear as conflicting in the practical everyday life, during political discussions we need to go back to the primordial unity of ethics and politics and appeal to universal principles like Justice which we can access, again, through rational discourse.

Marion Young identifies two main problems with this view: In societies like ours, which are pluralistic by default, there might not be sufficient shared understanding to appeal to when conflict arises in the search to solve collective problems. Think, for example, of how non-conciliatory are the different ideas and principle proposed to solve any political issue that presents itself (from economic inequality to abortion) in our society. In addition, Young writes, if we need to transcend our specific opinions in order to access a shared universal concept, we are denying one of the main principles of democratic discussion. We are denying the need to change our ideas and embrace someone else idea. Whenever we are transcending our view in the name of a general one, in fact, we are not correcting our ideas and our opinions to give room to different prospective that might not be our favorite. We are not including anything new; we are just embracing some sort of "divine" political principle that we have declared universal.

Some deliberative theorists, recognizing the problem with this idea of a pre-emptive unity, propose something different. They propose that unity should not be considered as a "starting point" but rather as a goal of political dialogue. In this version of the theory, participants transcend their subjectivity not in the name of a pre-existing principle, but in the name of what is the common good, the good of the whole system. Even though people start, necessarily, with cultural and personal differences they are able to locate through rational discussion a common good. Differences need to be overcome; their divisiveness is the poison of democracy. This version of the idea of unity is also problematic. It leads us to another mechanism of exclusion. If we assume, like these theorists do, a discussion where the participants are divided in different cultural and social groups it is easy to imagine that some group might have a greater privilege (symbolic or material) and consequently is able to "impose" its view as the common good and, therefore, to perpetuate the privilege of its members. The concept of unity seems not to be a viable one, at least articulated this way, when it comes to building a foundation for a model of democracy.

We can summarize all issues within the deliberative models of democracy as *the problem of the privileged speaker*. This model plainly fails to recognize that the norms of speech are culturally specific and that they must be learned in order to be expressed correctly. This model, therefore, privileges specific speakers and speeches: speeches that are dispassionate and controlled over speeches that are passionate and emotionally charged, speakers that don't use any significant gesture or body language over the one that do, etc. The inability to recognize this problem prevents the very goal of the deliberative model of democracy: equality and freedom among the participants in the democratic discussion.

11.1 Communicative Democracy

Iris Marion Young tries to mitigate the issues of the deliberative model of democracy by proposing an approach to it still rooted in communicative actions (i.e., dialogue), but that is able to overcome all the difficulties that we have discussed in the previous section. The goal of Young's proposal is to construct a democratic theory that is truly inclusive and fully functional.

The first consideration that Young makes is that we need to understand democratic theory as a practice. This means to understand it as a *situated and embodied* theory, that is, to understand it in the context of real people and historical situations. When we talk of unity, for example, we need to understand that the only reasons for differently situated groups to engage in political discussion are geographical proximity and necessity. The unity of a community is a precarious and weak affair that is, though, necessary for the existence of a democratic communication. People live in proximity and interdependently with each other; this means that people need other people to function properly. We can say that a political community, a polity, is made of people stuck together in a territory and forced to work together. The recognition of this significant interdependence coupled with the willingness to give everyone the rights to express their opinion, and with a series of agreed rules that regulate fair discussion and decision making are the bases of *communicative democracy*, the democratic theory proposed by Young.

These three minimum requirements of unity will allow, according to Young, for a better understanding of the value that differences bring in a democratic discussion. One of the problems that we have encountered when analyzing the deliberative model was that assuming unity (as a principle or a goal) we failed to accomplish one of the fundamental goals of discussion based democracies, which is to help people transform their ideas through communication. The truth is that, as we have observed, if we are looking only at what we have in common with other people we are not transforming our point of view, we are only trying to see ourselves in the others. If we assume, instead, that there are real differences—cultural and social—we will be aware of the fact that an *Other*, different from us, really exists. This does not imply that there are no similarities, difference, after all, is not total strangeness; this only means that we are aware that our position does not necessarily encompass the prospective of all the other "different" groups.

This way we preserve, in the democratic process, the plurality that is necessary even to have room for public discourses. One only speaks meaningfully to another, not to oneself. The more points of view are present in the public discussion and the more is possible to understand and accept different *social locations*. In turn, this process will reshape public space including a truly plural prospective. Once again, this means that communicative democracy will be a system where true communication across cultures, social positions, and social needs is happening. We need to be careful here, though. Fully grasping another social position, for example, will not mean identification. It will mean that the other was allowed to completely express her experiences and prospective, and that we were able to understand her without seeing ourselves mirrored in her.

A truly transformative discussion among participants in communicative democracies happens, Young writes, following three paths: (1) confronting different perspectives, which teaches us that our views and experiences are always partial. (2) being aware that we are part of a heterogeneous group where everyone has the right to challenge everyone's view, which will force us to make claims and arguments not for our own personal interest. This awareness will also teach us *not to make claims or arguments in the name of some general anonymous interest*; all claims and arguments will have to be made in respect and awareness of the *real* different groups existing within the community. (3) expressing, challenging, and discussing differently situated knowledge which will add to the social knowledge of all the participants in the democratic process. This leads to a wider understand of what a just solution to collective problems might look like.

In order to facilitate the decision-making process in a communicative democracy, we need more than the simple activity/ability to criticize different perspectives (including our own). According to Young, we need also other strategies to increase our ability to speak to a diverse group that shares different experiences and viewpoints when compared to our own. The first of these communicative strategies is called by Marion *Greetings*. She describes it as

A logical and motivational condition for dialogue that aims to reach understanding is that the parties in the dialogue recognize one another in their particularity. (Ibidem.)

This simply means that there is a moment in the dialogue with another individual (or group) in which we are not saying "anything", rather we are just acknowledging the other giving her respect and attention. Just like when we greet someone by saying "hello", or "welcome", etc. we are saying nothing but acknowledging their presence, when we can flatter someone during a discussion it implicitly shows them that we have them in mind, we are including them in our thinking process. And this is important when it comes to smooth the harsh differences that there might between different cultural groups.

The second communicative strategy proposed by Young is *rhetoric*. Using this term, she wants to stress the value that emotions need to have in our communication with others. She also wants to emphasize the role that listening rather than just asserting our viewpoints should have in our communicative democracy. Rhetoric, in fact, concentrates at least partially to the mode and the importance of listening to the audience and the others. Through rhetoric we situate the discussion: a good rhetorician knows to whom she is speaking. She knows how to express the real and practical place of existence for the discussions we are having, and she finally knows how to keep someone's attention. All these elements are fundamental in a communicative democracy.

The final communicative strategy that Young mentions is *storytelling*. We have seen how, in a communicative democracy, participants discuss to understand how to solve collective problems. Although it might seem more practical to use a plain assertive language in such situations, it is better, according to Young, to use a *storytelling* style. Narratives tend to foster understanding across differences in ways that assertive language cannot do. Narratives reveal, with their intricate combination of text, subtext, and metatext, particular experiences that are not shared and cannot be shared in "plain" language. Telling a story about a specific arbitrary obstacle in society that has taken away from us the opportunity to do such and such, it is a much more effective way to communicate difficulties and impediments experienced, than a dry "legal" description. Narrative also reveals the sources of values, cultural habits and meanings of beliefs that are not immediately available. Pluralistic society, in fact, suffer sometimes of lack of understanding when it comes to cultural practices or beliefs just because the others don't have access to the origin stories of such practices or beliefs. Telling the story of these origins might serve as a help to get a better grasp on what the others are thinking and why they are thinking it. Lastly, narratives also show us what position we have in someone else's story. Understanding that position is crucial to recalibrate behaviors and clarify positions that might lead to any sort of hostility. The imaginary described by a narrative reveals much of the ideas and rationale of other community to us, even when it comes to our role in those other communities.

To conclude, we can say that Young proposes an emended view of deliberative democracy that she calls communicative democracy. This model proposes to embrace the plurality of perspectives, speaking styles and expressions in order to achieve a much more realistic system of democracy in diverse contemporary societies like ours.

11.2 A Radical Critique of Democracy

We analyzed at the beginning of this chapter the etymology of the word democracy and, as you might remember, we established that the word literally means *power of the people*. It is legitimate to ask, then, if in today's democracies the people are really the ones that hold the power.

Some people argue that representative democracies, by definition, undercut the real value of democracy because they do take away from the people their power to participate in the political process. Direct democracy would be the only true democratic system. We saw that, for example, Rousseau considers direct democracy as the only legitimate form of government. But, Rousseau himself says, direct democracy is the best form of government among gods, but it cannot be realized among humans. In fact, if we look back in history such system, that is a system where *everyone* participates of the legislative and executive power directly, has never existed. And it cannot exist.

Another common idea regarding democracy is that it should be the political system that is supposed to bring us absolute *equality*. This idea has as its theoretical father **Tocqueville** (1805–1859) who thought that the real added value of democracy was the abolition of all statuses that were by default permanent (inherited political or social positions, no social movement, etc.), and therefore, in principle inaccessible to the common citizen. Tocqueville, nevertheless, intends democracy in a *sociological way* rather than a political way. For example, he never speaks of power within politics, but only of democratic societies where complete equality is achieved. He thinks, in a way, that as long as the citizens live in absolute equality, if they get bored and uninterested when it come to politics they can leave the power to some sort of a tutelar state that would take care of everything that has to do with the state. In other words, Tocqueville seems to believe that as long as people leave in equal conditions, we can trade a democracy for a liberal oligarchy.

Philosopher and political theorist **Cornelius Castoriadis** (1922–1997) believes that we actually already live in a liberal oligarchy in the sense described by Tocqueville. It is undeniable, in fact, that in Western societies there is this movement toward legal equality, but at the same time, Castoriadis writes, it is evident that our societies have become more and more un-equal when it comes to power. *Western societies today are liberal oligarchies and not democracies.* They are oligarchies because there is a specific group of individuals that dominates society, and they are liberal because they leave to the other citizens a certain number of negative liberties. The only freedom and power that common people seem to have is in today's societies is to conform to the rules established by the dominant group. A legitimate question here is, obviously, which one is the dominant group? The answer given by Castoriadis is complex, but we can simplify it by saying that the dominant group is made mainly of what we call today our political representative and the people that finance them. One of the main reasons for the existence of this oligarchy is, according to Castoriadis, the lack of reasoning regarding what we can call the *problem of representation.* To understand this point, let's make an example. In the Western world there are a series of situations in which we can delegate someone to do something for us. We can give someone power of attorney, we can make someone our medical proxy, we can designate someone as the executor or our will, etc. Now, we would think that, in all these cases, if there was a rule or a law that would prevent us, at any moment, from emending, modifying, or completely revoke the privilege to represent us to any of these people, this rule or law would be absurd to say the least. After all, we can delegate any of our powers just in our own interest and if we decide that our lawyer is not representing our interest anymore, we should have the power to remove her from her position. But when it comes to politics things seem to be different: we give to someone, in our interest, the opportunity to represent us for a period of four, five (in certain case even seven) years. But it seems that this power given to them is irrevocable during (at least) these years. This is particularly absurd when it comes to government because technically during the years in which the representatives are in charge, they can modify *permanently* the parameters and the conditions of their re-elections. Castoriadis here is not thinking of some sort of abuse of power, rather is talking about the ability that politicians have to predetermine the choices that the electorate can make. Early critics of representative democracies used to say that people, let's say in England, are free once every five years (when they go to vote); this is an optimistic view though, because even after five years the choice of the voters is drastically reduced because of the choices that not the people, but the representatives have made. Think of when it was the last time that the people directly, and not some group of delegates, have elected someone.

This is not the only issue here, Castoriadis writes. Think of the fact that in many democratic states there is a so-called *senate* which is practically (when not by law) the place where people become representatives for life. How can such institution be democratic? How can it be that there are a group of people that can be representing someone forever?

Lastly, we have another reason why we cannot call our current system a democracy, and it has to do with the fact that we seem to have crystallized the terms of our interactions. This means that there seems to be some sort of resistance toward any new forms of political coalition. The liberal oligarchy in which we live wants us to think that our historical reality is *natural* and therefore unchangeable. The truth is, though, that the society in which we live today is the fruit of a specific imaginary produced by the dominant ideas of the historical period (in our case capitalism and *not* democracy, Castoriadis thinks). What we fail to understand, for example, with the help of the system at large, is that capitalism and freedom are not synonymous, and, moreover, that capitalism and market are not synonymous. Capitalism is not necessarily the best possible market system and it is not the only system that can produce freedom (in fact, Castoriadis would say, Capitalism doesn't produce democracy, just oligarchy). Some would object, though, that if capitalism and our specific democracy (what Castoriadis calls liberal oligarchy) are still in place this means that they are what the people want, therefore they will say, we are in a democracy where the individuals are in charge of their choices. The flaw inherit with this reasoning is evident. The fact that individuals want something does not mean that they are freely choosing. Individuals are the product of the system that they constantly reproduce:

> *Islamic societies produce Islamic individuals which reproduce Islamic societies; the Soviet society produced soviet individuals that reproduced the soviet society.* (Castoriadis, *Which Democracy?*)

This is obvious. A society can exist only if the majority of the individuals subscribe, at least minimally, to its values and are willing to reproduce them. But if we think that the continuous existence of a system is proof that the individuals in it are freely choosing that system, then we have to admit all societies are democratic, which is evidently absurd. We need to understand, then, that our liberal oligarchies are not a natural form of government, or what people really want. We need to consider them simply as the provisional materialization of today imaginary. But we can and should think to reclaim true democracy. But what is that? What does constitute a democracy that is not an oligarchy? Is it direct democracy? Castoriadis is categorical here: true democracy is not direct democracy, it is, rather a democracy that has some specific characteristics.

Firstly, Democracy is the power of the *demos*, of the collectivity. What is the limit of such power? This power should have some limits, but it is obvious that technically, since politics is separate from religion (for example) and there are no more inherited powers and kingdoms, there is nothing that could establish intrinsically which are the limits of this collective power. Democracy is then the realm of self-limitation. Human rights are limitations that people put on themselves. A constitution is a limitation imposed by the demos on itself and it is therefore always emendable.

There is more: Democracy is the realm of *autonomy*. This means that it is the place where human beings can err by *hybris* trying to put in place limitations for themselves. Democracy is the realm where the power of the people does not accept external limits. It is power that self-institutes permanently, that can always chance itself. This, of course, does not mean that in democracy we change constitution every other day, rather it means that the people have taken all the precautionary methods to be able to change its institutions without a civil war or violence. This, unfortunately, does not mean that in democracy violence is banned for ever. It only means that violence becomes the exception.

The only kind of equality that is necessary for democracy is the equal possibility for everyone to participate of the legislative acts that have created the rules and laws by which we live by. In short, equal opportunity to participate of power. It is not just about having the right to vote. It is about also, for example, having the right to be informed, just like everyone else, about what we have to decide. When we talk of democracy we should distinguish, according to Castoriadis, between *oikos*, which is the sum of all private business and affairs, *agora*, which is the private or public sphere, and *ekklesia* the public or public sphere, namely, in a democracy, the place where deliberation and decision about public affairs happen. In the *agora* people talk to each other, buy fruits and bread. People are in a public space that it is also private: no political decision happens there. The ekklesia, which includes the public assembly, the government, the courts etc., is a truly public space where people—together—deliberate and decide about public and collective affairs. Democracy can be defined as the system where the public space becomes really public. To understand what Castoriadis is describing here think of Monarchy. In that system, the public or public is a private affair of the royal family. In a totalitarian society, instead, the public or public is a private affair of the party.

Today democracies, unfortunately are not materialization of the form of democracy just described that Castoriadis calls autonomy. It is evident, in fact, that the place where the deliberations happen, the place where the decisions are made are not public, but private affairs of the politicians. Most of the times, we are not informed about the why or the how certain decisions are made. And where information is not readily available to the people there is no public sphere. Equality should mean equality of information, so we can know what is happening; equality of education, so we can understand what is happening; and finally, equality of time, so we can spend time to actually participate in the decision-making. But this implies that we should rethink our education and economic system, which we seem to be uninterested to do anytime soon.

Castoriadis concludes that we can call our societies whatever we want, but surely, we cannot call them democratic: the political oligarchy is in power, in fact, not the people.

CHAPTER 12

Power

12 Political Technologies

In the previous chapters, we have encountered many times the word *power*. This word, and the concept that it denotes are of fundamental importance when it comes to political and social issues. It is necessary, then, to try to understand what power is and if and how it intersects other theoretical fields (we will see that knowledge and life are crucially intersected with the concept of power).

There is a sociological textbook definition of power that describes it more or less as "the ability of an individual or a group to act or have influence over others". This general definition obviously connotes power in a specific way. Power as the ability to influence others and/or to make them act like we want recalls closely the act of manipulation, which, in turn makes us think of unwilling people doing something that they don't want to do. In other words, power has been considered as an evil, negative force. The powerful are always somewhat evil and their actions are selfish and cruel. This seems to be our imaginary when it comes to power today. Although this way of understanding it might seem justified at times, it is reductive, if not plainly incorrect, when it comes to political discourse. We will see in this chapter how power can and has to be intended differently if we want to fully understand its role in our social and political life.

Philosopher **Michel Foucault** (1926–1984) in the twentieth century gives us an interesting account of power. He claims that, firstly, most general theories of power are inadequate because they try to define and catalogue an entity that cannot be theorized or catalogued properly. The reason for this inadequacy is that power cannot be understood abstractly, it always needs to be analyzed in its precise historical incarnation. For this reason, Foucault's account of power is not intended as a theory, but as what he calls an *analytics of power*. In order to understand power, in fact, we don't need an abstract definition of it, such a definition would be unworkable for our goals. Rather we need to intend power as a cluster of relations that are open and more-or-less coordinated; we also need to build a grid of analysis that we can use to analyze these relations. How do these relations work? What are they really? Again, Foucault cautions us to take the following statements as guidelines rather than academic theories.

1. Power relations are non-egalitarian and mobile. Power is not a commodity or a prize that someone holds. It is rather the act of the *political technologies* throughout the social body. It is the way in which these political rituals function that sets the relations to be non-egalitarian and asymmetrical. These political technologies are spread through space and time and that is what it makes them *mobile*. This means, in simpler terms, that power is not a "thing", or the "control of a certain situation or institution". Power is, instead, a specific set of historically constructed technologies that create our practices, that is, a set of theoretical and material tools that create the conditions for our beliefs and practices that function and operate in a specific way. Explaining what power is means to explain the domain in which these technologies are employed and to isolate the specific rituals that create the unequal and asymmetrical relation among the agents implicated in the relations of power. Understanding power means building a microphysics of relations to understand what makes these relations function the way they do.
2. From the previous point, we can derive a second one. Power is not exclusive of political institutions. It is, rather, multidirectional, productive, and it operates in everyone's hands. We see it deployed from the bottom up or from the top down. Power is not in a position of exteriority to institutions or relations that are otherwise "pure" or power-neutral. But it is also distinct from it; we can completely identify the institution or the relation with power. For example, we cannot reduce a school to the power relations that are fundamentally embedded in it. The content of Algebra is not changed by the way in which power is exercised in the classroom. Yet, many aspects of the school are different when certain disciplinary technologies are introduced: ranking the students, rigid scheduling, surveillance of sexuality, etc. We need to think of power as a general matrix of force relations existing at a given time. Power is in existence in institutions and all its participants are enmeshed in it. This does not mean that domination within the relationship of power doesn't exist. It only means that even the dominant group is not fully in control of the beast that we call power. The essence of power is not domination, and the existence of a dominant group gives us only the illusion that power is enforced by a group on another group. Power, in fact, is often exercised upon the dominant as well as on the dominated.

3. Power relations are intentional and non-subjective. We can understand power because it has aims and objectives. This means that all power is power toward a goal. This goal is often clearly recognizable, the logic employed to achieve this goal is evident, and yet, there is no one that can be identified as the "inventor" of these goals and logic. At a local level (politically, for example), we can see a high degree of conscious decision making, planning, etc. but in the large scheme of things the direction in which power is going is often beyond the local actor's knowledge. That is to say, in Foucault terms, that there is no subject of power. Power can be understood, in this context, as the name that we attribute to a *complex strategical relationship in a particular society*. It is possible, for most of us, to understand the logic of such relationship, but it is very difficult (if not impossible) the grand scheme of this relationship. This is the main reason why we cannot have a general theory of power, but only a local analysis of it. In plain language, we can only analyze the effects that power has on people's life at a specific time in a specific place, but we are unable to create a unified theory of power that would work at any time in any place.

12.1 Panopticism

Throughout his analysis of power Foucault chooses the *Panopticon* as the paradigmatic example of how power works. Specifically, he chooses the Panopticon as the perfect example of disciplinary power.

The Panopticon is a type of institutional building and control system designed by Jeremy Bentham, an English philosopher that lives in the eighteenth century. The architectural design of the Panopticon is thought by Bentham as the perfect form for a prison. The building, in fact, is designed to allow a watchman to observe multiple prisoners at the same time, while the prisoners can't know with certainty if they are being observed or not.

This architectural design and form of control embodies perfectly, Foucault writes, how power operates. It is a diagram that we can use and generalize (as much as a power technology can be generalized) to describe the different elements of power. The Panopticon, in fact, is not a utopian concept, but a practical

Paolo Arsie Pelanda/Shutterstock.com

plan for a specific mechanism of power; at the same time, though, it is so flexible that can be used and applied for various uses (today we find it in different versions: among other place, in prisons, hospitals, and schools). This mixture of specific practical design and generalizable use is paradigmatic of successful forms of power.

What was the benefit of the Panopticon according to Bentham? It was its efficiency: technically one watchman can be surveilling hundreds of inmates. To be even more precise, no watchman is necessary if the Panopticon is applied correctly. If the inmates are not sure if they are been observed or not, they will behave as they were watched at all times. This form of power functions, literarily, even if no one is enforcing it. The power at work here describes perfectly what Foucault thinks about power: it is continuous, it disciplines, that is it makes the observed behave in a set preordained way, and it is anonymous. The design can be used in all sorts of settings and the observed could be anyone: a prisoner, a patient, a student, a worker, etc. If the Panopticon works, all violence is eliminated, for example, from the observed places. Once again, if the observed is never sure if she is being really observed, she becomes her own guardian. That is not all. The observers, in fact, are also totally enmeshed within the mechanism of power as their life becomes fix, regulated, and subjected to administrative control.

The Panopticon is able to function the way it does, Foucault maintains, because it brings together knowledge, power, control of the body, control of space inside a visible technology of discipline. It is a means for the operation of power in space that aims exclusively to increase power. If we wanted to schematically summarize the fundamental components of power that we are able to recognize within the Panopticon, we could say that: (1) power is not just "held", it is exercised. This means that there is no such thing as a power that is "stored" somewhere, not in use. Power is always "actual", always at work. (2) Power has the tendency of being depersonalized, relational, and anonymous. It is difficult to establish who is observing and who is in charge when it comes to power. Think of how difficult it is to find the culprit whenever, for example, a mistake happens in a big company, or a document gets lost in a big institution. (3) Power is totalizing. It is a machine that englobes everything and anyone involved transforming everyone into a guardian of the system.

While living in a surveilled environment might seem in many ways something that one should not want, it is a fact that this system of power is efficient when it comes to its goals. In whatever institution where many people are together, we could agree, the Panopticon provides the efficiency necessary for operations to run smoothly without engaging in violent acts, holding responsible (we should probably say forcing to be responsible) each individual, in the most scientific and successful way possible. This is why, at the end of the day, thinking of power as a purely negative element is difficult. The distinction between good power and bad power gets even murkier the moment a political system preoccupies itself not with the simple discipline of the people in the sense of punishment, but with every aspect of the life of the individual. Political systems today claim to want their subjects not just to "live," but to *live well*. Such socio-political system starts to exercise power over the life of the people, promising health and happiness through certain practices. A new form of power is born, a form of power so pervasive and difficult to detect that permeates our every move. This form of power is called Bio-power, and its implementation is Bio-politics.

12.2 Biopower and Governmentality

Biopower is identified by Foucault as the form of power born in the seventeenth and eighteenth century and that it is characterized by life and its mechanisms becoming part of explicit calculations and political discourse. Biopower works on two axes: one is represented by the body, which becomes a machine to be made useful through discipline; the second one is represented by the regulation of the mass of bodies, what Foucault calls the *biopolitics of the population*.

The two axes form together a new system of power over life. The life of the individual body and the life of the population as a whole. Questions of usefulness, discipline and efficiency invest the individual body, while questions of demography, public health, and control invest the population as a whole. This new form of power, and the knowledge that is born with it, link for the first time in history the welfare of the individuals with the nation state and with politics in general. This means that for the first time the government will be fully involved in regulating every conduct of every individual that lives in a society. The sum of all institutions, apparatuses, and knowledge that regulate and survey the political domain involved with biopolitics and biopower is called by Foucault *Governmentality*.

With modernity a new way of governing is invented, Foucault writes, to respond to a specific need. The "discovery" of the concept of population, its control, and the consequent birth of what we can call the *social domain*, puts at the center of political action the problem of the welfare of the people. Political power is not content anymore with having power of life and death over its subjects, it needs now to have a grip on the way they live their lives. This distinction is a crucial one. We can see here how there exist *sovereign* forms of power (power as right, law, repression), and *normalizing* forms of power (power as the ability to organize, maintain and enhance life). The two forms of power are conjoined *in* the modern individual: we are citizens with rights, we are part of a juridical State, and, at the same time, we are the subjects of normalization, of the welfare society. When an individual is participating of both these natures, in fact, we can call her a *citizen*. Citizenship, actually, as a concept is possible only if we consider the state not just as a legal and sovereign machine, but also an instrument for the enhancement and the betterment of life. For example, the entire debate over the existence of borders, immigration, and access to a country, if we really think about it, is not about allowing or preventing individuals to be subjects of one or another set of laws or legal rights. It is solely about the access to the available techniques and structures to enhance and maintain life in a specific "country." The problem of the borders is a bio-political one.

The birth of a politics that is concerned with the welfare of its citizens comes with a cost. This cost is normalization. Since biopolitics has been deployed we have been invested with a series of norms that tell us to follow orders so we can fairly participate in the welfare state. These norms are not representatives of values, rather they are a rule of judgement. They produce homogeneity on one side—all people are comparable within it—and inequality on the other side—each individual can be in hierarchical order to another in relation to it. Thus, normalization implies on one side the formation, the creation, of a "society." Individuals that live in proximity of each other and that have common traits: they are all humans, free, and healthy, for example. While on the other side normalization produces a whole series of parameters to which said individuals have to conform if they want to keep their status of free healthy subjects. Therefore, the political system that is in charge of the welfare of these subjects has the necessity to ensure that the citizens of that state know how to exercise their rights, and that they know how, for example, to keep healthy. This kind of political system, which Foucault identifies as *liberalism*, is concerned with the liberty of the citizens and (foremost) with shaping these liberties within the horizon of the system itself.

Once again, we can see how power is some sort of double-edge sword. Biopower is effective in keeping people alive longer, in making them live better. At the same time, though, it demands total "loyalty" from its subjects, and it sets itself as the *normal*, natural way in which our society can be organized. Biopower shows us the way in which a welfare institution can work effectively, but it occults what it means, what is does. Once whatever biopolitical practice is set in place the entire debate around it becomes "which one is the best way of implementing it?" and never "what does it really mean to do what we are doing?" or "why should we spend energy and resources on this?" Foucaults example of competing implementations is illuminating, and it is taken from the discussion about the problem of isolating prisoners in the nineteenth century American prison system. At the time, there were two competing implementation models when it came to handle people that needed to be isolated in prison. One model implemented in Auburn and another one in Philadelphia. The Auburn model held that the best way to isolate the prisoners was to assign them a separate individual cell where they had to sleep by themselves. At the same time, though, they were allowed to work and eat together with the other prisoners. In both situations, the prisoners were strictly prohibited to speak to the others. The advantage of this model, according to the administrators in Auburn, was that it replicated the conditions of society where hierarchy and surveillance in the name of order are necessary to be a model citizen. The prisoner, this way, will be gradually prepared to return to social life. The Philadelphia model, instead, maintained that individuals needed to reform their conscience, and that the best way to do that was through isolation and self-reflection. Prisoners where, therefore kept in continuous confinement. This way the criminal would go through a deep and pervasive change in character rather than just superficially change habits and attitudes. The prisoner would discover his or her moral fiber away from society and would eventually be a better citizen.

It is interesting to notice how although the two systems genuinely sponsor different concepts of individual reform, of the way a society works and influence the individual, etc., neither of the two asks, not even for a moment, if isolation should be carried out. The only conflict is about the *how*, there are no ifs or buts. The biopolitical project is not in question at all. If we think that Foucault's example is outdated or exclusive of a specific domain like the prison system, we would be making a mistake. As for the outdated part: think of the prison system in itself: do we ever think that the whole concept could be wrong? No. The only thing that we try to do is to find better implementations of it: we want to be sure that the criminal is actually a criminal and not an innocent person, we want to make sure that incarceration happens "for the right reasons" and not, for example, because of some discriminatory practices; we even want to make sure that the conditions in which the inmates are kept are not cruel or torturous, but we never think that the whole system might be in need of elimination. As for the exclusive part, think of any other institution. Let's take college. We are always thinking of reforming college, of making it more "student-friendly," more technologically advanced, more progressive, less lecture-centered, etc. We are, in few words, looking for the "best" practices to implement this institution in the best way possible. There might be differences in the way we conceive these implementations, but, again, no one discusses the fact that colleges should exist more or less the way they do now. This is the power of normalization: it paralyzes us into the current state, and it prevents us to think of an alternative.

In conclusion, we need to stress once again that power, even if we have represented it at times as a coercive force, cannot and should not be considered a purely negative entity. It is true that power is involved when a government represses its citizens, or when an individual or a group of individuals oppresses and dominates another. But it is also true that power is necessary and it is involved anytime the citizens of a government rebel against it, or when a revolution is in place and the people that were oppressed and dominated find themselves in the position of making new rules to avoid further domination to happen. Paraphrasing Foucault, *power is a marvelous untamable beast*.

13

Revolution

13 General Characteristic of the Revolution

Revolutions have punctuated the political landscape from a long time, every once in a while, political turmoil happens and governments and leaderships are toppled. Today we seem to think that revolutions have always existed. People have always, one way or another revolted against the authority and quickly fast-forwarded toward a new era in politics and society. Revolution seems to be, at first sight, the political agents of change that has always been in place. If we think this way, though, we are wrong twice.

H. Arendt (1906–1975) at the beginning of her book *On Revolution* tells us, first of all that revolutions the way we intend them are a modern affair, and that, for example, the ancients, while acquainted with change in politics, were not familiar with the way we intend revolutions today. She also claims that revolutions are not concerned exclusively with problem of change, but also with the so-called social question. This means that revolutions are usually tied with the conflict between the rich and the poor, the oppressor and the oppressed. This contraposition, though, doesn't exist in antiquity because poverty is seen as a *natural* unavoidable fact of the human condition, few can escape the shackles of poverty, all others are inevitably and eternally destined to be poor and miserable. Work was seen by the ancients as the necessary burden that the majority of the people need to carry to survive. It is only with John Locke and, in pre-revolutionary America, with John Adams that we start intending labor not as "the toil of the poor" but as a source of wealth. America at this point in history, with the opportunity for work present on the new continent, becomes the symbol of a society without poverty. America becomes the place when men can break the chains of wants and basic needs that were considered for the longest time eternal and unavoidable. Only at this moment in history, the desperate rebellion of the poor can be a true revolution. Now the poor know that they don't have to be so. They know that another system is possible, that a nation without poverty exists and it thrives. This is why the "American man," the American way of life, becomes the aim of the European revolutions (starting with the French one). They want to emulate the absence of poverty, not the kind of government or the establishment of a new body politics that is in place in America. *They are looking for equality, not for politics.*

Arendt clearly tells us that the first revolutions are, without a doubt, the *American Revolution* and the *French Revolution*. Both of them, in fact, are concerned primarily with the emergence of a generalized freedom that was unthinkable before. Freedom and revolution are so intertwined, Arendt claims, that intellectuals of the time will declare that the only *true* revolutions are those whose aim is freedom. If we think about it even today, when we judge the constitutions of every political body, when we judge the "goodness" of a country, we do it by measuring the level of freedom perceived. This concept has its roots in the revolutionary period and, it is one of the few that seems to be shared by all revolutions.

It might seem strange that the political preoccupation for freedom could be only a modern idea born, basically, in the XVIII century. Weren't the ancients preoccupied about freedom as well? Don't they write often about freedom and free men? Of course they do, but their understanding of freedom is quite different. To be sure, the political concept of freedom is born in the Greek city-states, but it is intended quite differently from what we intend today, Arendt writes. The city-states are political organizations that are characterized by the condition of "no-rule": in a city-state people are free because there is no difference between the ruler and the ruled. They live in a condition of equality when it comes to the law. The word used for this kind of government was *isonomy*. A polis, a city-state, was supposed to be an isonomy and not a democracy. As a matter of fact, democracy was for them (as we saw in the first part of this text) a derogatory term to indicate the rule of the mob, a form of government where the many rule and therefore nobody rules. We need to careful here, though, the equality given by isonomy is different from the equality of which we usually think today. Isonomy is, for the Greeks, the place where equality is created, and not the notion that finally allowed people to be free. They thought *equality and freedom were not proper of the people at birth*, rather they are conferred to someone because they are citizens. Equality and freedom are *Nomos* (civil rights) not *Physis* (natural rights). One can only be free (and obviously equal) among her peers. The tyrant and the despot cannot be free, for example, because they have no peers. At the same time, citizens can only be free if they are not governed by anyone, only if they govern themselves. The city-state gave people the space to be free and equal; it more or less created these two concepts.

Modern revolutions on the other hand, change radically our idea of equality and freedom. Their freedom and equality are not civil rights, they are natural rights. The result of modern revolution is that life, liberty, and property become unalienable rights of human beings. There is more to this difference that it initially meets the eye. All the liberties granted by the revolutions are essentially negative. Freedom in fact is primarily freedom of movement, freedom *not to* be restrained (unless the law calls for restrain), while for the Greeks freedom consisted in being allowed to enter the public realm, to be part of the decision process when it came to the public interest. The distinction is important here, Arendt warns, because if we want to be free in terms of the Greeks, then we need to constitute, a republic in order for people to be free; if we care simply about the liberties of the people, then there is no need for a republican kind of government: a good monarch, for example, could guarantee its subjects all the negative liberties necessary, without permitting them to access the public real. We will see how revolutions can be catalogued in revolutions, like the American one, that seek mainly freedom intended as the ability o participate in government, and revolutions, like the French one, that get caught up in the search for private liberties and put on the backburner the search for government participation.

There are other differences between the American-style revolution and the French-style revolution, but the main one (if we exclude the one just mentioned) has to do with their legacy. The American one ends up being historically irrelevant, even though it will be the only one that, at least partially, realizes its goal: giving the people a constitution and let them participate to public life. No one will ever follow the footsteps of the founding fathers; no other revolution will ever attempt to realize, not even partially, what the American Revolution did. On the other hand, the French Revolution changed the course of our history forever. All revolutions will follow the pattern of the French one, in fact, all of them end up following a pattern where the people are first involved in the decision making, only to end up in terror and violence, and, eventually, in repression and/or tyranny (think of the October revolution in Russia or of the much more recent Arab Spring).

Despite these differences, all revolutions seem to share at least some characteristics, according to Arendt. All of them, for example, bring something new, add an unprecedented element to the history of the people involved; they also represent a new beginning, a blank slate, for the body politics created; they have a violent aspect to them, there is always some violence involved; lastly, they are irresistible: once they start they cannot be stopped. This last common element also illuminates us about the fact that the men of the revolutions, the actors of them, are usually unaware of where the uprising is going to go, and they are very often impotent when confronting the historical events happening in front on them. No revolutionary "leads" the revolution. All of them are led by the events. The revolutionaries are often the last ones to be aware of what is happening, they are, in a sense, the fools of history.

13.1 Happiness vs Freedom

The characteristic of the revolution that makes them inevitable, irresistible, made the people experiencing them think that revolutions, under certain conditions were historical necessities. This idea comes mainly by the observation—prompted by the renew faith in science, technology and ingenuity—that beyond the apparent diversity of human affairs, there was a reality that followed specific inevitable rules. Such reality is biological, physical, and it embraces everything, from the human body to the celestial bodies. A revolution, therefore, cannot be separated from these laws of nature, and it comes in existence only under certain conditions, according to the modern men living in revolutionary times. The revolution happens when the poor are driven by their bodily needs to start revolting against the rich.

In this sense it is clear, Arendt writes, why the French revolutionaries considered poverty to be the center of the revolutionary effort. Poverty is bad because enslaves people to their bodily needs. Poverty is the reason why people are unhappy, the reason why people are unable to think and live a decent life. Robespierre famously thought that freedom has to be surrendered to necessity; the rights of the poor are more important that the existence of freedom; this will be, eventually, the downfall of the French Revolution: necessity and poverty made the revolution a failure when it came to freedom. The aim of the French Revolution (revolution that started to emulate the American one that wanted freedom for its people) becomes at a certain point private happiness rather than freedom. This is the point when the *social question* is born into politics. From the French Revolution on, all revolutionary theorists (notably Marx) and all revolutions (Russian, Cuban, Chinese, etc.) will gravitate toward the needs of the poor and not the want of freedom.

The radically different historical condition present in America (the aforementioned "absence" of poverty) is probably to "blame" when we recount the radically different principles to which the American Revolution is tied and the different results that it achieves. In eighteenth century, America the oppression of the people does not mean the oppression of the poor and this is probably why the revolution is not social in nature on this side of the Atlantic. The American Revolution, in fact, succeeds in creating freedom, in opening to the people to road to public life (at least partially), but it also fails, as we have said, because it does not produce any historical effects. No other revolution will follow the path of the American one. The reasons for this failure are obviously multiple and we will analyze some of them later. For now, it will suffice to say that the sweeping statement that in America there was no poverty made seem the American Revolution as an absolute exception, where people had already solved the social issues and could concentrate on the political ones. The truth is that, obviously, poverty existed in America, but that misery did not exist, poverty was lived as a temporary inconvenience that will be eventually conquered. People were poor because they hadn't made it *yet*. The poor are not such because they are driven by wants, they are just in the process of working the land and all other resources in order to succeed. The truth is that the American Revolution is genuinely concerned ideologically with political issues and not social ones. The founding fathers are concerned with finding the best form of government and not with the order of society. For them, the acquisition of negative rights, the acquisition of wealth even, did not automatically open the political realm to the many. Wealth does not equal freedom. The American Revolution, Arendt states, was fought against tyranny and oppression, not exploitation and poverty.

The famous right to "pursuit of happiness" that appears in the Declaration of Independence, needs to be explained here. We have been saying that the American Revolution is not concerned with happiness but with freedom. How come, then that the pursuit of happiness is explicitly cited amongst the goal of independence? The confusion elicited by this inclusion in the Declaration might be considered, probably, another reason why the American Revolution did not preserve its spirit and was not influential in the world. It is baffling to try to understand why Jefferson decided to use the simple word *happiness* rather than *public happiness* when writing. It is clear that what the founders had in mind was public happiness, that is the freedom to fully participate in governmental decisions, and not private happiness, that is to say the possibility to be wealthy or whatever else one might have in mind when it comes to personal happiness. After all, the main complaint of the colonies was "taxation without representation" and not personal wealth or welfare. The murkiness of the pursuit of happiness and the elusiveness of it comes from the fact that everyone can make of it what she wants. What is happiness, after all? Why should a government guarantee to its citizens such an indefinite right? Again, it is clear that Jefferson intended public happiness, the freedom to participate in public affairs.

The French Revolution, conversely, did not even try to create a new form of government, or even a government that was in spirit different from the one before the revolution. It just tried to replace the people in power. The many are not liberated in a revolution simply because, in principle, this revolution was not about freedom but happiness. This is exemplified, for example, by the fact that the word "people" in French is "*le peuple*," which has a specific connotation. "The people" are not the ones that are excluded from the government or the citizens in general. The people are the *low* people, the one affected by misfortune and unhappiness. Compassion and suffering for the people has to be, according to the French revolutionaries, the main virtue of politics; this shift in emphasis was not caused by any theoretical preconception, but rather by the course of the revolution.

The distinction between the American Revolution and the French Revolution, according to Arendt, is also visible in the documents produced by them.

The Bills of Rights were meant to institute permanent restrains to all political power and presupposed a body politic and a functioning political power. The Declaration of the Rights of Man, instead, was meant to identify and enumerate a series of positive rights that are considered inherit in people's nature separately from political status. In other words, the Rights of Man reduce politics to nature by declaring that the body politics is supposed to rest upon man's natural rights and these rights should be the content and the goal of any government or political power. The fault of the ancient regime was not, for the French revolutionaries, that it had deprived people of freedom and citizenship, but that it had voided them of their nature and life. The emancipation that the French Revolution wants to achieve is not the emancipation of the citizens but the emancipation of the poor and the miserable, and it emancipates them as miserable not as citizens.

The efforts of the French Revolution, and of all revolutions that have followed its mold, were eventually frustrated, as we know, and the revolution ended up in terror. We can affirm that, with historical evidence, no revolution has ever solved the social question, but all revolutions have used the force of the people to topple the status quo. It seems, in fact, that the uprising of the poor against the rich is much more powerful than the one of the oppressed against the oppressor.

13.2 The Spirit of the Revolution

Arendt states that modern revolutions are all born with a specific aim. Aside from where revolutions end, she writes, all revolutions begin with the desire to give people freedom and to institute a republican constitution to exercise this freedom. The destiny of all revolutions should have been to create a government that is limited by law. Constitutions exist, by definition, not to display the power of the people, like someone might think, but to limit the government. The ground breaking idea of the revolutions is the concept that civil liberties and welfare can only exist within a society that is equipped with limited government. The rights of the people, in this sense, are not powers that this people can use to tend to whatever needs they have; rather they are exemptions from abuse of power by the government.

It is obviously difficult to put together revolutions and constitution's making; historically, again, only the American Revolution was able to (partially) achieve this goal. We have seen plenty of revolutions that did not produce constitutions but permanent revolutions (USSR, China, Cuba) or government that create constitutions without revolutions (like we have seen after WWI in European countries or in post-colonial country after WWII), but only one revolution that has created a true constitution. The difference between the "permanent-revolution" situation and the constitution making by the people during a revolution is evident; the one between the constitution making by the people and by the government might be less evident. Let's highlight the main issue with the latter ones. People are usually diffident, and with reason, when a government creates a constitution. Constitutions, as we have seen, should be limiting forces against the possible abuse of power of the people and the government. Who could trust the powerful to limit their power? If the government has already all the power, what can guarantee its citizens that they will create a constitution that would limit their power, and consequently, reboot the government? A constitution that comes by via of a revolution, instead, can be considered to be more trustworthy because it is created when there is no government and power is still in absolute flux. This can, of course, also be dangerous because a shift of power might lead the revolution—like it happened to the French one—to a terror state, but at least it gives a chance to the people to direct their interest to where they see fit.

This is the reason why beginning of every revolution is a very delicate moment and can lead to different consequence for its participants. There seem to be a constant about these beginnings, though. All revolutions seem to begin as restorations. People of pre-revolutionary periods, in fact, seem to be concerned with the loss of previously available freedoms and rights, and end up rebelling against the status quo not to get more freedom, but to gain back the freedom that they already had and of which they were eventually deprived. Once the rebellion starts, the central authority is compromised, and the people experience power in a different way, the revolution, with is novelty and inevitability, is on its way. This is the movement where every revolution has been taken by storm and catapulted, eventually, in a state of terror. The only time this did not happen, during the American Revolution, the revolution itself lost its appeal, its spirit and its influence.

Why, though? How is it possible that the only successful revolution ends up being the most irrelevant of all? And why is it that the disaster that the French revolution was becomes the example for all other revolutions? The difference comes after the revolutions ended. America becomes politically insignificant and it ceases to be the land of the free to become the land of the poor, the land of economic opportunity. The United States pays the price for a sort of self-imposed ignorance and oblivion about the revolution. The American people and the American intellectuals have long forgotten that the republic was born to found freedom and not to aid free enterprise. The founding fathers knew that economic growth did not equate to freedom, and that political participation is *the only* road to freedom. But no one, after the revolution seems to care anymore making, consequently, the entire American experience sterile. On the other hand, the French revolution becomes the example because there are all sorts of thinkers remembering it and idolizing it.

But aside from all the differences that we have pointed at during this chapter, a tragic similarity can be ascribed to both revolutions: they failed to keep alive the *spirit of revolutions*. In America, we can see that we have now moved from political issues to social issues; in France the traditional principle of its revolution continues to maintain that the urge for freedom present in all revolution at their onset has to be repudiated and that the only important issue is poverty and welfare. Considered the examples it is not a surprise that all the revolution of the nineteenth and twentieth centuries have also failed. Even though they know, they can tell in advance the exact evolution that the revolution will follow (see the path of the French one), people are inevitably driven by compassion and frustrated sense of justice rather than true thirst for freedom and end up inevitably in a failed revolution, if not in a tyranny.

Again, all revolutions seem to betray the Revolutionary Spirit. The reason for this betrayal might be that this spirit is composed by two elements that are difficult to think together, for us: (1) the act of founding a new body politic which would lead to stability and durability of the new structure, or the new form of organization; in other words the satisfaction of the longing for some stability proper of human beings; (2) the awakening of the human capacity to begin and create something new, that is the quenching of the thirst for novelty and change also proper of human beings. These two instances that seem contradictory to the point that are now separated in two different "political currents" (conservativism and liberalism) are now thought in opposition while they were considered complementary at least until the end of the American Revolution: the founding fathers thought these elements to be so natural that they felt no need to include in the constitution any article regarding the possibility to exercise these two elements together again in the future. They believed, not after some discussion, that the people would eventually reclaim creativity and stability and, eventually, renew the constitution. That means that, in a certain sense, a new, possibly nonviolent, revolution could/would happen again. Revolutions after all are nothing but reboots of democracy. Unfortunately, Arendt concludes, the revolutionary spirit seems lost, and within our representative democracies we seem to have also lost any chance to fully participate in true public life. We might be closer to achieve some sort of private happiness, but we are light years away from public happiness.

Bibliography

Althusser, L. *Ideology and Ideological State Apparatuses*. London: Verso, 1971.

Arendt, H. *On Revolution*. London: Penguin, 1963.

Aristotle. *Nichomachean Ethics*. English Translation. Perseus Digital Library. http://www.perseus.tufts.edu/hopper/.

Aristotle. *Politics*. English Translation. Perseus Digital Library. http://www.perseus.tufts.edu/hopper/.

Ashenden, S. and Owen, D., eds. *Foucault Contra Habermas*. London, Thousand Oaks, New Delhi: Sage, 1999.

Bentham, J. *Panopticon or the Inspection-House*, Moscow: Dodo Press, 1787.

Butler, J. *Sense of the Subject*. New York: Fordham University Press, 2015.

Castoriadis, C. *Le Monde Morcelé*, Paris: Edition du Seuil, 1990.

Chomsky, N. *Problems of Knowledge and Freedom*. New York: Pantheon Books, 1971.

Chomsky, N. *Language and Problems of Knowledge. The Managua Lectures*. Cambridge: MIT press, 1988.

Davidson, A. *Foucault and His Interlocutors*. Chicago: University of Chicago Press, 1997.

De Martino, E. *Il Mondo Magico*. Torino: Boringhieri, 1973.

Dreyfus, H.L. and Rainbow, P. *Michel Foucault. Beyond Structural and Hermeneutics*, Chicago: University of Chicago Press, 1982.

Foucault, M. *Surveiller et punir*, Paris: Gallimard, 1975.

Foucault, M. *Sécurité, Territoire, Population. Cours Au Collège de France 1977–1978*, Paris: Seuil/Gallimard, 2004.

Foucault, M. *On the Government of the Living. Lectures at the Collège De France 1979–1980*, New York: Picador, 2012.

Hardt, M. and Negri, A. *Assembly*, New York: Oxford University Press, 2017.

Hobbes, T. *Leviathan*. (1651). https://www.gutenberg.org/.

Hooks, B. *Feminist Theory. From Margin to Center*. New York: Routledge, 2015.

Lewontin, R. *Biology as Ideology. The Doctrine of DNA*. Concord: Anansi Press Limited, 1991.

Locke, J. *The Second Treatise of Government*. With an Introduction by Joseph Carrig (2004), New York: Barns and Nobles, 1690.

Machiavelli, N. *Il Principe*. English Translation. The Prince (1998), Chicago: Chicago University Press, 1532.

Marx, K. *Oekonomisch-philosophische Manuskripteaus dem Jahre*. (1844). English Translation https://www.marxists.org/archive/marx/works/download/pdf/Economic-Philosophic-Manuscripts-1844.pdf.

Marx. K. and Engels F. *Manifest der KommunistischenPartei*. (1848). English Translation. *The Communist Manifesto*. London: Penguin, 2002.

Montesquieu, Esprit Des Lois (1892)

Plato. *Laws*. Eng. Trans. Perseus Digital Library. http://www.perseus.tufts.edu/hopper/.

Plato. *Republic*. Eng. Trans. Perseus Digital Library. http://www.perseus.tufts.edu/hopper/.

Plato. *Statesman*. Eng. Trans. Perseus Digital Library.

Plato. *VII Letter*. English Translation. Perseus Digital Library. http://www.perseus.tufts.edu/hopper/.

Plessner, H. *The Limits of Community. A. Critique of Social Radicalism*, translated and Introduction by Andrew Wallace Humanity Books, New York: Prometheus Books, 1999.

Ricardo, D. *Principles of Political Economy and Taxation*, London: Albemarble-Street, 1817.

Rousseau, J. *Discours sur l'origine et les fondements de l'inégalitéparmi les homes*. (1755). English Translation. https://www.gutenberg.org/.

Rousseau, J. *Du contract social. OuPrincipes du droit politique*. (1762). English Translation. https://www.gutenberg.org/.

Schmitt, C. *Der Begriff des Politischen*. Berlin: Duncker &Humbolt, 1932.

Simondon, G. *L'individuationPsychique et Collective. À la Lumière des Notion de Forme, Information, Potentiel et Métastabilité*, Paris: Aubier, 1989.

Smith, A. *An Inquiry into the Nature and Causes of the Wealth of Nations*, London: Penguin, 1776.

Virno, P. *Naturalismo e Storia: Cronaca di Un Divorzio*, Rome: Deriveapprodi, 2005.

Wittgenstein, L. *On Certainty*. Oxford: Basil Blackwell, 1969.

Young, I. *Intersecting Voices*, Princeton: Princeton University Press, 1997.